TIGERS IN THE DESERT

First edition
published in 2009 by

WOODFIELD PUBLISHING LTD
Bognor Regis ~ West Sussex ~ England ~ PO21 5EL
www.woodfieldpublishing.co.uk

ISBN 1-84683-047-8

Tigers in
the Desert

A Reservist at War in the Middle East
Operation 'Telic' ~ 2003

IAN H. WILLIAMS

Woodfield

Woodfield Publishing Ltd

Woodfield House ~ Babsham Lane ~ Bognor Regis ~ West Sussex ~ PO21 5EL
telephone 01243 821234 ~ **e-mail** enquiries@woodfieldpublishing.co.uk

Interesting and informative books on a variety of subjects

For full details of all our published titles, visit our website at
www.woodfieldpublishing.com

Dedicated to Linda and all of those who watched and waited, and to my comrades in arms who have given their today for Iraq's tomorrow. Also, to those ordinary people of Iraq who crave a democratic peace after having suffered and endured so much for so long. And, last but certainly not least, to the memories of the two men who long ago 'did their bit' and more – my Father and the man who inspired me to write this, my Uncle John.

My Father with his RE Bomb Disposal Unit, Florence, Italy 1943.

My Uncle, John Fryer with the R.A.S.C. – Arras, France 1944.

~~~~~~~~~~~~~~~~~~~~~

Only the dead have seen the end of war.

~~~~~~~~~~~~~~~~~~~~~

Plato

~ CONTENTS ~

Disclaimer

It is important to note that the views, opinions and feelings expressed throughout this piece of work are purely my own and do not necessarily reflect those of the MOD and Forces.

Much of the text captures the experiences and feelings of the time period, having been transcribed from a daily journal, which has been expanded upon where necessary for reasons of readability.

I would also add that where there may be some inaccuracies, I have left them in rather than correct them, as information and events were believed to have been correct at that particular time, so I therefore apologise for any omissions or errors which may be present.

Introduction

For my part, this is not a piece of work full of heroic bravado or particularly daring deeds. Those individuals who literally went through a baptism of fire, have their own dramatic stories to tell – and there are many. This is merely one volunteer soldier's account of events as they unfolded during another historic chapter that marked the beginning of a new millennium, and the end of a tyrannical regime.

As to whether our part in the conflict and subsequent aftermath was justified, I'll leave history (and other more informed individuals) to be the judge of it, as this work only encapsulates a given five-month time span and I make no attempt to comment on later events. The rights and wrongs of the decision for Britain to become involved in the removal of Saddam will no doubt be debated for many future generations to come.

I will say however, that I was proud to have served alongside my countrymen and those of the American, Australian and Polish Armed Forces, and honour the memories of those who have made, and who continue to make the ultimate sacrifice for no easily won right… for peace, freedom and democracy.

Ian H Williams – 2009

Iraq 2003

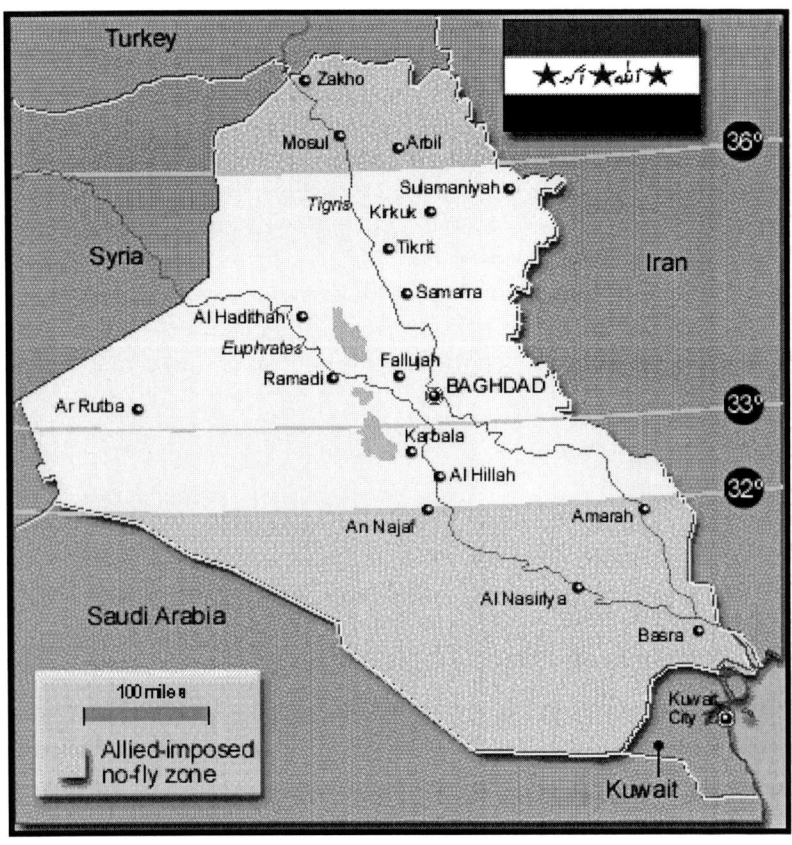

1.   The Die is Cast

With my weighty Bergen and army grips squeezed tight into the luggage rack, I found my seat in the almost empty carriage. Minutes later, the train shunted forward and started to pull out of Lime Street as I moved along the carriage to make sure that I could see Linda, as she made her way back to the parking area. I just had to get that last goodbye in, and I was anxious in case I missed my chance. I waved like an idiot as I caught sight of her. Fortunately, she looked over towards the train as it started to head out, and spotted the carriage with me waving frantically through the window, returning my wave with a brave smile.

We'd given ourselves plenty of time in order to be able to sit for a while in one of the station's coffee outlets. I didn't want to have to rush to board the train at the very last minute, and I certainly didn't want to be dashing down the platform with my 'house' on my back whilst lugging two heavy bags that threatened to pull my arms out of the sockets with every additional second that I defied gravity with them.

I would imagine, that in these situations there are those who prefer a quick, surgical, last minute goodbye, with no fuss, well, we're all different I suppose. This moment had been coming for weeks, and this time, my leaving was somewhat different to my previous departure for a Peacekeeping tour with the UN – attached to '32 Regiment Royal Artillery' patrolling the 'Green Line' (*aka* the Buffer Zone) that split the island of Cyprus in two. Greek soldiers on one side, Turkish soldiers on the other, and us, good old UNFICYP, stuck in the middle between the two of them (the UN had played its part in this particular theatre of operation for nearly 30 years).

The prime mission order which had barely changed in all that time was basically thus; to prevent either side from having a go at each other, while endeavouring to maintain the *military status quo*, and at the same time also remaining impartial. In some instances it was a little like trying to keep naughty school kids apart, except that these 'school kids' were armed (and potentially dangerous). But if nothing else, it had been a valuable lesson in the art of learning how to deal diplomatically with OPFORS[1] that constantly wanted to test your patience. That said, I took every opportunity that presented itself in order to make the most of this particular tour of duty. Overall, I could look back with mostly good memories of a job well done.

Now, I realised that again I was leaving behind everything that was familiar, only this time the stakes were slightly higher, as this was not just another operational tour, this was a 'war' tour. Although at this point in time, the major build-up of troops preparing to move on Iraq at a minute's notice, were a precursor to conflict, given that 'Big Bad' Saddam Hussein was now at the eleventh-hour stage with regard to the UN deadline for declaring his weapons of mass destruction (as specified in the UN Security Council Resolution 1441). But, then again, he'd been stringing everyone along for such a long time and his 'sell-by date' was definitely up.

In the January of 2002, President George W. Bush introduced his concept of an "axis of evil"- those countries with regimes "arming to threaten the peace of the world". Those he referred to most notably were, Afghanistan, Korea, Iran and of course Iraq. As the President declared in his State of the Union address, the terror camps of Afghanistan had been put out of business, and yet many more training camps existed in at least a dozen other countries, where terrorist groups such as Hamas, Hezbollah and Islamic Jihad to name but a few, continued to flourish. The President went on to say that the "United States of America would not permit the world's most dangerous regimes to threaten us". So in effect, he had taken the gloves off.

Some nine months later, he would state:

> "The time for denying, deceiving and delaying has come to an end. Saddam Hussein must disarm himself, for the sake of peace, or we will lead a coalition to disarm him."

The US Commander in Chief, being totally frustrated with the UN, felt that America had every right to go to war with Iraq, especially after the events of '9/11', a date that will forever be etched in the minds of everyone around the world, and one which marked the day that a terrorist organisation perpetrated the most spectacular attack on the world's most powerful nation.

But, this also brought home to ordinary US citizens that they, more than anyone, would never be safe again. At 08.45 a.m. (US

---

[1] OPFORS = Opposing Forces.

Eastern Standard Time) on the 11th September 2001, in a four-pronged attack, Flight 11, a fully laden Boeing 767 plunged into the North Tower of New York's World Trade Centre, followed by another (Flight 175) which plunged into the South tower shortly after. Whilst a third, (Flight 77) hurtled into the Pentagon, a fourth (Flight 93), believed to have been on a direct trajectory for Washington and the Whitehouse, was deliberately crashed into a field south of Pittsburgh, through the heroism of some of the passengers who managed to tackle their hijackers – everyone on board perished, thus preventing a catastrophe of even greater magnitude.

> "Prior to the well-orchestrated attacks on the US, Saddam Hussein had placed his troops on "Alert G," the highest state of military readiness. In fact, it was the highest state of alert that Iraqi soldiers had been placed on since the Gulf War in 1991. And although it is believed that he had no direct involvement in the events of '9/11', Saddam had prior warning of what was to befall the US. It is impossible to say as to why he'd placed his troops on such a state of readiness (as he retreated for a bomb-proof shelter in Tikrit), but Washington's deep mistrust of the Iraqi dictator was sufficient to raise grave suspicions. Although the US Secretary of State had previously cited links between Saddam's government and aligned al Qaeda terrorist group Ansar al-Islam, led by one Abu Musab al-Zarqawi."
>
> *Saddam: The Secret Life* – Con Coughlin

Prior to my own mobilization and deployment to the Middle-East, a British Naval Task Group and Amphibious Ready Group had already deployed for the Gulf via the Mediterranean in early January, pre-planned originally to take part in an exercise in the Far East, headed by the aircraft carrier *HMS Ark Royal*, with some 3000 Marines on board.

There was already a UK presence established in the area of the southern marshlands of Iraq – a coalition operation; 'Operation Southern Watch', which had been in place to monitor and police the southern no-fly zone, thus giving protection to the Marsh Arabs from Saddam's forces. (In conjunction with the Americans, Iraq's northern and southern no-fly zones had been policed since 1992).

By the end of January, the first British ground troops were already in theatre, comprising of: the Desert Rats: the HQ and Signal Squadron, the Royal Scots Dragoon Guards with Challenger 2 Main Battle Tanks, the 2nd Royal Tank Regiment (also with 'Chally 2's), the 1st Battalion, Black Watch (with Warrior Infantry fighting vehicles), the 1st Battalion, the Royal Regiment of Fusiliers (also with Warriors), the 3rd Regiment, Royal Horse Artillery, equipped with AS90 self-propelled guns, the 32nd Armoured Engineer Regiment, the Queen's Royal Lancers (with 'Chally 2's), the 1st Battalion, Irish Guards (with Warrior's) and the 1st Battalion Light Infantry (also with Warriors). It was still winter in Iraq as the Battle Group – 1 UK Armoured Division, prepped for war, housed in tented camps out in the desert of northern Kuwait. In reality, I, and those like me, would only be a matter of weeks away from joining them.

Saddam had now declared that he was ready for war, accusing the UN weapons inspectors of being spies and calling his enemies the "friends and helpers of Satan". And, as if to put a top hat on it all, France, Germany and Russia had made clear, their opposition to war.

The US however, now reserved the right to act without a second UN mandate, with George 'W' stating; "The United Nations Security Council has not lived up to its responsibilities so we will live up to ours".

And so it appeared that the whole situation looked rather dire, and as time on the 'crisis clock' ticked away, an anxious world held its breath.

As Linda receded from view, I was filled with a number of mixed feelings: obviously a little sadness at leaving home, some apprehension, but most definitely a tinge of excitement too. I gave thought to all those servicemen and women in decades past who'd boarded trains to join Regiments and units that would eventually take them overseas and closer to war.

My Father and my Uncles on both sides of the family did just that when the British Prime Minister, Neville Chamberlain, announced to the nation that Britain was now at war with Germany in the September of 1939.

With me having been born to older parents, it gave me a better appreciation of what they had been through, what with their own experiences being a generation closer than that of most people my own age.

I suppose this all sounded a little fanciful really, but there were all manner of thoughts running through my head at this point in time. As I was jolted back to reality, I checked the information I'd scribbled down in my note-book regarding my connections through to Nottingham.

I'd arranged to meet Tony at Crewe and travel the rest of the journey with him. Tony and I had been friends through 15 years of

TA Reserve service (12 of which were spent together in the then 5/8th King's Regiment), and over the last few years, he'd completed several operational tours of the Balkans – on and off with 'Tiger Team'.

It was in fact he who had planted the seed which culminated in me eventually disappearing off for several months on a Full Time Reserve Service posting under the auspices of the United Nations. For some time I'd fancied the idea of a tour in the Balkans, with Kosovo as my originally intended destination. I'd made tentative enquiries with my parent unit, but my employment situation also happened to be a little tenuous at that time, despite my long years of service with the company, and I needed to ensure that I didn't jeopardise it by "disappearing" for several months. There was also a gradual drawing-down of troops out in Bosnia and Kosovo, and so it appeared as though there weren't a lot of opportunities available for myself at that particular point in time. However, a year later, I'd finished with the company where I'd spent most of my working life ... now things had changed.

An operational tour was now not such an unlikely proposition.

As it would turn out (and following a slight change of plan), I found myself proudly wearing the blue beret of the United Nations in Cyprus, instead of flying the flag as it were, for NATO in the Balkans.

When I returned, following my 'FTRS' stint in the June of 2002, it wasn't long before I'd begun to get 'itchy feet' again, and had started to think about another operational tour. All that I now had to do was let my intentions be known to my other half ... not as clear cut or as easy as it may have sounded. Mind you, Linda had sussed that I had started to formulate some ideas regarding another overseas tour. Maybe I'd blabbed in my sleep?

Anyway, time marched on, Christmas had come and gone, and I was thinking that I would have to resort to 'plan B' (whatever 'plan B' was), when my buddy Tony, phoned. He was coming to the end of his POTL or post-operational tour leave, following his latest escapade in the Balkans and had just been informed that 'HQ Land Command' were again looking to fill slots for 'Tiger Team' rather urgently, and was I interested? This was now January and things were looking decidedly serious in the Gulf – compulsory mobilisations were now more than just a vague possibility at this stage.

I had considered the possibilities of signing up with 'Tiger' previously, but now this seemed too good an opportunity to miss, and to my way of thinking, wasn't it better to have a 'willing horse' than individuals who are mobilised against their will? As the old saying holds true, "One volunteer is worth ten pressed men," or something like that.

On a number of occasions, Tony had told me of his involvement with 'Tiger Team', and mentioned that whilst doing what to some, may appear to be a not particularly glamorous job, the role certainly allowed for a fair amount of mobility in whatever Theatre that 'Tiger' operated. It had already proved itself in the Balkans over a period of several years. Well, if it allowed me the opportunity to experience even a little of another country, albeit with the prospect of almost certain conflict, then so be it. And to be honest, I was never one to pass up the opportunity to travel somewhere that was new to me, although I must admit that it was one hell of a way to collect air mile points!

In simple terms, 'Tiger' (or Theatre Information General Equipment Register) is an auditing tool by which the whereabouts of every 'asset' or piece of military equipment – whether it be, vehicles, tracked armour or containers for instance, can be traced by means of a unique bar code to identify it. Once the bar code has been laser scanned by hand-held scanner with all relevant asset details logged in, the data is then down-loaded to laptop computer, where the information is then relayed electronically to 'HQ Land Command's database. Thus, allowing the National Audit Office (and HQ LC) of the exact location of thousands, and in many cases, key assets to be known.

So with this in mind, it appeared that the likelihood of 'Tiger Team' being deployed somewhere "hot and sandy" was now extremely high, and although nothing was definite at this stage, the destination would most likely be Kuwait for starters, and depending on the outcome of the next several weeks, Iraq (or 'Ibiza' as we discreetly called it) was becoming increasingly likely too. 'Tiger' would certainly prove its worth over the coming months.

And so, armed with the contact phone number, and following a chat with the 'Tiger head-sheds' down at HQ Land Command, I found myself signing on (at least verbally at this point) for mobilisation to the Middle-East, discreetly known as 'Operation Telic', which sounded quite sedate compared to the US moniker given for it: 'Operation Iraqi Freedom'. But then again, the Americans do like to do stuff with plenty of bluster.

The word 'Telic' sounded to me like it had a Greek or Latin connotation, although normally, for reasons of 'OPSEC', most code-names for British military operations are chosen at random by computer, so as not to alert a potential enemy as to the nature of an operation in any way, shape or form. However, my early thoughts on the matter were correct, as I later discovered that 'Telic' does indeed come from the Greek which means 'directed or moving towards a goal purposefully'. And, although our particular designation didn't exactly inspire in the same way that 'Operation Iraqi Freedom' might, some people may well argue, "What's in a name?"

2. Iraq – A Brief History and the Rise of Saddam Hussein

It would be remiss not to touch upon a little of the background of this ancient, historic land, once known as Mesopotamia (Greek for 'the land between the rivers'), and also to give a short chronicle of the man who would again have the Western World and indeed, the Middle-East, balancing on a knife edge.

Whilst taking other hallowed traditions and religions into account, Iraq can claim to be the birthplace of Adam, Eve and Noah, the descendant faiths of Abraham; Judaism, Christianity and Islam (Islam being the official religion in Iraq). Today, Muslims make up 95% of the population, with considerably more Shi'ites than Sunni. The Shi'ites tend to live in the south of the country, and the Sunni mostly concentrated in the central and northern districts, with the largest group of non-Muslims being Christians, belonging to several sects. The other religious minorities are the Yezidis, the Sabaeans, or Mandeans – who are followers of John the Baptist. In terms of the general populace, Arabs make up approximately 80%, with the Kurds at around 15% (who live mainly in the northern provinces). The other minority groups are the Marsh Arabs, Turkomans, Assyrians, Chaldeans – the nomadic tribes who live in the western desert region, and the Jezira Bedouin who live in the highlands of the north.

However, long ago, this great civilisation flourished with its artistic and intellectual advancements ranging from writing to philosophy to algebra to banking to social justice to war. Iraq, it would appear (which also transcribes as 'the country which is firmly rooted'), has been quite significant in the course of human events.

Long before advanced civilisations blossomed in Egypt, Greece and Rome, there were the Sumerians, who flourished around 4000 B.C. These innovative people who farmed the lush fields in the fertile lands between the Tigris and Euphrates rivers, developed the wheel, a mode of writing and recording, and a mathematics system based on the number 60 that remains the basis for time and measurement in today's world.

Historical Iraq was a more democratic "civilised" place than the nations rising around it. But these things would not last.

Despite being overcome by a Semitic people from the Arabian peninsula in the 3rd century B.C., several centuries later, King Hammurabi reunited and extended their domain north and west. This was now Babylonia, (ruled from Babylon) where the rule of law was just and fair, with justice for the poor and where punishment fitted the crime ("an eye for an eye, a tooth for a tooth" was written in stone – literally). After the death of Hammurabi in 1750 B.C., war returned to the region we now know as the Middle-East. It is fair to say that Babylon, and later, Baghdad, contributed enormously to the rise of civilisation that we know today.

Centuries later, Nebuchadnezzar also ruled from Babylon as did Nebuchadnezzar II, who built one of the seven-wonders of the world – The Hanging Gardens, during the golden age of his reign. Imagine the city, where a quarter of a million people lived (this may well have been the largest city that the world had seen at that period in time) with outer walls some ten miles long and wide enough for two teams of horses to pull chariots side by side. Add to that the thousand or more temples, with the most prominent being the tower of Babel rising to around three hundred feet.

This was a colossal place.

The sad thing is that virtually all traces of the original city have all but vanished today, due to insensitive modern-day building, some of which Saddam himself was partly responsible.

Alexander the Great conquered in 331 B.C. And, a while later in 1258 A.D., Gengis Khan's grandson, Hulagu, swept across from Central Asia, murdering all in his path en-route to Baghdad, and stormed the city with 200,000 Tarters where it is believed that three-quarters of a million people were slaughtered.

He celebrated his victory by erecting a mound of skulls … those of his victims. (This would be mirrored several centuries later when Saddam Hussein would pay homage to this grisly exhibition by having nets full of defeated Iranian soldier's helmets affixed to the bases of his crossed-swords monument in Baghdad – many of the helmets bearing shrapnel and bullet holes, I might add).

This then became an outpost of the Mongol empire and was ruled from Iran. Sultan Suleiman the Magnificent overpowered Baghdad in 1534 and established Ottoman rule that endured into the 20th century. During the next two centuries, rule in Baghdad passed back and forth between the Turks and Persians, but by the eighteenth century, Iraq was finally beginning to re-establish itself as an important economic centre. However, in 1831, Bubonic plague took hold in the capital as the Tigris River burst its banks, flooding the city. The population decreased by two-thirds, dwindling to a mere 50,000.

During the 19th century, Turkish rule was actually a little more enlightened than anything the country had previously experienced, but Iraq suffered as a result of the general decay of the Ottoman Empire. And so, as Ottoman rule ended with the onset of World War One, the occupying British cobbled together present-day Iraq and King Faisal I's monarchy was established under British protection in 1921, with Iraq gaining its independence in 1932 (as the unwanted British marched out).

Between 1937 and 1941 there were several coups, which ended with the pro-Nazi, anti-British regime of Rashid Ali Kailani. The British now faced defeat in the Middle East and sent in a force which captured Basrah and occupied the country once again. Up until 1958, the country was run by the pro-British Nuri Said. But, Nuri would eventually pay a heavy price for his pro-British stance. Prior to this, King Faisal's successor, his son, King Ghazi remained as figurehead until he was killed in a car crash in 1939. His son, Faisal II became king at the age of three. With much bitterness also aimed at Faisal II, two men, Brigadier General Abdel Karim Kassem and Colonel Abdul Salam Arif moved against Faisal in 1958, whereupon the young King, and several members of his family were brutally murdered. It appeared that the old rules of whoever was the most daring and ruthless, won the day.

Then the most infamous and despotic of all stepped into the arena … Saddam Hussein. Saddam, which according to one translation means, 'he who confronts', was cited as being born in 1937 in the village of al-Awja, a hundred miles north of Baghdad and five miles south of Tikrit itself.

The dirt-poor village of al-Awja, which means, 'the turning' (or bend of the river) stands on the western bank of the Tigris. This unremarkable place of around a hundred dwellings – mostly mud brick huts, was a place that Saddam came to hate (which was one of the reasons in later years that he cited the larger town of Tikrit as his birthplace).

He faced a harsh, poverty stricken existence, where he was neither wanted by his new step-father, Hassan al-Ibrahim (as his own father, Hussein al-Majid had simply disappeared). "I don't want him, the son of a dog," Hassan would shout, and according to other villagers, the young Saddam would quite often end up being beaten and abused, and thrown out of the house.

Saddam eventually escaped from it all at the age of ten and found sanctuary with his uncle Khairallah Tulfah, a cashiered army officer, in the village of al-Shawish. Just as he had learned anger and violence at the hands of his stepfather, he learned bitterness at the knee of his uncle, from whom he also gained his political grievances. Saddam was grateful for his uncle's wisdom, who he eventually made an honorary Iraqi general and then Mayor of Baghdad when Saddam himself later became President.

In Saddam's secondary school, known to be an incubator of nationalism, he became involved in the Ba'ath Party (Ba'ath meaning renaissance), a socialist group founded in Syria during the 1940's, which was also formed around the cause of Arab independence.

When he was around 19, he took part in a coup attempt against Faisal II, which failed, but marked the Ba'ath Party worthy of note, and Saddam as a political activist. Shortly after, he killed his brother-in-law for being a communist, although some believe that Saddam himself invented this story as he was a consummate, calculating fabricator of legend, who would later ensure that there would be nobody to challenge him, and most certainly not in public. Once the young Faisal and his family had eventually been 'removed' in 1958, military man Kassem took control.

Saddam, by then, a thug of some experience, then attempted a daring daylight ambush on Kassem's car killing several others but not the Premier. Later, an authorised film would be made of the story called *The Long Days*, with Saddam's cousin (who would later actually be put to death by Saddam) playing the lead role.

Again, this would bolster the legend that was Saddam Hussein.

However, with a death sentence now on his own head, Saddam holed up with a like-minded group in Egypt, whereafter he finished his preparatory schooling and enrolled into the University of Cairo Law School.

In 1963, Kassem was successfully assassinated, which left the door open for Saddam to return to Iraq where he then married his first wife, Sajida in an arranged marriage – she was the daughter of his Uncle, Khairallah Tulfah, and it would prove a good move for him (Saddam).

He immediately got busy assisting Kassem's former sidekick, Abdul Salam Arif in the execution of more than seven hundred people. Following a later shoot-out, he was captured and imprisoned where his reputation further grew, and he was elected to a Ba'ath Party leadership post. His star was fast ascending, and there was no one to stop him. In 1968 he escaped and plotted whilst in hiding. The Party finally toppled the government and Saddam donned a military uniform for this *coup d'état* and rode victorious like a conquering hero back into Baghdad on a tank.

Now at age thirty two, in reward for his bravery and service, he was made Iraqi vice president, as well as deputy chairman of the new government's ruling Revolutionary Command Council. That same year, he gained his law degree (one report maintains that he showed up for his final exams sporting a gun in his belt and flanked by four bodyguards). So, whether he'd actually earned his degree is open to much speculation. This particular incident appears little different from an earlier episode when, as a young boy he would carry an iron bar around everywhere he went, even at school. It had reached the point where the headmaster had threatened him with expulsion for being such a troublesome pupil, only to have the young Saddam reply, "I will kill you if you don't withdraw your threat." Needless to say, he didn't get expelled. His violent streak was already beginning to surface.

During the following decade, Saddam certainly put the hours in with regard to 'the cause', emulating one of his idols, Joseph Stalin, by working 18-hour days. Over time, he came to be regarded by those around him as the real ruling power, taking control of many areas of the government – he appeared to be involved in everything during this period of time.

Strong now, he flexed his muscles, though perhaps not in quite the way for which he would later be known. However, during the 1970's, he was actually seen as being something of a progressive. And now, with control of the world's second largest petroleum reserves he enriched himself and the lives of his family. The little peasant boy-cum-hoodlum, had come a long way.

But whilst the Hussein clan revelled in their luxurious, regal lifestyle, he not only funnelled enormous sums of money into a modernisation programme for Iraq's infrastructure, but also in the launch of a nationwide literacy programme. And, believe it or not, set up one of the best public health systems in the Middle-East. Beyond the border of Iraq, his reputation was positive and growing (despite whatever plans he may have been secretly harbouring). He was without doubt a gifted actor who could be unbelievably brutal on the one hand, yet don the mask of the caring (future) President of the people, and whoa be tide anyone who was heard to be uttering anything other than to sing his praise. In Ba'athist Iraq, no one could be trusted.

One story which may or may not be true (but I would wager is more than likely true) will bear this out. Saddam, upon one of his many trips around the country, would literally drop in on a village at random to get the general consensus of opinion about what "his people" thought about him.

He stopped to ask a child, "Do you know who I am?"

"Yes" came the reply – followed by "Every time you come on television my father spits on the ground and switches it off!" Apparently the whole family disappeared – including the child.

And yet, it was around this time, that the United Nations awarded him the UNESCO citation for his humanitarianism, and he was actually having cordial meetings with the Washington diplomats as well as those from the other Arab nations. By 1979, when he'd 'eased' the ailing al-Bakhar out of office and wasted no time placing his relatives and old hoodlum cronies in key government positions. These were known as the 'Tikrit Mafia'.

Once he had assumed the presidency, his authority was without question and his ruthlessness legendry. If any doubted their new leader's power, their doubts were soon dispelled. He wasted no time, for example, when after having succeeded General Ahmad Hassan al-Bakr, Saddam called a party meeting. Whilst quite casually smoking a cigar, he began to name the "traitors" among Ba'ath Party cohorts and potential rivals who were present. They were escorted from the room, one by one, some 60 in all.

Weeks after, 22 of the alleged plotters were executed. This was only the first of many such purges – between 1978 and 1979, some 7000 Iraqi's disappeared (believed to be mostly communists).

Having previously signed a pact with Iran which secured the Shah's promise to end his support of the Kurds, this cleared the path for their later genocide. In 1980, firmly in control, but with a Shi'ite Ayatolah having replaced the Shah, Saddam simply made the pact null and void, whilst also having reneged on the 1975 boundary agreement over the Shatt Al Arab waterway – Saddam wanted a return to total control of it.

Because the Iraqi Government had always been dominated by Sunni Arabs, and even though Shi'ites form a majority of the population, Saddam was concerned about the real threat of a Shi'ite revolution in his own country. Clashes broke out along the border, and in September of 1980, Iraqi forces entered Iran along a 500

Kilometre front. Thus, the ensuing eight-year war had begun, only to end in a stalemate, and for very little territorial gain, yet a million lives had been lost on both sides.

But, this also brought him favour with the US, who where more than happy to supply shipments of arms with which to fight the Ayatolah. Saddam had visions of a pan-Arab universe dominated by him alone, but things had already started to unravel. Eight years of war with Iran had taken its toll on this once proud, "civilised" country, and the progress that Iraq had made under Ba'ath Party rule was completely eroded, leaving the country thoroughly broken – but still (it was believed) with the fourth largest army in the world.

It was with this military might that he focussed his attention on its small, oil-soaked, all-but-undefended neighbour, Kuwait. Things had quickly began to sour with the Kuwaiti's – Saddam accused them of waging 'economic warfare' against Iraq by attempting to artificially hold down the price of oil, and stealing from the Iraqi portion of the Rumaylah oilfield that straddled the border of both countries (although the accusations were not entirely without merit). As Arab attempts to mediate a peaceful solution to the dispute failed, Saddam had decided to take matters into his own hands, and prepared to move on Kuwait, believing that the world would raise little more than an eyebrow. He could now be seen for what he really was, a power-mad, megalomaniac.

This man, who claimed to be a direct descendant from the prophet Mohammed, and who had himself committed countless atrocities during his rise to power, not least when having given his subordinates the order to gas 5000 Kurds at Halabjah without a second thought, was now on the brink.

At 2a.m. on the morning of Thursday 2 August 1990, Saddam defiantly ordered his 100,000 troops and 300 tanks into Kuwait, and was so confident about the outcome of his actions that he was already calling it Iraq's 19th province. With armed forces of only around 16,000 personnel, Kuwait could do virtually nothing as the Iraqi army rolled across the border.

But reaction was swift as Saudi Arabia's King Fahd petitioned Washington and the UN for protection from the madman, and in response, President George Bush (Snr) deployed 'Operation Desert Shield' to defend Saudi lands. Within days, the Arab league voted to send troops to assist the US effort. With Iraq ignoring the deadline to withdraw, on January 16 1991, the US President gave the go-ahead for the most devastating strategic air assault in history: 'Operation Desert Storm'.

Early in the conflict, Saddam had termed it a holy war, and prophesised "the mother of all battles". Ground fighting was indeed intense but brief, as the coalition overwhelmed the Iraqi's. In the final two days of the conflict, the largest tank battle since World War II was waged. Two hundred Iraqi tanks were destroyed; the coalition lost not a single one. In all, 148 of American ground forces were killed in the 42-day action, with 159 lost in non-combat actions, (35 of which were attributable to 'friendly fire') and 467 wounded. During the British phase – 'Op Granby', we suffered 19 losses, with nearly half of them also to 'friendly fire'. However, it was estimated that somewhere in the region of 100,000 Iraqi's were killed, with 300,000 wounded, 60,000 captured and 150,000 desertions.

And yet for several years after the Gulf War, the UN Security Council sanctions that had been imposed on Iraq under the presidencies of George Bush senior and then Bill Clinton (which were believed to be the most useful means of controlling Saddam), actually killed more people by means of a policy that was slowly strangulating the country eg; war damage had caused the breakdown of the country's sanitation and drinking water, and Iraq was now dependant on the importing of equipment that could assist with the repair of the sewage, purification and pumping systems.

Basically, if Iraq was kept poor, then Saddam would not have the financial means to develop the kinds of weapons systems that he would otherwise have at his disposal. It was as a result of this deep-rooted fear, that one fifth of the originally agreed engineering and supply contracts were nullified. And, whilst the west waited for Saddam to comply with all 10 points of UN Security Council Resolution 687,[2] diarrhoea, malnutrition and acute respiratory diseases were killing four thousand to five thousand children each month.

So, here we were, just having barely broken into a new century, with Saddam having survived to taunt the West and those other nations who wanted rid of this tyrant who would not acquiesce.

---

[2] According to UN representative, Denis Halliday, who had been sent to Iraq to monitor the 'oil for food' programme, ordinary Iraqis, who were supposed to be protected by it, actually benefited very little.

The War Against Saddam' – John Simpson

Now, in the early months of 2003 some twelve years on from the liberation of Kuwait, we again waited for the 'green light' to go to war.

Tony Blair, the British Prime Minister, had already promised the United States that the Brit's would be their coalition partners, standing shoulder to shoulder as and when required. To be honest, there was no reason for the US of A not to believe that we wouldn't be right behind them when things started to get tough and the smelly stuff started to accelerate towards the fan, right? I mean we'd always been there for them in the past hadn't we?

I could just hear the Whitehouse advisors: "Yes siree Mr President Sir … there mightn't be many of 'em but them Brits is always good to have on your side in a ruckus!"

Apart from those regular serving Regiments and units already on standby for the Gulf, a call up of TA/Reservists had begun, the scale of which had not been seen since the Suez crisis back in 1956.

It was somewhere in the region of 5,000 call-outs and deep down I had a feeling that I'd end up getting mobilised officially – perhaps previous operational experience was taken into account in the call-up process, or maybe each individual was just a number chosen at random?

But I'd already made my mind up that I would follow my instincts and get myself sorted. I believe that there is some merit in taking control of your own destiny sometimes, and it was with this in mind and a strong sense of duty that had me pre-empting the situation. But, also with a pre-determined posting, I would then be a little more prepared for mobilisation and deployment as and when Her Majesty, via the Government, required my humble services, and it would leave me a little less in the in the dark with regard to my own particular role in the whole scheme of things. (I would later be informed that I'd still receive the standard compulsory call-up papers as a formality). And, so I waited for the buff-brown envelope to drop through the letterbox.

Up to this point, I hadn't particularly weighed up the argument as to whether Iraq may or may not have had weapons of mass destruction, but the one thing that I did believe in at this point in time … Saddam Hussein had to go.

To the unwitting, the arrival of the 'dreaded brown envelope' would come as quite a shock, as a fair number of individuals were given very little notice in which to sort their lives out – for some, they had as little as a few days.

And many would have little clue as to what their operational role was liable to be, until that is, they went through the mobilisation process at RTMC – the Reserves Training and Mobilisation Centre at Chilwell near Nottingham.

Tony and I spoke several times as we both waited for the postman to arrive each morning. And even though I'd offered my services freely (and yes, I realise that back in those long-ago days when I was first attested, that by doing so, I had already given myself up to defend Queen and country in whatever form that took) but when the A4 envelope did eventually arrive a couple of weeks later, I still opened it with some trepidation.

One of our other mutual TA buddies, had also received his call-out order a couple of days earlier, and would be heading for RTMC on the 17th of February. Anyone who'd ever mobilised for operational service over the last few years, whether Territorial or Reservist, would have been through the RTMC system prior to deployment, and in many individuals cases, several times.

Anyway, prior to 'Postman Pat's surprise, a little inside information had alerted us as to the fact that we would more than likely be processed for mobilisation on the 20th, so there was no turning back now.

Amongst all the legal documentation regarding mobilisation, there was a packing list, which was just a very basic guideline on what to pack, (which if I'm not mistaken, was identical to the one I'd received prior to my Cyprus tour) but this particular list stressed that you could only take what you could carry, meaning that we wouldn't have the luxury of 'MFO' boxes filled with home comforts as on other operational tours, for obvious reasons.

So, packing was a nightmare, as it was a case of trying to cover every eventuality for what would most likely be desert conditions with cold nights and red-hot days? Also bearing in mind the strict weight limits on baggage.

Fortunately for me, I'd been able to sign out all my 'PLCE' from my unit, which meant I could at least pack properly, filling my Bergen with the necessary essentials (but no kitchen sink, which really would have been indispensable later on!). As it turned out, quite a number of people would end up having to sign out all of their 'green stuff' from the RTMC (mostly Reservists who were 'diffy' in current military kit). This was an additional pain in the butt for many, as they now had a mountain of stuff that they somehow had to pack for the Gulf. Fortunately for me, all that I would need to sign out was a weapon, ancillaries, and … body armour.

Anyway, with Tony having joined the train at Crewe as planned, we settled in and talked of past tales, mostly funny ones, with pensive talk about the future.

We eventually stepped off the train and lugged our bags onto the military transport bound for Chetwynd Barracks, where Tony found a couple of familiar faces he'd known from previous tours. We'd made the journey in good time, giving us a little breathing space – getting in at around 1230, as we weren't required to be at RTMC till 1400 hours latest.

I thought back to the last time I'd entered the main gate here at Chilwell, but this time the future prospects of what lay ahead were a little different to say the least.

The Barracks itself, named after Lord Chetwynd of Chilwell, had previously been a munitions factory during the First World War, and after a period of only 18 months, had established itself as the largest munitions store in Europe. So much so, that it became the 'National Shell Filling Factory'.

Even when a massive explosion killed 134 people (many of which were never found) in the July of 1918, a month following the disaster, the factory was up and running again, with an even higher output. The King himself recognised the factory by awarding it the 'Victoria Cross', and from which time, it was known as the 'V.C. Factory'.

The old black, white and sepia photographs that were dotted around the various departments gave some idea as to what Chetwynd Barracks was like in those far off days, and of the vital role that it played during WW1.

This place certainly had an interesting history.

As it approached the appointed turn-up time, the arrivals brief began.

The processing staff reckoned on us being through the whole mobilisation process in around 48 hours at most, which would include a night's stop-over before heading across to Grantham's Prince William of Gloucester Barracks for the 5-day's pre-deployment refresher training, courtesy of the Royal Green Jackets. That was of course, for those who'd successfully completed the mobilisation process. There were no foregone conclusions here, despite the fact that numbers were needed.

With bags finally dumped, people were 'herded' into numbered groups for the different sections of the admin 'sausage machine', whist others waited in the main holding area, trying to amuse themselves as best they could. This entailed the drinking of countless brews whilst attempting to keep a little warmer in this large, draughty building. There were a hell of a lot of people to mobilise. One of the staff had mentioned that they had been processing around 250 people per day over the last few weeks, working week-ends and long days to keep the numbers of individuals rolling through. (As I said, this was some mobilisation). From the outset, we'd all been told to hang on to a good sense of humour for the next couple of days, as this whole process took its toll on nerves, and we'd need it. They weren't wrong.

There were some anxious faces when it came to the medicals, with a few individuals who were more than happy to fail and be de-mobbed, but even the de-mobbing process took time. However, there were others that were totally devastated upon being told that they would not be mobilising for whatever medical reason and in some cases, dental problems.

There were also a number of border-line cases who were deferred, pending further medical evaluation, after which, there were some individuals who got the 'green light to go' and those who didn't. And then, there were others who's employers had put in a grievance over the possibility of losing their employee for an unspecified period of time, which at this stage, could have been anywhere up to 12 months. (Employers had a seven-day window in which to lodge a grievance, in order to attempt to "reclaim" their employee).

At one very low point, whilst waiting for what seemed an intermi-nably long time for anything to happen, I said to myself, "Well, if I don't get through, I don't get through, no big deal," but this feeling didn't last long at all.

Then, when I finally found myself at the medical stage with the first round of examinations about to begin, I was saying "Don't fail me now, don't fail me now!" If I was being honest with myself, I reckon that I too would have really been devastated at being told that I could not deploy, especially after all the mental preparation and psyching up that I, amongst many put myself through.

What was funny though, was that by the time everyone came to the blood pressure checks, most people were already stressed, giving off elevated readings, not least myself. For those waiting to sign up to head off for possible war, the whole build-up made for quite an intense experience. So by the time my name was called for the round of medical assessments, my own heart was beating ten-to-the-dozen.

The hearing tests were no less stressful, particularly when you're having to listen for the faintest of tones in the headset, and all you can hear is the thumping of your own heart like a bass drum in your ears, whilst pressing away on the damned button like a Second World War Spitfire pilot trying to bring down a Messerschmitt.

But finally, those who got through the various tests and examinations successfully, got the stamp of approval; "Fit For Service". I did wonder about my own sanity once I'd got through it all. Maybe I should have had an in-depth psych consult, surely I must have had a screw lose, right?.. volunteering for this lot?! Having said that, it would be some while later when my sanity would decide to go 'AWOL'.

We were then 'jabbed' up like pin-cushions with the various inoculations. Fortunately for me, I'd made sure that I'd had one or two of the jabs at my local health centre, a week or so earlier, so as not to end up having half a dozen vaccines entering my bloodstream all at once, with the obvious downside of possible reactions to any and all of them. God help those poor buggers who panicked at the mere sight of a syringe (or those who felt ill just thinking about it). Although injections didn't particularly bother me, there was one that caused some concern amongst my fellow 'mobilees', and which would not be administered until just before deployment … .this was the Anthrax jab.

The thought of which, conjured up all sorts of things in everybody's minds. Not least, the reason for which soldiers were advised to be inoculated – Biological Warfare, which gave rise to what other 'nasties' a crazed dictator could throw at his enemies. Now, that really kind of focussed the mind!

When it came to the visit to the main stores where, amongst other things, we were all issued with all the ancillaries for the modified 5.56mm SA80 A2 assault rifle, which were fresh off the production line, well almost.

I'd spent 6 months patrolling up and down the 'Buffer Zone' in Cyprus with its predecessor – the A1. But it would remain to be seen if we'd need the A2's upgraded reliability. There were still many who weren't sold on this particular weapon, especially since the blueprints and actual design had been around for some considerable time, and not to mention the well publicised reports of the early models falling apart. The cry of, "I'd rather have a good old SLR any day!" rang true with many people. Only too well do I remember the demise of the 7.62mm and the conversion and familiarisation training with the A1 back at my TAC. I was safely confident on the ranges with it, but ask me to put the bloody sling on a second time? That was something else.

However, times change, so with the amount of money that the MOD had ploughed into the A1's re-modification, everyone hoped that it was money well spent. All the information reports that had come back from the Research and Development people and the various units that had been given the opportunity to test fire and assess the "new" weapon under different operating conditions, seemed favourable. On the outside, it looked virtually the same, apart that is, from the cocking lever. Add to this the four slightly heavier duty magazines capable of holding a combined total of 120 rounds, cleaning kit, speed loader, and last, but not least ... one multi-functional bayonet which doubled up as a wire cutter amongst other things.

But, if it came to the point where soldiers were told to, "Fix Bayonets!," then things were really starting to get serious because it meant that close-quarter fighting was next up on the agenda. And to be honest, when it came to it, no-one knew how "their war" was going to work out.

It had been the same with many of the veterans of (mostly) World War Two that I'd spoken with in times past, including my father – for some soldiers it was the best time of their lives, whereas for others, the horrors and the memories of their experiences were, and are still too painful. During such times, who can say what fate awaits you?

Later, we'd sign out what would be our own personal 'bundook' – weapon (as my dad used to call them) from the armoury. These would be our 'best buddies' for the duration. And apart from those occasions later on, when secure weapon storage facilities were on hand, where we went, they went too, and that's been the soldier-weapon relationship for hundreds of years.

Along with the other items that the stores personnel were ticking off their check-lists, everyone also signed out additional respirator canisters and vacuum packed NBC suits – otherwise called 'Noddy Suits'. It was at that point that it started to hit home even more ... WE WERE ACTUALLY ABOUT TO GO TO WAR!

Or, as things stood at this moment in time, we were on the very brink of it.

Next, was the body armour, which was heavy enough without the addition of the protective front and rear ceramic plates, which half of us weren't issued with anyway. (As far as I understood it, only front line infanteers and other key bods were issued with plates, if of course there were enough to go round).

In terms of actual clothing, there was no problem in getting enough 'green' kit to bring everyone up to scale, but there was not a stitch of desert gear anywhere to be seen, but that had been expected. It had been mooted that we (along with those who had already been out in the Gulf for some time, and desperately needed desert kit more than us) would at some point get some sort of issue "out in theatre".

In the meantime, we had had to stow the body armour in our Bergen's, along with additional ration packs, which added greatly to the overall weight, thus reducing whatever personal kit we could carry. This proved to be the case later, when it came to clearing our baggage through 'MCCP' at Grantham, prior to deployment. What's more, I wasn't the only individual whose kit was over the limit by several kilos, which meant having to ditch some gear. Any kit to be left behind was to be boxed up and would be sent back to Chilwell, where it would remain until its owner collected it some several months later. So, it was to be hoped that everyone who did leave kit behind, would indeed return home safely to retrieve it.

In the meantime, most of us who were to form Op Telic's 'Tiger Team', started to break the ice a little, during the lulls between the admin and information briefs. As I mentioned earlier, a number of the guy's hadn't previously known what their role would be when called up, well, not until they got to Chilwell and were hitched up with us. So, there were a variety of cap-badges and different levels of experience amongst us all – Signallers, Engineers, Infanteers and Artillery, with several having been on 'Tiger' before, whilst there were other individuals who'd never mobilised for an operational tour before. So this was a different kind of proving ground for all concerned, as the task at hand was to be conducted in a 'live' situation as it were, what with the more than likely onset of conflict.

Although we only needed enough overnight kit to take over to our accommodation, most of us left the main bulk of our military gear in one of the hangers. But, because I had stuff split between hold-all's, I still had to lug a couple of bags across the camp, whilst working up a sweat in the process. It was no wonder that a shower was on everybody's 'to do' list, followed by a beer or two in 'Fletchers Bar'.

But for me, as with a number of others, this was to be no late night. As I sorted out the kit that was required for the next day, I groaned with the realisation that my freshly stocked wash-bag was still hanging behind the bathroom door at home.

So, after berating myself about the fact that I knew I'd forget something, I set about seeing if I could scrounge some kind of disposable razor from somebody, as the supermarket across from the barracks was closed for renovation, giving me no chance to re-purchase the stuff I'd need.

I did eventually get a 'Bic-bleed-a-lot' razor from one of the guys, accompanied with a blob of shaving gel. The problem was that I only had to hold one of these face-disfiguring implements near my skin and I'd instantly lose a pint of blood!

(However, Linda would eventually send my shaving bag out to me in Theatre).

After an early-up, the day's admin trail was completed and finally, by 9pm the following evening, those who were to deploy were ferried to the Prince William of Gloucester Barracks in Grantham (home of the Royal Logistics Corps) by coach, where we would spend the next four to five days conducting refresher training. We had been informed that we would be flying out to Kuwait between the 26th and 28th of February, depending on troop deployment and available flights. This was just over a week away, and not that long in the whole scheme of things, and still no sign of Saddam complying with the UN.

By the time we'd got into 'PWG' Barracks, everyone was dog-tired, but before we could be bedded down for the night, we were required to listen in to the five-day plan brief given by the Royal Green Jackets Adjutant and resident Sgt Major.

Sometime after midnight, everyone swooped on the area were all the baggage had been dropped, and then trudged around trying to find their allotted accommodation. Gear was hastily stowed and kit readied for the first of the day's refresher training, which consisted of First Aid and AFV recognition. Most people didn't waste any time getting some shut-eye, it had been a long one.

Following a hasty breakfast where every available seating space was filled as soon as anybody moved, (a bit like military musical chairs, but no music) all of the training groups assembled at their required locations for the day's lessons.

During the AFV refresher, Iraqi armour and other associated hardware featured quite heavily. Were they trying to tell us all something, I wondered?

There were quite a lot of '34 Field Hospital' personnel training with us, and we'd managed to break the ice and have a laugh as the day progressed. There were one or two 'characters' amongst this lot too, which made for some interesting diversions, not least in the First Aid lesson. It was quite interesting sitting alongside these highly trained specialists as one or two appeared to be quite put out at not being able to apply the full range of their medical skills in battle casualty scenario's. This is because nowadays, basic battlefield first aid is taught, where no time is allowed for elaborate life saving drills. It's a case of follow the aide memoir and do what you can as quickly as you can, then move on so as not to risk becoming a casualty yourself, particularly if hot lead is flying all around you.

The weapons handling skills test took place after evening meal had finished. These took longer, due to the fact that some of the guys were Reservists and hadn't maybe touched a weapon since the days of the SLR, so it was unfair to blame some individuals for taking longer when the SA80 as a weapons system, was unknown to them. So whilst the first batch of people had gotten through their assessment, the rest of us waited outside the classroom, freezing our 'nads' off, as the bitter February wind cut through us. It was right at this point that I wondered what the temperature was like in Kuwait. It definitely had to be a lot warmer than here surely?

It would now only be a matter of days before we found out for ourselves.

Finally, with everything successfully completed for the evening, we immediately went in search of warm brews (or cold beers, depending on your preference) the minute we'd finished. I always made sure that my mini auto- jug was ready to hand, so that brews could be had anytime – electrical sockets permitting of course. During the evenings, after things were squared away for the following day, people would congregate in the 'PWG' bar, but trying to get served wasn't the easiest of things to do, so I would grab a quick beer, after which I'd head back to our accommodation and stretch out, listen to a bit of music or discuss the day's events or some funny incident with whoever happened to be about, or chat about the slightly more serious subject of our inevitable spiral towards conflict. But generally, with the exception of one or two individuals, most people weren't too late in getting their heads down. The days were long enough as it was.

Next up, we were on the firing ranges at Beckingham, where the weather remained quite reasonable, which made grouping and zeroing weapons all the more enjoyable. As we lunched, with good old range stew as our guest, those of us that had completed our 'shoot', had some leisurely time to strip and clean our weapons in bright, surprisingly warm winter sunshine. There was a great deal of banter going on, which kept everyone's spirits up (even for those individuals who happened to be the butt of some joke). But once everyone was back on the coach with the heater going, it was 'gonk city', which was probably just as well really as most individuals needed to revive the batteries a little, as again, on this particular night we had another activity to get through – mind you, that was the scenario most evenings.

After evening meal, respirator function checks (aka gasperators) were being carried out ready for the 'NBC' refresher the next day, which was also to include a session in the respirator testing facility. Now, 'NBC' training is every soldiers most loved topic – Not! (apart that is, from those individuals who are trained as instructors in the subject). However, I didn't think there would be anybody in the tutorials next day who would not be giving the instructors their full attention, especially with the destination we were headed for and the very likely threats that it was believed that we would face.

But, that's not to say that we didn't have a number of light hearted moments during training, eg, when having to assist your 'buddy' in the semi-removal of his/her 'Noddy Suit' "to go potty" as it were. And last but not least, everyone laughing at everyone else as they exited the chamber after having to remove their 'gasperators' and recite their army details as eyes watered and lungs heaved. I must admit that it took me some time to stop my eyes and nose running from the effects of the 'CS' gas. Thank goodness that you only had to go through it once a year when undergoing 'ITD's (Individual Training Day's) with your own unit. Although in all fairness, changes were due to be made to the whole testing procedure, including a new moniker for NBC … .CBRN – Chemical, Biological, Radiological & Nuclear. Not exactly a million miles from Nuclear, Biological & Chemical, but whatever its designation, I just hoped that this wouldn't be required for real, that much was for sure. However, after all that at least I now knew that my 'gasperator' fitted, sealed and worked correctly.

In between the practicals, we had various briefings. But the one which really stuck in my mind, was the use and effects of chemical and biological weapons. Footage of the aftermath of a smallpox attack by Saddam's regime upon the Kurdish population of Halabjah was being shown. It was grim viewing to say the least. Some of the sights on the auditorium screen elicited a few sniffs and snivels from several of our female training companions, which I'm sure could not be attributed to coughs and colds.

When the brief was over, nearly everyone walked out of the auditorium in relative silence. The wearing of 'IPE', would take on a more serious meaning after that.

One of the last briefs we received was all about the Anthrax jab and why we should have it. Many people were none too happy about having this one at all, despite assurances from one of the Senior Medical Officers, who stated that practising veterinarians throughout the UK have this inoculation frequently when dealing with livestock and such. But for which particular strain we wondered? as there are several.

The after-effects, we were told, could range from a sore arm, symptoms similar to a cold or raging flu, or both … Nice! And, although there was no hard evidence, as far as I knew, did this particular inoculation have any direct link to the condition known as 'Gulf War Syndrome'?

During a recess, this was a major talking point, with a number of people remaining unconvinced about the reasons for having the jab, not to mention the additional boosters that would be required later. At mid-day as we were receiving the last couple of briefs, an announcement was made for the attention of all 'Tiger' personnel. All the team members waited with bated breath for their names to be called out. What if my name's not on the list, I thought? Then what? Finally, it got round to 'W' and I was ok. "Phew!"

Everyone on the list was being pulled out at short notice to prepare to deploy ASAP. The flight had indeed been brought forward by two days, to the 26th. The 'head-sheds' wanted us out in the Gulf fast. Had it been possible, 'HQ Land Command' would have had us out on the ground sooner.

I think my heart skipped a few beats as all we picked up our bits and pieces, mouthed hasty goodbyes to our fellow 'mobilees', who, in one way or another, would be joining us overseas in the not too distant future.

As we moved out, some of them were wondering, "Tiger Team"? Must be some sort of specialists to be called forward suddenly?"

Well, we weren't going to disappoint them anyway, and I suppose we were a specialist team after all.

A while little later, once we were established on Kuwaiti soil (or sand), one of the team thought up a rather catchy *nom-de-plume* for 'Tiger'; 'Tactical Information Gathering – Eastern Region'. Well, we were data gatherers and we were operating in the Middle-East, so no mistruth's there.

It was a bit of theatrical fun that got people thinking, 'Okay, Ssshhh, mum's the word!' Once we were embedded with our American 'Cousins' in Kuwait, one or two of them were to enquire as to what we were about, given that we were a relatively small team of Brit's amongst their vast numbers.

After a furtive glance around they also got the same reply in whispered tones, followed by a wink and a knowing look. It was something else that kept us amused anyway, and it added an air of mystery to our mission.

After we'd been pulled from the last round of briefings, we then had to clear all our baggage through 'MCCP', that afternoon, as the next day, we were on our way, heading out to what was originally known as the Persian Gulf (the Kuwaiti's called it the Arabian Gulf). I'd got a right sweat on after lugging my heavy kit over to the hanger where baggage clearance was taking place, but at least it was another important task accomplished, after which, a couple of us hurried over to the camp laundry to collect our last bits of 'dobied' bits and pieces that we'd handed in the previous day. Thank goodness it was ready and bagged up, which was just as well really, because if we had handed our laundry over first thing this particular morning, we would no doubt have ended up having to leave it behind, due to the rather hasty departure (or advance to contact?) that we were now having to make.

And so, with task number two complete, all of 'TT' where to remain and bed down in the camp gymnasium, ready for move early next morning. So, after a shower and evening meal, everyone settled down and made sure that they had all of their final deployment documentation completed, with all 'parrots and monkey's squared away. Our "new" Sgt Major informed us that reveille would be at 0400 with Anthrax jabs following at 0500, the thought of which, wasn't the nicest thing to have to wake up to.

Despite any misgivings, everyone in the group would have the jab, whilst wondering what reactions any and all of us were liable to have.

A couple of weeks earlier, I'd scoured bookshops and the like, in an attempt to find a map which focussed mainly on the Gulf region. But in my search, I'd only managed to find a rather large map of the whole of the Middle-East.

Well, for the moment, that would have to do.

As we settled ourselves down in the gym, with roll mats and 'gonk' bags laid out, and kit for the morning at the ready, I laid the map out on the floor, trying to get a handle on where we were about to deploy to.

The only problem was that this particular map was about 2 metres square and required a Master of Origami to be able to fold the damn thing up correctly. As I poured over the area that I was most concerned with, I couldn't help thinking about the place names I'd remembered from the first Gulf War. Places such as Kuwait City, Basrah, Baghdad, to name but a few.

The reality was, that we would be calling the few grid-squares that I was looking at, "home" for God knows how long. Previously, my history of the Gulf region stretched as far as knowing that ancient Iraq was once a part of Mesopotamia, and that Babylon was believed to have been in the Baghdad region. As I pondered, a few of my comrades were also scanning the map with some interest, probably churning over the same thoughts as me.

It clearly brought back the memories of those weeks, watching the daily television bulletins and news coverage on TV – not least when several hundred Westerners in Kuwait City had been taken hostage directly or indirectly as "human shields". I remembered that there was one particular boy called Stuart, who Saddam singled out to speak to on camera in a rather awkward exchange. It was as though Saddam was playing some major propaganda stunt, but if that's what it was, then it was quickly condemned by the US, Russia, France and Germany. And now, it was hard to believe that it was 12 years ago.

Next morning, after a not particularly restful sleep, I, and the rest of the Tigers had packed up all of our gear and had been 'jabbed-up' before sun-up.

Although it was gradually growing lighter, the grey, ominous clouds were determined to let as little winter sun through as possible as we continued to load up the waiting coaches that would take us to South Cerney – the Air Mounting Centre, where our baggage would then be sorted and processed – ourselves included.

This was just the beginning of our long, stop-start journey to the Middle East. When we eventually arrived at Cerney, we only had about half an hour to wait for the cook-house to open, so we'd timed it just right for breakfast, as we'd been up and rolling for four hours by then and were all getting decidedly hungry. And, despite me having shoved one of my by now, slightly squashed 'Nutri-Grain' bars down my throat at 'half-past stupid', it had done little to ease the building hunger-pangs. So, an RAF fry-up with a couple of extra rounds of toast, washed down with a couple of mugs of tea, would soon sort that out. With furnaces fuelled, we were then able to re-load all of our kit and baggage onto the freight vehicles that would head for RAF Brize Norton, with us following not too far behind.

That would be the last time we would see our gear until we touched down in Kuwait. We, along with I don't know how many hundred other 'Gulf-bound' individuals, had to remain in the holding areas whilst we waited for onward transportation to Brize, a few hours later. Despite the fact that everyone here was heading for the Gulf region, there weren't that many people wearing desert clothing, and those that were fortunate to have it stood out against the sea of green clad bodies milling around.

We chatted, drank tea and coffee in an attempt to kill some time, and watched the large TV screens which happened to be showing the film 'Windtalkers', followed by episodes of 'Blackadder Goes Forth'.

The general consensus of opinion was that this seemed an odd choice of viewing, seeing that we were off to almost certain war. Still, we laughed at what can only be described as 'gallows humour,' something that the British soldier through the ages, has been renowned for.

As some people played pool, and amused themselves as best they could, I queued at the brew station again, which happened to be a little kiosk selling the usual sweets and munchies, but also a small variety of military bits and pieces, and it appeared to be doing a roaring trade.

Well, we were a captive audience, and it would be the last chance for a while to buy that handy little 'gizmo' that would improve your well-being out in the 'boonies'. While I was standing in line, I noticed desert shemagh's on the shelf. (A shemagh is a large wrap around head-dress, face veil and scarf rolled into one, which is ideal for covering up against the elements, and in this case – sandstorms). The very thing! Now, I'd been trying to buy of one these in past weeks and it appeared that there had obviously been a mass purchase of them (as was the case with other essential pieces of kit – boots etc) by anyone and everyone who were going anywhere slightly 'deserty'.

"Better buy it now," I thought. Shortly after, they'd sold out too.

As I was making my way back to my seat, I noticed four or five familiar faces nearby. These were some of the guys from '32 Regiment Royal Artillery', that I'd served with on my UN Cyprus tour the previous year. Their RSM, who was in the vicinity, also remembered me and said hello as I passed him to head back to my much coveted seat. "Small world" I thought.

Word had gotten round that we were to fly out at 2130 hours, (only five hours late). With what little time remained, I made a couple of goodbye phone calls. Not long after, an announcement alerted everyone that we were to mount the coaches for Brize – the wait was over thank goodness. This had been a very long day and it still wasn't over yet.

We still had an hour or two to kill once we'd finally made it through into the departure lounge at Brize, so after yet more coffee I made the final call home. I paced around, fed up with sitting, and let's face it we'd have a number of hours stuck on our posteriors during the flight. So I briefly went for a breath of fresh air (away from the smokers trying to get their last nicotine fixes) just outside the glass partition of the airport lounge, and wondered how long it would be before I returned to Blighty, and stepping (safely) back through these doors, headed for home. None could tell, that much was for sure.

Eventually, after the usual scenario of 'hurry up and wait' (something that the army system is renowned for) the announcement came over the tannoy system for us to prepare to board – senior ranks, first of course.

Our plane was an Egyptian job – 'Luxor Air' (or 'Crab Air' as others called it). I could understand the attachment of such a name if it was an RAF crate that was delivering us, what with Army's affectionate term for RAF personnel being 'Crabs', or did it intimate that the flight was a little less than hygienic? Well, just as long as it got us to our destination safely.

Next stop, the Middle-East!

3. "Toto, I've a Feeling We're Not in Kansas Anymore!"

27th February – 7th March

After an unremarkable flight we stepped onto the tarmac of Kuwait International Airport at 0730 hours into an already warm morning – this was still only February and it was still classed as winter in the Arabian Gulf. I was glad I'd had what was probably my most severe haircut since I was a child – a bit close even by my standards, but not exactly 'down to the wood'.

Our present time zone also meant that we were now three hours ahead of UK time.

As I glanced around, there were large tents and US military vehicles all over the place. We eventually found the truck that was about to dump our baggage and once everyone had searched for their kit like bargain hunters at a jumble-sale we were bussed across to another part of the airport where those of us who were new 'in-country' were ushered into a large Bedouin-style tent. This was the Theatre Reception Centre at Centurion Lines, where everyone received their induction and registration into Theatre, which meant that when each individual was logged in, his or her pay and medical details would (hopefully) be activated, thus removing the need for an admin paper-chase. This was where we all received our 'Welcome to Kuwait' brief, in conjunction with a crash course regarding the customs and 'do's and 'dont's whilst in our host country. One of the major do's being the intake of plenty of water, probably the most important thing in this kind of climate, not to mention the desert conditions (it worked out that each individual was scaled for ten litres of water per day on average). The don'ts were; not showing the sole of your foot to a host, never offer or accept objects with the left hand and never stare overlong at Kuwaiti females, as the first two were considered insults, and the latter was extremely rude. Sitting there, trying to take in all these little snippets of wisdom, made me wonder what the likelihood was of actually falling foul of any of the aforementioned transgressions out in the 'boonies'. I didn't think there would be too many Kuwaiti females to upset by staring … maybe a few camels!

However, the rigours of the trip, combined with the heat, started to take hold and a few of us started to do 'nodding dog' impressions, whilst doing our best to stay attentive. With our registration and processing into theatre finally complete, we boarded the transport, which would take us to Arafjan troop base, about 45 minutes drive south. As we set out for Arafjan, I think most of us fell asleep, waking only as we neared the camp.

Driving off the main route, we passed a sign that read 'Mubarak 15th Armoured Brigade'. As we headed through the heavily-armed checkpoint and onto the part dust-track, part tarmac road that led to the camp, it reminded me of a US State Penitentiary, with its gun towers dotted along the perimeter fence. This place was huge.

There were sand-coloured military vehicles going here, there and everywhere, as well as desert-suited US soldiers, all of different shapes, sizes and creeds, wandering about the place. We'd passed one vertically challenged guy who's rifle was almost as big as him (and an M-16 rifle from stock to muzzle ain't that long either). Only in America – or rather, Kuwait!

This Kuwaiti-American base was currently home to around twenty five thousand US soldiers and as the build-up continued there were now around 220,000 US troops and 40,000 Brits spread across the camps in the northern deserts of Kuwait. The numbers would increase further, but basically, we were outnumbered by about six to one by our 'colonial cousins'. By March 18th the British contingent out in the Gulf, taking into account members of all three armed services, would number around 46,000.

We were outnumbered by some of the other indigenous inhabitants of this region too – sand flies, mosquitoes, scorpions, venomous snakes, packs of wild rabid dogs … and the one to really watch out for … the camel spider.

Now this palm-sized critter injects its prey (large or small) with anaesthetic before nibbling away on its numbed, often sleeping victim. The stories surrounding this beastie are open to exaggerated rumour, but I for one didn't want one of these eight legged monsters inviting itself to dinner with me as the main course!

Finally, the bus came to a halt and we dismounted alongside a rather large hanger, being one of several in a row which had previously housed all manner of armoured hardware.

The large roller-shutter doors that ran the length of the building were up, allowing some light and a little air to circulate inside. We grabbed our kit off the baggage truck and lugged it inside.

"Well boys, welcome to Hanger 10!"

As we looked around for a likely spot to claim in the name of Her Majesty, I could see that a good two-thirds of the floor space was taken up by American soldiers or 'Spams' (the processed tinned meat was their war-time invention after all) with their camp cots all laid out in neat rows. It looked more like a refugee camp, with bodies as far as the eyes could see, the only giveaway being that these 'refugees' were covered in US desert kit. There must have been, at the very least, a few hundred people dotted about, which serves as an idea as to the size of the building. Most of the Americans billeted in this particular hanger were part of a chemical and biological warfare unit who would be staying put for some considerable time. Apparently, if this lot ended up having to move further north it would mean that "things were in deep shit" according to one of the lieutenants I would speak with on occasion.

Anyway, we found ourselves a likely space and laid out our stuff. Some time later we would get the chance to re-locate to a better spot.

The Defence Secretary, Geoff Hoon, had been out here just a few days previously on a whistle-stop tour. He had visited the troops up near the Kuwait-Iraq border and told them that their (our) threat of force was vital if Saddam Hussein was to be disarmed. He'd outlined that if last-ditch efforts failed to resolve the crisis through diplomacy, then we would have to fight. But, for the time being, this was home. It was hard to believe that just over a week ago, around a million people had marched through the streets of London to protest against the war, making it the largest ever protest in the UK. And now, here we were … Kuwait.

Arafjan was also the HQ for 'JFLogC', otherwise known as 'Joint Force Logistics Component'. Whilst the main part of the Battle-Group was ensconced further north, for the time being, everything logistic-wise came through here. Once the green light was given, 'JFLogC' as part of Group Support, would also head north (along with some of our team too).

In order for us to be properly administered to, we, Tiger Team, needed to be attached to a main unit, which was, for the moment, '2 Signals Regiment'. In the meantime, we'd been informed that the ship carrying our team vehicles was somewhere afloat on the briny and would not be arriving for several days, so this was to be home for maybe a week or two. With that in mind, we set out our gear in an attempt to make ourselves as comfortable as possible, but until we could beg, steal or borrow camp cots, we would be spending the night on our roll-mats. My back was already wincing at the thought of a night spent just half an inch from a concrete floor but "them's the breaks" as they say.

The senior ranks briefed us regarding the next few days' activities but what with a little travel tiredness and the need to acclimatise, it would give us some time to adjust and familiarise ourselves with the kit we needed to do our job.

We'd been informed that 'the Boss' – our OC – would be joining us a few days later, as he'd either caught a bug of some sort or had a severe reaction to one or all of the jabs we'd all had. There were one or two team members who looked like they were starting to suffer the first effects of 'flu-like' symptoms, not least the Sgt Major, who was looking none too good. Anyone suffering just had to bed down for a couple of days and sweat things out unless, of course, their condition deteriorated. Boy, when this thing started to react it took no prisoners. I just hoped I would get through the next few days without the cocktail of stuff flowing through my system kicking off.

Across one of the main roadways from 'Hangerville' there were several portakabin laundry units, which proved to be a god-send while we were based there. The chance to 'dobi' some kit, including a now grimy sleeping bag, made such a difference. But it was all a matter of timing, in that if someone had just finished with a washing machine and you had your kit at the ready, then you were sorted. Sometimes it meant having to leave your stuff on the top of a machine and hope that the next user would be kind enough to throw your stuff in for you while you were absent. As a rule, someone would help you out and vice-versa. It was a reciprocal arrangement really, and if you'd found a 'Spam' a dryer as you threw your gear in his 'ex' washing machine, it kept us all on good terms.

Of course there was always someone who had no scruples and you would return to find your stuff dumped, with a 'queue-jumper' having hi-jacked your washer or dryer. On those occasions where we did have some time to wait in situ for the use of a machine, it also gave us the opportunity to chat to our American neighbours and get their thoughts on the "Big Picture".

Because our team members were from a variety of regiments, there were one or two different styles of head-dress amongst us. We had Billy proudly sporting his 'TOS' with 'Black Watch' Hackle, myself with an Artillery 'Glengarry', Terry the Sgt Major and Daz with their distinctive 'Fusilier' hackles, and the remainder of the team sporting an assortment of unit cap badges. This in itself also attracted some interest from the Spam's, which tended to be a bit of a conversation starter, and in particular, the long histories associated with our respective Regiments and Corps, not to mention the few collectors amongst our American comrades, who were looking for any spare badges we may be willing to trade (I do believe that a couple of deals were struck, too). Arafjan was definitely a far cry from the Brit camps further north. In terms of the welfare facilities, this was sheer luxury in comparison. As we went walkabout to check the place out, we couldn't believe our eyes. There was a Burger King trailer, along with Baskin Robbins, Subway, Pizza Hut and not to forget the good old American PX, where you could by almost anything, if of course you were willing to queue. These guys certainly didn't want for much, and to be honest, I don't think that there are many places in the world where the US Army serve that don't have access to a PX, whether mobile or otherwise. It certainly made us the 'poor relations', that much was for sure.

A point that also bears this out is that the Brit contingent out here had been nicknamed 'The Borrowers' and in some cases (some might say rather unfairly) 'The Flintstones', which wasn't really surprising, judging by the lack of desert kit amongst a number of other things. However, this would not affect the Brits' overall fighting capability, if and when the time came.

Certain parts of the camp where the Spam's resided resembled 'M*A*S*H* 4077', with makeshift signposts positioned between tented green canvas alleyways. The signs were pointing to and from the likes of Baghdad and elsewhere to various states in the US, with the accompanying mileage distances. The adjoining vehicle park had all manner of US military rolling stock – tank transporters, trucks and countless Humvee's lined up in rows. I'd never seen so many vehicles except maybe at a car manufacturing plant. Beyond that was the airstrip, used mainly for helicopters, which were constantly up and down, flying missions at various times of the day.

At the centre of the camp was the gigantic mess hall, which would feed thousands every day (and night). As with everything else, long queues for meals became the norm, which wasn't surprising with the amount of soldiers coming through the place. Having said that, the 'chow' queue moved at a reasonable pace, which was mostly due to the sheer size of the place. Compared to the '24 Hour Rat Packs' that our own troops up north were having to survive on, the food was pretty damned good (although, there were one or two amongst the Brits that would have preferred to have eaten the ration packs). Each to their own, I suppose. But having said that, it would only be a matter of time before we were wishing we were back there, enjoying the American grub. Next to the mess-hall, was a water tower that looked like a giant 'spring onion', which was what we, or I referred to it as.

It also made for a good landmark which you could see from several miles away. There was even a makeshift volleyball court, which we used when it was decided we would do some sport. At least this was a much more fun way to keep fit and keep the blood pumping, as well as a little team building.

With the March temperatures steadily climbing up the thermometer (mid- 20's) we could acclimatise little by little. The real test would be when the summer heat really kicked in, allowing of course, for the fact that we would still be out here by then. An old familiar turn of phrase from 80-odd years ago sprang into my head, "It'll all be over by Christmas!" But, look what happened there … ..another 4 years of war ensued.

We were informed that a smaller tented camp ('Kohima') for the Brit's would be completed in a couple of weeks, just to the side of the perimeter, giving us our own facilities, although we would still have access to 'Spam Central'. Just across from the PX and 'Snack Central' was the welfare tent which was always a hub of activity too. One half of it had a few tables set up for reading and board games, including table tennis, whilst the other half was partitioned off and had a large satellite TV set up (and wonderful air-conditioning). The TV made for compulsive viewing, as we would make every attempt to catch up on world news and the latest military developments that were going on around us. Where possible, myself and one or two of the guys would shoot in after breakfast to get an update on the latest happenings. This was interspersed of course, with the intelligence briefs that were disseminated down to us.

Usually during evening hours, a DVD film would be shown, and you'd have to find a spare seat rather quickly. This became a bit of a diversion from the more serious things that were happening around us. That, and the fact that the only alternative was to stretch out on our newly acquired camp cots back in 'Hangerville' and read books and magazines that were doing the rounds, play cards or just simply write 'Blueys' – the free-post Forces air letter.

Not really being a card player, I would read or write.

With regard to our new sleep furniture, a day or two after we arrived, we'd managed to sign out enough of these excellent pieces of kit from the Americans, allowing us all to do away with the roll-mat option. These particular camp cots were good heavy duty jobs and high enough off the ground to stow your gear underneath … ABSOLUTE LUXURY! especially with the roll mat acting as a thin mattress just underneath your 'scratcher'.

In addition to this, the PX had started to sell fold up canvas chairs for $7, which were selling like crazy. So, first chance we got, a few of us hastened over and joined the ever-increasing line that snaked its way towards the PX tent. This was to be a no-nonsense operation.

Once in, we made a bee-line for the dwindling box of chairs, nothing else mattered, success of the mission, was everything. Just a little further back along the queue from me, the lot had gone. Those wanting one would have to wait until the next delivery. "Phew! That was a close run thing!"

What a difference the chair made. It was probably the best five quid I think I'd ever spent, and it was something else to drape damp towel on or your fresh kit. The camp cot and chair would prove invaluable for the whole of the tour. (I eventually left the chair for someone to use, but my trusty camp cot would come home with me). The sand-coloured bag that the chair came in would also prove to be invaluable later on, when doubling up as a protective weapon bag.

The PX appeared to be the Spam's second home. These guys would come out with arms full of munchies, cans and bottles of juice – buying as much stuff as they could carry. *Gatorade* was a big seller, they loved the stuff, but I found it revolting and couldn't quite figure out what the fascination was with it. It was more like Gator Pee in my humble opinion! However, there were all manner of electrical goods that could be purchased too: anything from DVD players to head torches and everything else that you could think of. 'Inova' micro torches, in particular, were very popular and it took me several visits to actually get hold of one these very small but brilliant pieces of illuminating technology. I stocked up on a few of the little bottles of baby shampoo, which were perfect for stowing in your kit, with just enough in each bottle for about three hair washes. These would do when we moved up north, providing, of course, that water would not be a problem once we were out in the desert.

The camp tailor shop was also doing a roaring trade, particularly with the Americans. You could have your desert 'boonie' hat embroidered with any kind of logo, name or comical design. Not that any of us had a 'boonie' hat between us (yet). Name badges with the Arabic alternative, seemed to go down well, and one or two of our guys managed to get theirs done, but as with everything else, you had to be prepared to queue. Next door, 'Baskin Robbins' was even more popular. But then again, coffee and doughnuts are high up on many a US soldiers daily 'must-have' list.

However, on those occasions when we were stood down, or when a case of the 'mid-morning munchies' struck, we too would rush to get in line for these belt-busting delights. Either that or we'd take it in turns to do the 'sticky and coffee run'. Well, everything in moderation as they say. But then again, who knew how long it would be before we'd get the chance to sample 'comfort food' again?

A couple of days later, local traders came onto the base and set up a "Bling" market in the central gravelled area, tempting potential customers with shouts of "Bling, Bling!" – a word which I'd heard even more when I eventually came back to Blighty, and which now has a place in the English dictionary. A lot of stuff on sale was real tat; rugs, fleecy blankets with animal prints on them, and a good deal of other crap to waste your dollars on. But last, and certainly not least amongst all the dubious looking ornaments were the carved wooden camels – a big hit with some of the Americans who seemed to love 'em, but then there's no accounting for taste. I had a mental picture of a young American soldier arriving home, handing over one of these wooden dust collector's to his nearest and dearest, with the words; "Gee Mom, look what I brought you from the Middle East!" There were one or two useful items for sale, not forgetting the usual imitation designer sunglasses, with the logo miss-spelled of course – I did actually get myself a pair of snazzy looking 'Oakeys' into the bargain.

Daz, one of the guys, bought himself a small digital camera for just over a hundred quid and we did wonder whether this thing would actually work, but the extremely good images it produced later, when down-loaded to one of the team laptop pc's proved that he had indeed got himself quite a little bargain. I too, was tempted, due to the fact that my 'cheapo' wind-on camera, which had served me well on my previous tour, let me down as we'd started the refresher training back at Grantham. It meant I'd have to make do with the disposable cameras from the PX.

So, in the meantime whilst we waited for the team vehicles to come ashore, we eat, slept and familiarised ourselves with the expensive pieces of hardware we needed to do our job.

There were so many bods in 'Hangerville' that general chatter would sometimes get a bit annoying, particularly as the Spams get so excited about things, which could be especially aggravating when we were trying to get a little shut-eye and more especially annoying when one particular group would start up with some harmonized rap type stuff … boy they'd pick their times!

One thing that improved our circumstances somewhat was that a central power point had been rigged up for people to charge their laptops and mobile phones. My main use of this facility was to boil my mini-kettle, enabling us to get a brew going during those hours when the mess hall was closed.

This also became the central 'barber shop' area, where Herbie, our have-a-go-barber (who I nicknamed 'Marcel' when in hairdresser mode) would plug in his clippers and oblige anyone who wanted a 'hack and whizz' (although he certainly didn't require one himself; his own dome was shaved squeaky clean!)

We also had a late night bonus in that the mess hall would be re-opened at 2330 hours for those who were on a late duty to get something to eat. Occasionally a few of us would traipse over for tea and toast or a hot meal, although usually most of us were asleep by that time, tuckered out by the heat.

In the to-ing and fro-ing up and down the hanger, in the aisles between camp cots, I got to speak to a few of our Colonial Cousins regarding our current state of affairs as we headed for war. The general consensus of opinion was that the US were "gonna get some" fuelled by memories of '9/11' and that they were more than delighted to have the Brits standing shoulder to shoulder with them, despite us being around a sixth of their number. It seemed to me, as far as the Americans were concerned, that there was an air of 'unfinished business' about the whole Gulf scenario. What George Bush Senior hadn't finished 12 years previously, 'Dubya' would.

We required a spare NBC kit issue, but it was a matter of 'Hobsons Choice' in relation to sizes. So, we signed out whatever we could and would hopefully exchange whatever needed changing when further stock came in. That seemed to be the way of things.

Ammunition was something else that we desperately needed. We managed to get enough rounds for each for us to be able to fill a magazine near enough, but it wasn't until we headed up north, that we would be able to properly 'bomb up' all four mags with 120 rounds, or 'Shiny Friends' as somebody had called them. If we were to travel the highways and byways of Kuwait before heading into Iraq (if that indeed was the case) then we needed to be able to protect ourselves. Despite being in the relatively safe environment of our host country, there was still the threat, no matter how remote, from terrorist insurgents that were believed be operating in and around Kuwait.

After a few days we were given the mission brief. The boss called all the 'Tigers' together and gave us a 'heads-up' regarding the plan of action for our immediate future. The team was to be split into two sub-teams, one half in the north and the other in the south. We all listened in as the boss read out the names assigned to each sub-team. For my part, I was to be heading north as part of the '1 (UK) Armoured Division' Tigers, simply known as '1 Div'. Those that would be remaining in Kuwait would be covering the airport, shipping ports and central Brit camps.

I was obviously a little apprehensive as I thought about the fact that we '1 Div Tigers' would be heading up nearer the Kuwait-Iraq border, with the strong probability that we'd cross into Iraq once things had kicked off and the Battle Group had established itself. Of course, at this stage, nobody knew anything other than the Battle-group was poised, ready to move at a minute's notice. We were also expecting up to around 10 more guys (who were currently operating in the UK and Germany) to boost team numbers to around 30 bods, at least, for several weeks, anyhow.

In the meantime, we'd been told that there would be regular airborne attack drills, or 'incoming alerts' to get everyone used to throwing respirators on as quickly as possible. During training, 9 seconds was the accepted time in which to don a respirator. Once deployed, we were expected to have them on and fitted correctly in five seconds! But we did actually become quite adept at getting these life saving pieces of kit over our heads within the five seconds. Upon hearing, "Lightning!, Lightning!, Lightning!," blaring from the camp tannoy system (at any time of the night or day), the drill was that we were to get under cover, into the concrete scud shelters if outside, or close to a wall when we were in the hanger, where the roller shutter doors would be lowered until the all clear was given.

There was one occasion however, when the 'incoming' alarm sounded as I happened to be half way through a rather pleasant, if hurried shower. But the fact that the shower units happened to be built into steel ISO containers made them a reasonably safe environment in which to stay until the supposed danger had cleared (except of course, for a direct hit). So, even when going about normal ablutions, NBC gear was close to hand. Everyone had to get used to carrying all of their gear around with them wherever they went, which was a damned nuisance initially, but it soon became the norm.

After a while, if you didn't have your 'rezzie' pouch hanging off your hip, you missed the weight of it.

When sleeping, 'rezzies' (or 'gasperators' as we liked to call them) would be within an arms reach and more often than not, the 'rezzie' pouch would be left open with mask ready to grab, even in half asleep mode. The only problem with the drills was that we (the Brits) had been briefed only to don rezzies at this point, based on the current alert state. However, upon hearing the alarm for a simulated attack, the Spam's had obviously been briefed otherwise and would start to dress themselves in full NBC gear. During some of the first alerts, one or two individuals hadn't as yet, removed the brand new suits from the vacuum sealed packaging, which made things really interesting to watch. Albeit a drill, this was not the time to be trying to get new kit out of the plastic, which was a hard enough task when not having to rush to do it. In a real situation, every second lost when 'suiting up', meant a greater chance of being exposed to some possibly deadly contaminant.

So, there we were, waiting for the all-clear with rezzies, helmets (and later on, body armour), which just took seconds to remove when given the "OK," whilst some of our Colonial Cousins were still half way through 'suiting up'. When word was finally given for them to remove the damned stuff, they would then continue to spend the next half hour debating about the drill that had just taken place. On more than one occasion, a glance was made between us, and we either laughed or shook our heads in frustration.

That's not to say that such incidents summed up the entire US Army, as I can't speak about what I don't know, but their way of going about things was definitely different to ours. And, it would also be fair to say that there were a few amongst the team who had little time for our coalition partners.

But on the whole, most of those US soldiers that I spoke to appeared to be decent enough and extremely polite, even if some were a bit over-zealous.

Word got round that we would deploy to our pre-determined locations sometime in the next few days, as the vessel with our vehicles on board was about to dock.

On the morning of the supposed move, everything was packed up and we were ready to head down to the port by 0530, only to find that, for whatever reason, not one single piece of kit was going to be unloaded for another couple of days.

"Well, bugger me with a fish-fork!" was all I could say (to coin a certain Lord Melchit's phrase). So, it was to be 'Hangerville' for a bit longer. Well, it was actually to be for one more night as it turned out. With our gear eventually loaded onto a '4-tonner' we did actually move the next afternoon.

Once down at the port we checked over our assigned vehicles – mine was at least half-decent, being a 'Wolf', with more comfortable seats, punchy engine and overall, a much better ride than a standard gas-guzzling, crappy-handling '110' Land Rover, and as a convoy, headed north for 'Camp Fox', where we would be spending the next few days. This was the home of '6 Supply Regiment RLC' and was the main logistics distribution area.

All of the in-theatre ammunition, vehicle spares and masses of other stuff were to be found there. 'Fox' was some 40km slightly south-west of Kuwait City in the Umm ar Roos region of the desert – the nearest point of the Saudi border was only around 20km further south from here too.

I was paired up with another 'Long Range Sniper' called Nick, who was to be my vehicle commander for several weeks. We'd left the port area exactly at the pre-determined time of 1500 hours, but the trip north took longer than anticipated, due to the fact that we had to follow small Tac signs that would eventually take us to 'Fox' – but not before a couple of roadside stops were made behind the lead vehicle, to check out our route.

As we skirted the suburbs of Kuwait city, heading north, I noticed a sign which simply said "Desert," accompanied by an arrow pointing straight on. The fact that the wide open desert was already visible just a little way beyond the sign, made it all the more amusing.

As we swung east, we overshot the barely visible turn-off and promptly u-turned, with a Kuwaiti Police patrol vehicle pointing us in the right direction, whilst stopping all other civilian traffic to let us on our way (not that there was that much in the way of civilian traffic). Perhaps they thought that we had some high-ranking military bod in our convoy or something. But then again, this was probably the most exciting incident to happen to them all day.

As dusk approached, we slipped off the main carriageway onto the sand track which would take us 20km out into the desert. Each driver had to ensure that a reasonable enough safe distance was kept between vehicles, due to the clouds of fine sand being thrown up, but not too far that you couldn't see the vehicle in front manoeuvring – basic good convoy skills really.

With eyes straining through windscreens, our convoy bobbed, weaved and bumped from left to right along the track where, in parts, exposed areas of bedrock rose out of the sand, requiring a little care on approach, whilst ensuring that we gave room to a stream of oncoming headlights that were making for the MSR.

Finally, we pulled up to the camp perimeter and it was now totally dark, which masked the layout of the whole area, apart from a few glimmers of light from the various areas of this tented village.

As we waited for the OC to return after having alerted the necessary personnel that 'Tiger Team' had arrived, a few of us decided to nibble on some of the contents of our ration packs, namely, the rather bland paté, spread on the accompanying crackers. This was the quickest and easiest thing to open in order to halt the rumbling in our bellies, as there was no certainty that we'd be able to get hot chow at this point.

Someone came over with the Boss and walked us in to the main parking area by torchlight. With the rovers parked up for the night, we grabbed our kit and headed off for the tent we had been allotted for a couple of nights. It turned out that we were sharing it with the camp 'Fire Defence Team' and the only thing that helped us find our billet during those night hours was the damned great fire truck parked outside. We set our camp cots up, which space-wise, were just six inches away from each other. It was definitely Sardine City but, as was becoming the norm, we just had to make the best of it – 'adapt and overcome'.

We had to leave half of our kit in the vehicles as there just wasn't enough room for it.

Up next on the agenda … Food! Apparently, we'd timed it just right, so we stumbled off over to where the mess tent had been. I say *had* been because the previous night a tremendously violent sandstorm had literally picked up both the mess tent and the welfare tent and deposited them some distance away in a tangled heap. And we're not talking about some 12ft x 12ft frame tent here, we're talking about a rather large Bedouin-style affair. All that was left were the base-boards and walkways. To add to this, half the power was out, which meant trying to get our bearings whilst wandering about with torches in hand.

The chefs were still managing to dish out hot grub from the mobile kitchen, which meant that we could get some welcome chow down our necks. It was then just a case of trying to find somewhere to stand, lean or squat whilst trying to eat it. Whatever, the hot chicken and veg in a foil container was a veritable banquet, with several rounds of bread to mop up. I remember there being very little conversation, as everyone concentrated on polishing their meal off. At least now I could get my head down without my stomach talking to me all night.

I was back in our tent trying to sort out some clean kit for the next day and having a laugh about our luxurious, well-spaced 'dez-res' when the tent flap was pulled aside and who should greet me but my other long-time TA buddy, Gordon, who'd arrived just a few days previously. He was out here with the RLC.

We smiled and shook hands. It seemed that he'd heard that 'Tiger Team' personnel had arrived and he'd found out where our tent was. We had a quick natter about the events that had brought us to this point and agreed to catch up properly over the next few days, over a brew. But as things would turn out, our paths wouldn't cross again until many weeks later…

Bed was calling by this time and the slight nip in the desert air necessitated the wearing of shorts, t-shirt and trusty old woolly hat. I then clambered into my maggot, zipped myself in, leaving my nose barely poking out. Next thing I knew, it was 6a.m.

Because the camp was not yet in a state of completion, in terms of amenities, we had to rely on the age-old water heating field equip-ment called 'Puffing Billys'. But at least these old yet reliable pieces of kit gave us hot water to wash and shave in. It was just a case of, find your spot at the trestle table, fill a bowl and away you went.

The Kuwait mornings were still rather cool a little after dawn, as you removed your t-shirt in order to have a body wash, but I could never fail to be impressed by the sight of the sun slowly rising up over the vast expanse of the desert, as it gradually warmed the air, degree by degree. "People would pay good money to do this," I thought (being in the desert, waiting for sun-up that is, not actually preparing for war). Something about this outdoor ritual reminded me of my early days camping. But with sand substituting for grass … and a hell of a lot more of it too!

7th – 15th March

It was necessary for us to have the vehicles that we had inherited, inspected before we had any hope of moving further north to 'Hammersmith' (the British forward group support operational area). The more the REME guys looked, the more faults they found. Plus the fact, that there wasn't a single vehicle that had a complete tool kit, which was a definite 'No-No'. Chris, better known as 'Geordie', for obvious reasons, was one of our two 'VM' Corporal's, who was doing his best to help sort out the vehicle document nightmare and all the other associated problems that came with the vehicles. His 'VM oppo' was – 'Taff' (again, for obvious reasons), who would eventually remain with the southern team. At one point it looked like we would have to have the REME escort all the vehicles south to Arafjan, what with half of the Rovers being in no fit state to pound the highways or the desert plains of Kuwait and beyond. This really hampered our deployment, as we needed to be embedded into our AOR as soon as possible. So, in the meantime, all would be done to at least get the rovers "passable" for use.

As we progressed with the familiarisation and use of our scanning equipment, we'd been warned that "Fox" would be calling incoming missile alert drills over the next few days … … and today was one of them.

At 4p.m. prompt, repeated blasts of vehicle horns sounded.

"I guess somebody's trying to tell us something!" I said to no-one in particular. This was a full 'IPE' drill.

It was bad enough donning a 'rezzie' in the afternoon heat, never mind the suit, over-boots and gloves. Then it was a dash for the scud trenches which the engineers had recently dug around the edges of the camp perimeter. Every time somebody jumped down into the trench that I happened to be in, half a ton of fine sand would also be kicked around, creating its own airborne problem. It was just as well that virtually all of those already in the trench had their rezzies on before being covered further with more fine dust. What's more, it stuck to sweat just lovely – just like the good old 'Blue Peter' project again, where you paste your glue onto the chosen surface and then sprinkle your glitter, sand or whatever onto it. And, *ét Voila* … .coated!

I wonder whether Saddam had ever managed to catch 'Blue-Peter' on 'Al Jazeera' – the Arab TV station, because judging by his earlier scud missiles, they looked like they were more or less home-made, that much was for sure. Not dissimilar to the space rockets that you would make out of washing-up liquid bottles when you were a kid. That is, after of course, having patiently waited and waited for your mum to finish with the damned bottle of what seemed to be never-ending washing up liquid! Except that Saddam took his 'BP' project one step further by adding a motor, filling it with propellant and explosives and letting 'em go … and in no discernible direction either.

Referring back to 'IPE', the one thing that had concerned me from the instant that I knew I was heading for the Gulf was the thought of having to remain in a 'Noddy Suit' for any amount of time (it was no doubt the same thing that countless others were thinking too). To wear full 'IPE' is draining at the best of times. But thankfully for us, on this particular occasion, the "all clear" was given after about 20 minutes.

Had the alert been called earlier in the afternoon, the heat would have made things even more uncomfortable. I definitely didn't want to have to put this gear on at the height of summer, where tempera-tures could reach in excess of 55°C. Even though NBC kit would save your life, it was no fun to wear.

Everyone peeled themselves out of their protective clothing, and allowed the rather warm afternoon breeze to dry their sweat soaked combat shirts and trousers. Even though 'Combat 95' clothing was better than the older stuff in these conditions, the much thinner and comfier desert kit would be very welcome, if indeed we ever saw it.

I pulled off my outer rubber gloves, allowing the perspiration to drip from them before stowing them in my 'rezzie' pouch, ready for the next time.

The inner cotton gloves were as sodden as a face flannel. I then rolled up my suit, glad to be out of it. And, I was in no doubt at this point that there would definitely be a next time, whether it be a drill or not.

As the sun started to rapidly set, everyone geared themselves up for evening meal, and prepared to wait in the queue that wound into the mess tent.

Food and all that it entails is a key point in any military day, no matter what the environment, operational or otherwise. And, all in all it was pretty good, despite the conditions. Once served by the 'slop-jockeys' (meant *in the best possible taste!*, as Kenny Everett used to say) everyone would slide along the wooden slatted benches and park their weapons and 'IPE' somewhere close to hand on the floor.

Looking back now, I'm surprised that there weren't many more meals launched as individuals caught their feet in someone else's rifle sling or simply tripped on the military clutter around people's feet. Of course there was always the odd accidental dig in the bonce from the end of a rifle barrel as someone tried to squeeze past with his or her hands full of weapon, IPE pouch, plate, mug and KFS. Just simply going in for meals could be quite a hazardous task in itself sometimes.

On this particular evening, it was no small wonder that meal-time conversation centred around the subject of having to don full 'IPE', and what a bitch it was to wear. But there were also a few funnies to laugh at, such as the odd individual who had got stuck getting kit on whilst trying to hop, skip and jump to some form of protective cover.

No matter what the circumstances, there was always something that could be turned from a calamitous situation to an amusing one, and if you could do that, then you would get through all this with your sanity reasonably intact.

The boss briefed us all on the latest happenings, and the team objectives, for the next few days. We then dispersed to do our own bits and pieces.

My finest and fondest moment of the day was being able to wash myself down as best as I could. This task was carried out under a star-spangled sky with a bowl borrowed from someone else and filled with three inches of barely lukewarm water.

I even managed to wash my hair, which felt so good. This simple luxury was so invigorating, but even more so, it was nice to know I'd be climbing into the old 'scratcher' knowing that given my circumstances, I was as clean as I could possibly be. One thing I'd promised myself was that if we ever got back to Arafjan, I'd throw my sleeping bag in a washing machine for good measure – and there can't have been many individuals that could have imagined being able to gain access to a washing machine at this point in time – apart that is, from the camp-bound Americans.

As I headed back for our tent in the blackness, I could make out the red-orange glow of the oil processing burn-off flares at various points on the horizon. In some ways it was quite an eerie sight, and it was one that would be simulated later, a good way north, when coalition bombs started to fall.

At home, the foreign secretary, Jack Straw, was proposing that the UN gave Iraq an ultimatum that unless it demonstrated "full unconditional, immediate and active cooperation" by March 17th, then it should be invaded.

The earlier words of the Iraqi foreign minister, Tarik Aziz, formed in my mind, "American soldiers will not be received by flowers, they will be received by bullets" – Iraqi ordnance was not going to distinguish between a soldier of the Queen and a soldier of the US of A.

Next morning, whilst shaving with the aid of my little travel mirror, I could see the desert behind me. Through a gap in the sand-berm, I could make out a number of moving shapes way out on the flat plains, and it was definitely too early for a mirage. It turned out to be a herd of camels – 'Ships of the Desert' ... more indigenous wildlife. Well, that was a first, for me anyhow.

We cracked on with the various tasks we needed to get done, not least, assisting in any way that would ensure our vehicles would be heading north to our 'AO', rather than having to return south to Arafjan with our collective tails between our legs.

In the end, enough was done to satisfy the REME guys that we could take the rovers up to area 'Hammersmith', where the support elements of '1 Div' were dug in. The OC called the Tigers together for a brief.

We were indeed heading out at 1530. Corporal Jones words ringing in my ears; "Don't panic Mr Mainwaring ... Don't Panic!"

Then, just as we'd completed the task of loading up the vehicles, another incoming alert was called – repeated vehicle horns blaring and shouts of "Gas! Gas! Gas!". "Oh Not Again! Bloody typical!"

Everyone scrambled this way and that for cover. Rather than the scud trenches, my nearest shelter was in the back of my 'Wolf', where two of the guys were already pulling on their gear in the front, which was no easy task in such confines. So I clambered in the back, with 'gasperator' already on, although I didn't have much room either, as the sweat continued to pour off me, whilst I tried to get my damned suit on. I was half way through 'suiting up' when the all clear was given.

Despite having already lost precious bodily fluid, it was such a relief knowing that we wouldn't have to spend any more time than necessary in 'Noddy Suits'. (The five minutes that we were under full NBC conditions was enough. It just seemed longer).

With gear stowed, we wasted no time in leaving 'Fox', just in case another NBC drill was called. We high-tailed it for the highway, and headed north, the 50 or so K's nearer the Kuwait-Iraq border.

As it turned out 'Hammersmith' happened to be a mere 40K's from the border, within even closer strike range of Saddam's 'Al-Samoud' and scud missiles.

I could only wonder as to the sheer scale of the coalition build-up as we passed endless convoys of US hardware: transporters loaded with M1 Abrams Tanks, Bradley Fighting Vehicles, countless trucks, Humvees and fuel tankers. And, not to forget the few convoys of British gear that were rolling north too (albeit very much in the minority – numbers wise).

Even though we kept to the speed limits, we passed the Americans as though they were standing still – their convoys were moving that slow.

So I jokingly commented to Nick that we would probably see those that we had passed, up north sometime next year.

Honestly, a snail on Sanatogen would have overtaken them. But, having said that, the whole experience was rather awe inspiring, and it made me realise that our own mini convoy of rovers heading north was part of some momentous event, and that whatever the outcome, it would long be remembered by those who played a part in it.

Within a couple of K's of the turn-off for 'Hammersmith', two large battle-damaged (courtesy of the first Gulf War) satellite dishes could be seen from the main highway.[3] These were good visual landmarks against the skyline for anyone trying to find this part of the battle-group, which was spread across a 6K grid square. As dusk fell, we followed the track into what was the home of '2 CS Regiment RLC', and once at the guarded entrance, identified ourselves and proceeded to park up. This was to be our new home for the next couple of weeks. Some 20 or so K's slightly north-east of us lay the Sabriyah Oilfield with the Ar Rawdatain Oilfield directly north of our position, and from there, it was just a matter of a hop, skip and a jump to the Iraqi border.

Once it had been established in which direction our accommodation was situated, we lugged every bit of kit we possessed across open area of the camp to our designated tent, trying to carry as much as possible in one or two trips.

---

[3] I had the story related to me of how the personnel who operated the Sat dishes, had been taken out and shot by the Iraqis during the rout of Kuwait.

As I pulled back the heavy doorway flap of our rather spacious abode, I thought "Now this is more like it". It had a boarded floor and strip lighting which required power via generators that were still being installed.

This was a massive Bedouin style tent that would probably have housed around 30 or more people quite easily.

Just outside the front opening, the base-board flooring extended for 4 or so feet, running the width of the tent and giving the impression of a wooden patio. This would become a very useful space, where we would later put our chairs outside, strip and clean weapons or just relax for a while at the end of the day. We didn't exactly have the most picturesque view from here, just the rise of the sand berm some 5 to 6 feet high. Beyond this, lay another regiment, spread out and suitably 'cammed up'.

As darkness descended, we had to rely on torchlight, and this was where head-torches were invaluable (mine had been nicked previously, prior to deployment) but that didn't matter, a hand torch would suffice. We'd been informed that the lighting would be working in a few days, fingers crossed. We had as much room as we wanted as we were the only occupants at the time. However, a little while later, a small team from '11 EOD Regiment' took up the lower third of the tent. But we still had enough space to swing several cats without them hitting each other. With camp cots, floor mats and folding chairs in position, we were as "happy as Larry". And in addition, there were power sockets too. My travel kettle + 240v + water = hot brews! It's funny how the smallest improvements within your environment can raise your comfort level dramatically. And, as any soldier knows, a brew is such a moral booster. Food on the other hand was a different matter. The chefs were doing the best they could with the only food supplies they had ... compo rations. It would take time for things to improve, but to my knowledge no-one complained (well, not loudly). We acknowledged the situation we were in and most of the time, approached it with a reasonable amount of humour.

The breakfasts were the best (or worst) meal of the day, depending on which way you viewed it. It was better just to mash everything in together – growlers, hash browns, beans and whatever else, then sprinkle a little salt, add a bit of ketchup and *Voila!* ... sorted. However, I later swore that if I never saw another compo sausage again, then that would be too soon.

Whether or not anyone liked the American cuisine back at Arafjan, and as I'd said, there were a few who didn't, you did have a choice and it was plentiful.

The massive food hall back there seemed a distant memory now.

Still, the heavily armoured boys and Infanteers on the start line further north were much less fortunate than us, so we knew better than to labour the point too much.

As with all of the other camps, the ablutions – as in portaloos or 'thunderboxes' as they were affectionately (or unaffectionately) known, were none too friendly in the building heat. Or similarly, when the desert wind picked up sufficiently to upend one or two – enough said. But, fortunately for all, they were emptied and pressure washed on a regular basis by local contractors, at least on this camp, otherwise the situation would have been unimaginable. They were also a fair distance from our tent, particularly if the need 'to go' suddenly crept up on you. So, if there was that sudden need to make a dash for it, then you could be up there with the best of the hopefuls for the 400 metres in the next Olympic Games.

But, for that 'middle-of-the-night' pee, there were the good old plastic-pipes or 'desert roses' sunk into the sand – great for guys, not for gals, obviously. And at least we had some positioned just far away enough from our tent, but no distance that required 'GPS' navigation. Many's the time when the day's water intake would have me clutching my bladder and cursing the fact that it had got me up in the pre-dawn hours.

It was as the heat stress info card read, "Pee clear once a day!   ". Yes, but why did it have to be the middle of the bloody night?!

However, things would improve further when portakabin ablution and shower units were to be installed during the following week. "Boy!" I thought, "This place just gets better and better".

It didn't really make much difference, having to have an outdoor wash and shave in a bowl near the water bowsers, but the thought of standing under a proper shower head again was one to savour. Although, I must say that, the 'Solar Shower' bags which some people were using, were a very handy make-do alternative. All that you needed to do was fill the bladder with water, leave it hanging in the sun and you had an instant shower complete with mini-sprinkler, which held more than enough water to shower with. Again, back in the UK, this was another 'must have' item which had been flying off the shelves of military kit specialists, and not surprisingly either.

Once evening meal was done with, the team then usually changed into 'trackie's at this point, which was indeed a luxury. It was just pleasant to be out of the green stuff for a little while.

This particular evening, Herbie decided that he would 'unleash' his alter-ego; 'Marcel the Barber' again. A couple of willing victims had decided to go for the 'Velcro look' and sat in the chair waiting for the hair to fly like clippings from a hedge trimmer. 'Marcel' certainly didn't disappoint, and pretty soon there were another half-a-dozen individuals sporting 'No1's' – not least our new 'EOD' buddy, Gaz. I didn't mind having my own hair short, but an all-over 'No1' was just a little too severe for me.

Once darkness descended (which came on very quickly) I grabbed a plastic bowl and wandered round to the water supply, managing to get the last vestiges of warm water from the near empty 'PB'.

It was now so dark I could barely see my hand in front of my face. But standing in a few inches of water and ladling it over my head felt wonderful. At least the daily ingress of sand was now dislodged and I was clean from head to toe, hair included (thanks to my little bottle of Johnson's Baby Shampoo). It's amazing how far you can make a couple of litres of water go.

Anyway, just as I was about to dry myself down, a diesel engine roared to life somewhere behind me and I was suddenly bathed in light as the spot-lights of a JCB forklift flashed on. What a sight I must have looked!

But hey, I didn't care, as I was clean and smelled human again.

However, in the not too distant future, the showers would be up and running.

This place was fast becoming a 5-star oasis, complete with camels, but with power pylons instead of palm trees.

Up here in the northern sector of the Kuwaiti desert, the 10 of us were a reasonably content bunch, all things considered, and made the best of our situation. Alex, our very own 'RMP', let it be known that it was his birthday. He looked positively disconsolate, no doubt with thoughts along the lines of, "What the hell am I doing out here?" mixed in with a touch of home-sickness. Anyway, in an effort to brighten the guy's spirits, both Herbie and I made him birthday cards out of the sides of the ration pack boxes, drew something amusing on them with an equally amusing bit of nonsense scribbled inside, and handed them to him. This seemed to do the trick, at least for a while anyhow. I wonder whether he ever kept his war-time memento?

The QM's department was now issuing boxes of US 'MRE's – Meals Ready to Eat (or, 'Meals Rejected by Ethiopians' as they were more affectionately known) which were to be kept in vehicles when travelling, along with copious supplies of bottled water. This meant that when we were out on the ground during the day, our lunch was sorted. It was jokingly commented upon that we, the Brit's, were a 'cheap date' with regard to the American forces. For example, they give us unlimited supplies of MRE rations and we stand shoulder to shoulder when war looms. Plain and Simple.

As we started to find our feet as to where the other parts of 'Group Support' were to be found, we got used to following the track routes to the different locations. There were British camps everywhere in this sector, including a US base located a couple of K's away.

Perimeter sand berms had been shovelled in place by Engineer bull-dozers, helping to disguise whole camps when viewed on reasonably flat desert.

But they mainly acted as a giant wind break, although there wasn't much that would stop a determined desert wind.

The Kuwait sand up here appeared to be even finer, like a talcum powder, which could find its way into every 'nook and cranny', whether it be on a vehicle or human orifice, and driving on the stuff could be an interesting experience. Four-Wheel Drive was as much a godsend out here as it was when running about the muddy training areas of the UK or Germany. Although some of the well-travelled routes were in the process of being flattened and compacted by the Engineers using road rollers on water-soaked sand. This helped in as much that it reduced a little of the bumpiness of some of the tracks around the local area between camps.

There was one particularly busy 'intersection' up here, and where the routes crossed, this was marked up as the 'Old Kent Road'.

It looked rather funny seeing signs pushed into the sand in the middle of virtually nowhere, with familiar road markings on them. This was exactly what it was like in WWII when my forbears were running around the deserts of Tunisia and other such places – some things don't change.

Over at '33 Field Hospital' we worked our way through the vehicle park, gathering the data required for HQ Land's Database. We reckoned on a few days work in this particular area of 'Hammersmith', and so kept to a similar routine. We were in two-man teams to cover certain parts of the units. Usually, someone within their 'cammed up' enclave would have a brew on the go, and we'd get the occasional invite. As far as I was concerned, it was all vital fluid intake. That's my story and the one I'm sticking to.

Besides which, it was rude not to accept anyhow! To get the data we needed, it meant clambering up, over and under cam nets and vehicles – thirsty work.

Around mid-day we'd stop for lunch at our usual 'RV' point, and break out the MRE's. In my humble opinion, the 'MRE Rat Packs' were more in interesting than ours. By using the special heater bag, it meant that you could quickly and easily have a hot meal ready in a few minutes without having to resort to the use of hexi burners. You simply tore the top off the heater bag poured in an inch of water and let the chemical reaction between liquid and heating component do its stuff, making sure of course that you had inserted the sachet meal of your choice. But, you needed to ensure that you left the heater bag bubbling away in a reasonably ventilated area, or the fumes given off were rather unbearable.

One particular favourite of the 10 available meals that I enjoyed, was the Teriyaki Chicken. The meat-loaf wasn't bad either, and there was even a pork chop in there too! It was better to swap them round or you'd soon get fed up of the same meals. Crackers, cheese paste or peanut butter usually accompanied a cookie or pound cake. One of the cheese spreads had Jalapeno's in it – which required a bottle of water on stand-by! And not to forget the ubiquitous little bottle of Tabasco sauce for those occasions when your food needed spicing up (again, the water came in very handy!)

Probably the worst of the contents for me was the powdered fruit juices, to which again, you just added water. The 'OJ' was ok, but the grape juice was yeeuck! As was the vanilla cappuccino type drink.

On the whole though, they did the job. Most of the guys ex-changed the meals with each other until they had the combination of things that they liked.

When we'd finished the tasks for the day, we headed back 'home'.

For, home was where you unfolded your camp cot. The remaining daylight allowed us time to do some basic vehicle maintenance, such as tap out any sand lodged in the air filter element, checks the levels etc, and brush the desert from the foot-wells. After which, it gave us the chance to clean weapons, sort kit, and dobi our bits and pieces over at the wash area, which in the warm Kuwaiti breeze would dry in no time on the guy ropes of the tent. The 'patio' became a little communal area of activity, with those of us going about our own admin tasks or writing 'Blueys' home. As I listened to the radio whilst stripping down my A2 ready for a de-dust, the news revealed that one of the cabinet ministers, Claire Short had threatened resignation if the PM sent the Brits to war without a second UN resolution (Robin Cook would follow a couple of days later), and France's 'head honcho', Jacques Chiraq announced he would veto any new UN resolution that authorised the use of force against Iraq. Well, all I could think was that we were teetering on the very edge, as it were. Donald Rumsfeld had stated that the US was willing to attack Iraq without the aid of the UK, but that British involvement would "be welcomed". Wasn't that nice of him! (However, the statement was later withdrawn). Turkey couldn't decide whether to allow 62,000 US troops onto its territory, which would give the US a back door through which they could attack Northern Iraq. Pakistan couldn't decide what to do and Russia would follow France's line to exercise its veto.

But that was OK. We'd just sit here in the sand whilst half the bloody world argued about it!

After a few nights where all 'in-tent' activities were conducted by torch light, the generator powered lighting was finally up and running. And within a day or so, the showers would be on-line ... Outstanding!

The cookhouse-cum mess tent doubled up as a gathering place a couple of hours or so after evening meal had finished, where it was possible to buy a few additional munchies such as Pringles, Choccy bars and the odd tin of fizzy whatever. Over time, it was possible to purchase more 'exotic' things, but these little diversions really helped, particularly when evening meal had not quite filled the void. Put it this way, the queue to buy stuff was always as long as the queue at chow time. It was great to chat, write (yet more) 'Blueys' or watch the small TV that for some reason featured films with Wesley Snipes nearly every night. I, along with everyone else, drank endless brews. Well, that's what we Brit's do isn't it? The camaraderie coupled with people's sense of humour during the run up to war was especially good. Different names by now had been adopted for the gathering place such as, 'The Naughty Hell-fire Club' or the 'Blue Oyster' (anyone knowing their 80's comedy films would identify the latter).

One morning, the 'Staffy' brought up a stash of 5.56mm rounds, along with the post. At that particular point in time, I don't know whether I cared more about having enough bullets to fill the rest of my magazines or the fact that every time the mail was delivered there was never any for me.

Anyway, we each signed for a total of 120 rounds. So, now with mags fully 'bombed up', we'd do a round check each week to ensure that we could account for every single one. Whereas when the war kicked off, we were briefed that no one would be penalised for missing rounds – as it was considered a serious offence in peace-time situations, and it was quite easy for a round to spring out of a mag, what with all the constant movement of kit. And although full magazines obviously added a little more weight to kit, it was infinitely better to have more rounds than less.

During one of the night's, a tremendous downpour came out of nowhere, but it did help to keep the top layer of desert sand damped down and relatively dust free, but only until the sun baked the surface dry again, which took no time at all really. The next time we saw any rain was during a very brief storm back at Arafjan, but I think that was it for my whole time out in the Gulf.

After another day spent roaming the areas of 'Hammersmith' and climbing in, over and under vehicles, we headed back to base, a tad more sandy than when we'd left that morning. The major difference this time, was that the shower units were up and running! There were strict showering times for males and females, but that was ok, the wait made it all the more special. So, after everything was squared away ready for the next day, everyone was on the starting blocks for the luxurious feel of running water – a sensation I'll never forget.

After evening meal which consisted of an 'all in stew' of sorts, a few of us sat on our 'patio' and gazed at an amazing sky. As the sun sank towards the horizon it appeared to be one of the nicest evenings we'd witnessed since landing in theatre … or so we thought.

As usual, we traipsed over to the 'social club', brewed and chatted in between writing blueys. Without warning, the wind suddenly picked up flapping the sides of the tent, as a fine dust started to blow in, creating a haze. This was time to abandon the 'Naughty Hell-fire Club' in rapid fashion. In the minute or two that it took for everyone to file through the canvas opening, a *shamal* – seasonal sandstorm, was raging full force. It was impossible to see and I, for one, had never experienced anything like it. It was so bad that most people could only guess as to the direction of their own tent. A few paces on and it was totally disorientating.

Even though our tent was in a dead straight line some thirty yards or so from where we now stood, we had to lead each other hand-to-shoulder like the blind leading the blind whilst trying to shield our faces and eyes. After some time we made it back, only to discover that everything inside; beds, kit, absolutely everything was coated in a fine sand. I'd already started with the 'Kuwaiti Cough', and what with all the fine sand being kicked up, it just exacerbated the problem. The only thing we could all do was 'batten down the hatches' and climb into our 'scratchers'.

I put my woolly hat on and pulled it all the way over my face like a sightless balaclava. It was the only way to filter out any further dust.

The next morning, I literally felt like I'd swallowed half the desert and was desperately in need of anything that would suppress this damned cough (which was the same story for hundreds of other individuals).

As the team prepared to move out into our AOR, the wind was beginning to build again. There were three of us requiring some sort of medication and headed for one of the med stations – to find … NO SUPPLIES!

Oh well, I'd just have to cough myself stupid.

Out in the open spaces of the desert, as we attempted to get through the day's tasks it became harder and harder, what with the sand being whipped up. Shemaghs were always on hand. One or two of the guys had proper ski masks (another item of much needed kit), whilst the remainder of us struggled on with sunglasses for eye protection. By early afternoon, 'sand stopped play'. Due to the fact that smoking (for obvious reasons) was not allowed anywhere near the tents, taped off smoking areas were dotted around the perimeter of all camps. This was the kind of day that definitely required goggles or a ski-mask, with Shemagh wrapped around the bonce in order to be able to venture out and about without being engulfed in sand. It made for a strange, but interesting sight to see these guys standing or squatting in one of the designated areas, whilst trying to have a smoke with sand and dust whipping around them. During the worst moments of the desert *shamals*, sky and ground were virtually indistinguishable, with your surroundings (or whatever you could see of them) taking on an other-wordly 'Mars-like' red/orange atmosphere. But the other thing which fortunately, we hadn't (and wouldn't experience, thank goodness) where the desert rains which could turn the sand into a nightmarish quagmire. The desert storms had to be experienced to be believed. Certainly, over the next couple of weeks, some of the worst *shamals* for many, many years would hit the region.

It was as if Saddam himself had personally summoned the storm to hinder the coalition – and given that he considered himself all-powerful, that was probably what he would have his loyal supporters believe – that it was of his doing. It was in conditions like these that the modified 'chair bags' came in very handy, as they minimised the amount of daily sand and dust getting into the working parts of our personal weapons. I simply dropped my A2 into the bag, pulled the draw-chord tight, and slung the carrying strap over my back … sorted. Whilst out in the areas around 'Hammersmith' this practise was OK, where there was no immediate threat, but once over the border in Iraq, that was a different matter, as weapons would have to be 'locked and loaded', to borrow US terminology, in case there was a need to quickly react to any given situation.

Word had gone around like wild fire that there was now a seventy two hour run-down to 'kick off'. This was really starting to get serious now. But still, most people remained quite chilled about the whole thing, outwardly anyway.

It was, no doubt, a slightly more-tense situation for those, further north, who were ensconced with the forward battle group, watching the crisis clock tick down to zero. And, the French were still adamant that they would not form part of the coalition against Saddam. In the meantime, it seemed likely that we would get back to Arafjan for a brief spell. We each exchanged glances and read thoughts out loud; "Subway! Pizza Hut! Burger King!"

It was now the fifteenth of March and I realised that it had been exactly fifteen years to the day that I'd been attested and signed on the dotted line as a 'Territorial Soldier' – "Just another day in paradise!" I thought. There were probably many TA soldiers who had never envisaged the prospect of actually going to war. There were contrasting views on the matter. For some, this was the ultimate 'test' as it were – a pinnacle for which their military (and also many full-time regular soldiers) career's had been heading. That's what a committed soldier trains for at the end of the day, even though many may never have conceived of a war happening during their time of service.

But for other individuals, this was no doubt the furthermost thought from their mind, and quite possibly enough for them to literally hand in their kit and sign off. I suppose that for me, it was just something that I had to do – one way or another it was there in the genes, regardless of my never having joined the 'Regulars'.

So, on this fifteenth anniversary, another equally important event happened … my very first letter from home arrived. After having watched and waited, (for about three weeks) as mail from Blighty was handed out to everyone, barring me, made for a rather disheartening experience.

It reminded me a little of the situation I'd found myself in when I was serving in Cyprus, just prior to the Christmas, some 15 months before. A few of the TA guys in my troop had been sent letters from their CO's and other interested parties who wished them well, whilst one or two others received Regimental Christmas cards from their parent units. And, what seasonal greetings did I get? … Bugger All! It really teed me off, simply because I was the only individual from my Regiment who at that time (as far as I'm aware), happened to be away on an operational tour … out of sight out of mind, I suppose. I really felt let down over the lack of correspondence between the Regiment and myself, and yet here I was again, proudly flying the flag for my unit. Later, when the war-fighting phase in Iraq had eased off, I decided I'd take up the gauntlet and make the first move again, whereupon I penned a 'Bluey' to one of the officers, who didn't even have the good manners to reply, so maybe my criticism wasn't entirely without merit. This is not meant to come across as a grumbling session, but a little acknowledgment to reinforce the fact that what you are doing, particularly in a time of war, carries some pride with your Regiment. And, as only those who have endured long periods of time away from home on operations will appreciate, each and every additional bit of post is such a morale booster.

However, gripes aside, right at this moment in time, it appeared that the 'curse' regarding my non-receipt of post was now broken.

As the latest bulletins regarding the build-up to war became available, I caught up on the everyday news reports to find that one of my all-time hero's had died. Barry Sheene, the twice World 500cc Motorcycle Champion had passed away after losing his battle with throat and stomach cancer. He was only 52. He was known just as well for his two spectacular crashes at Daytona in '75' and Silverstone in '82' and, even more-so for the amazing recovery that he made from both. Barry was a magnificent ambassador, which did no end of good for the sport, not least in increasing its popularity. I had seen him race on a number of occasions and was always impressed by his prowess and style on the race track. Even when he was first diagnosed with cancer, in his typical 'cheeky cockney' style, he said, "Although this is a complete pain in the arse, it happens to a lot of people, and a lot of people get over it". The world had lost an outstanding sporting icon.

16th – 23rd March

The sand storm of the last couple of days had abated slightly, and with a little less dust blowing around, visibility improved too. We definitely didn't want a repeat of the first night that the storm kicked in, that was something else, and it was certainly an experience that will live long in the memory.

As the clock ticked away, air and road activity appeared to have increased, and was obviously more noticeable at night. As I lay in my pit in the total darkness, complete with woolly hat rolled down to my nose, I could here the rumbling of vehicle convoys on Kuwait's MSR, interspersed with the sound of all manner of aircraft flying at different altitudes, but all on a trajectory heading north. There's something different about the sound of military vehicles and aircraft heading for their objective – not like trying to get to sleep in the vicinity of a motor way or civilian airport. It's hard to describe really, but I suppose in a way it felt comforting. Later, over at Ali Al Salem AB, we'd have GR4 Tornadoes to lull us to sleep … .or maybe not.

The British Prime Minister had met with his Spanish counterpart and George 'W' in the Azores to prepare for a crucial debate with the Security Council. The President announced that the outcome of the Iraq crisis would be decided within a few days. But after ninety minutes of talking between those present, it became obvious to all concerned that there was actually little left to discuss. The meeting ended with the following statement from the US President, "Tomorrow is a moment of truth for the world. Many nations have voiced a commitment to peace and security and now they must demonstrate that commitment in the only effective way, by support-ing the immediate and unconditional disarmament of Saddam Hussein".

It appeared that he now believed that war was almost inevitable.

Saddam and his sons had been given a final ultimatum: to leave Iraq within 48hours. But, the ever defiant Saddam stated that if Iraq were attacked, he would take the war to anywhere in the world, "wherever there is sky, land or water".

At the various units we'd been visiting in recent days, the yell of "Gas! Gas! Gas!" was becoming more and more frequent with 'gasperators' now being donned as though it was second nature.

Another key point which marked this period of time was when the order had been given for everyone to be issued with 'Combo Pens' and Morphine Ampules, which were to be carried everywhere from this moment on (or until word came down from higher up the chain of command). 'Combo Pens' as every modern Soldier knows, are an integral part of the 'NBC' survival package. In simple terms, these are to be used when an individual believes that he or she is suffering the incapacitating effects (or someone else spots the tell-tale signs) after having been contaminated by a nerve agent, which may have been released by ariel bomb or shell for example. Once ready to use, the 'Combo Pen' needle is required to be jabbed into the thigh (for a slow count of ten), where the Atropine is then released into the system. If the symptoms still persist, then only a maximum of three can be administered every fifteen minutes thereafter. The down-side of course is that if an individual has mistakenly assumed that he or she is suffering such effects and injects the Atropine, then 'Atropine poisoning' can occur, which would then, most probably entail the individual being 'cas-evac'd to where an antidote could be adminis-tered. All in all, not a very comforting thought really.

And so, the simple act of having been given these particular pieces of kit, confirmed further, people's suspicions to the fact that the blue touch-paper could be ignited at any given time now. We did wonder how many people would mistakenly jab themselves over the coming weeks when reduced to "panic" mode. I did hear later, that some officer had been the first to accidentally inject himself, and was believed to have been ok afterwards.

But then again, it was most probably just hear-say – 'mountains out of molehills', or, as per our current situation, 'sand dunes out of shell scrapes'.

Anything's possible in a time of war I suppose.

Just over the other side of the sand berm, 'Gimpys' could be heard rattling away on a makeshift firing range as their gunners prepped and zeroed these time-served weapons. They are a formidable piece of firepower, capable of fast accurate fire up to 800 metres in its light role, and up to 1800 metres in its 'SF' or 'Sustained Fire' role, and can also be used in an anti-aircraft role, as was so aptly demonstrated during the Falklands conflict. This was, and is still the main fire support weapon for any infantry section, but it is not without its logistical problems in that it requires countless amounts of heavier, belted, 7.62mm ammunition, plus spare barrels to accompany it.

A number of the units out here had the Minimi machine gun at their disposal, which offered a lightweight, robust, and highly efficient alternative that used British Army standard 5.56mm ammo (same as the A2), but with 200 rounds under-slung in a plastic box, or alternatively, it could be belt fed. Not only that, but it had an interchangeable housing that could accommodate American M16 magazines. Overall, it was a nifty bit o' kit.

Everyone was in a state of alertness and preparing for what lay ahead, despite the fact that we were not exactly at the "pointy end" of things, although we were well within range of ballistic missiles, should any be launched in our general direction. And at this stage, nothing could be ruled out.

Personal weapons were kept as dust and sand free as possible, with just the right amount of oil coating the working parts (in line with SOP's for this kind of climate) but it appeared that's just what our weapons required to prevent stoppages.

Most of the camps spread across Kuwait by now had a satellite TV set-up, making current events seem even stranger, when watching them unfold on screen. This was an even larger media 'circus' (I use the term loosely), than the first Gulf conflict. This would be the first major war of the 21st century, and to record it as it unfolded, over 700 journalists were embedded with many units, with access (security permitting) to all areas all the way up to command level. So, no doubt, the folks at home would be getting wall to wall coverage of the war, with many families of serving soldiers leaving the news channels on '24/7'.

Where possible, I and my fellow Tigers gleaned as much info as we could, when we could. And right at this moment, the hourly news reports were stating that "war was imminent" with or without a UN resolution.

It was around this time that all British and American Nationals were being moved out of Kuwait, pronto.

As we roamed the northern desert of Kuwait, moving onto each unit within our current AOR, the daytime temperatures were steadily rising.

In other words, it was starting to get damned hot! We simply couldn't wait for the first hint of desert kit coming our way. Whilst we operated in one particular area, our vehicles all converged on our usual RV spot for lunch and despite the baking heat, the good ol'e MRE's were still going strong.

Wherever we would stop for lunch, Jacko our resident 'Light Inf' member, would jump out and crack open his 'Hexy' burner to get his brew on. Now, there was no problem with that whatsoever, and I loved a brew as much as the next person, but we were usually near enough to a unit to be able to literally go and politely cadge a brew – but he seemed to get a kick out of it anyway.

The OC and Sgt Major rocked up to brief us with regard to the next few days tasks. Two small teams were to head off to Shuwaikh sea port and Ali Al Salem AB for a couple of days, leaving the rest of us to do the business up here. It was planned that we would then RV with the whole of the team at Arafjan, in three days time, which would give everyone a chance to catch up and generally chew the fat. It looked like I was staying up here with the slightly decreased team – "Maleesh" (never mind, it didn't really matter).

For reasons that I couldn't fathom, I liked being in and around the desert. Maybe it was the open spaces, I'm not sure. And to this day, I can't really explain why ... ..I just liked the desert. Although, I may have thought differently about it if I'd experienced the kind of conditions in which you could find yourself, some way north in the Iraqi desert – where the winter rain could turn the sand into a muddy quagmire, and making things an absolute nightmare.

One particular day, I did have quite a fortuitous bit of luck with regard to another much needed piece of kit – something else that we'd been told would be issued. I'd just tipped out the contents of our make-shift litter bin into the camp skip when I spotted a Ski mask lying amongst the rubbish. Now, I'm not prone to rooting around skips like a 'skip rat' (or as someone else would say, a 'skip licker'). As I retrieved the mask I thought, surely nobody would throw it away without good reason, and so I figured that it must have been unserviceable. However, upon further inspection, the only damage that I could see was a few minor scratches on the lenses, but were completely intact. So, I gave them a wash and they were 'A1'. Needless to say, that from then on, I didn't have to worry too much about the occasional face full of sand, now that my 'mince pies' were well and truly protected. That was definitely a piece of luck. This was not unlike the later episode when I lost a pair of sunglasses, only to literally stumble across another pair out in the desert near one of the units that we were visiting.

That night we were unofficially informed that the clock was now counting down to a 48hour deadline, so we watched, listened and waited.

It was a perfectly clear night with a full moon ... a 'bombers moon', to coin the phrase. It was after I'd been asleep for maybe a couple of hours that I woke with a start (as did Herbie in the next cot) as a low flying jet thundered overhead. We both sat bolt upright, still in half sleep, half panic mode as I automatically flicked on my torch, imagination running wild and muttering exclamations of

"What the hell was that?!" Although it was an over-exaggeration, to a half-awakened brain it sounded like something as big as a B52 bomber flying extremely low. Whatever, it was enough to give us both a start. As our heart rates returned to normal we settled down again in the darkness. The memory of the look on Herbie's face was enough to make me chuckle as I tried to get off to sleep again.

Next day, we headed off across the desert to where the remainder of '16 Air Assault Brigade's light, tracked armour was to be found, in order for us to get the vehicle data we needed. After having clambering up and down on a few dozen pieces of armour, with IPE gear to hand and A2's slung across our backs, we were glad when we'd finally finished our sweep of the area and headed back 'home'.

As we gave the sentry our half of the password (which changed constantly) to get back into camp, we could see that a fair proportion of the unit based here had moved on.

So with my A2 stripped and cleaned, followed by a 'de-sanding' in the shower, we made ready for the gastronomic delights of the mess tent.

Only this evening, the meal was a bit of a revelation. Instead of the usual, "we've disguised and re-hashed the compo as much as we can" kind of meal, we were greeted with a little piece of steak and chicken, which had most of us rather bemused. I wasn't the only person to wonder as to whether there was something that the big 'they' were not telling us.

Thoughts of 'last supper' crossed the mind. Feed the boy's up, sort of thing. Well, whatever, it was better than 'all-in' stew. Anyway, now that I was fed and watered, I was a happy bunny. I was about to head across to the 'Blue Oyster' with the rest of the Tigers, as two 'A10 Tank-Busters' flew over, racing north. Next minute, the damned alarm went off. But fortunately for us all, this was a short drill, without the need to 'suit up'.

"Phew! Valuable brew time could have been lost there!"

To add to the realisation that serious events were about to happen in the very near future, the order came round from on high, that 'NAPS' tablets were to be taken from 2200 hours. We all looked at each other with a kind of "Oh, what next?" expression. This was just a little something else to add to the concoction of chemicals floating through our systems. Not to mention the Anthrax booster jab that we were booked in to have, over at '4 GS (Group Support) Medical Regiment' the following night. Oh, and I nearly forgot about the Paludrine and Nivaquine anti-Malerial tablets too.

With war now imminent, the UN now ordered the withdrawal of its weapons inspectors from Iraq, as there was serious risk of them being taken hostage if they remained in situ. There was now no question of whether there was to be a war, just a matter of when. A peaceful solution to this crisis was so remote, it was non-existent.

Late into the evening, around 50 dhows had arrived in the waters of the Gulf from southern Iraq, in somewhat suspicious circumstances. And, given the fact that the fear of suicide bombers were well founded, warships intercepted them to carry out search and seize operations, where fortunately, nothing of significance was found. They were released to go about their normal business. But it was a case of, "better safe than sorry".

Herbie, being a west-country lad and all, just happened to be singing some familiar little ditty which I'd not heard for a very long time. I said, "That's an old Wurzels tune ain't it?" "Aaar, that it be," he replied. From that moment on, Wurzel tunes sort of became anthems for the rest of the tour. According to the 'Herbmeister', it was actually quite hip down in the west country to still be into their music. And, they'd apparently played his rugby club in more recent times too. So if you wanted to lighten things up a little, then just start singing a Wurzel tune. I'd later find myself uttering the words, "Oh Blackbird oi'll 'ave ee!" from another of their hits.

Anything that made us laugh and kept our spirits up was most welcome. Some while later, someone would end up sending him a 'Wurzels' CD at his request. That would definitely keep us amused.

4. Out of Time

Wed 19th March

It was 0600 and time for another bloody NAPS tablet. So now, all of us had to ensure that we took the damn things as part of a strict eight hourly regime until further notice. If you missed taking one, then you were not fully protected. If you took two tablets at too close a time-span then you were quite possibly open to a number of side effects. The least of which, was a feeling of nausea. How lovely!

Anyway, with breakfast out of the way, we were kitted up and ready to roll. All of a sudden, a *shamal* picked up without warning. One minute the skies were beautiful and clear, and the next, a wave of dust rolled in across the desert like a *Tsunami*, completely engulfing the camp. And, as if to make matters worse, a 'gasperaor' drill was called again. … only this would be the last. Next time the alert was sounded for 'incoming' it would be for real! The only good thing was that the 'gasperator' kept the fine sand out.

In spite of the storm, it was decided that we would make an attempt get to one of our intended locations, although a few K's out from camp, the storm was even worse. We were driving with respirators on, as the all-clear had still not been given when we left camp. With the decision made to U-turn, we crawled back to base to do some 'admin'. (The all-clear would eventually be given some two hours later). It was a relief to take 'gasperators' off, even after only a couple of hours. There may be those out there that take great pleasure in the wearing of tight, rather uncomfortable rubber pieces of kit, but I'm not one of 'em.

Later, with gear stowed again and the Kuwaiti sand cleared from personal weapons, we waited for the storm to recede, whilst attempting to get any information from the 'World Service' on the radio. After evening meal, we headed off in the direction of '4 Group Support' for our 1930 hour appointment with a needle … the dreaded Anthrax booster.

Once we'd been inoculated again, our small convoy set off again into the now pitch black desert night. Fortunately, we only had a couple of K's to travel along our much used and now familiar route. The rovers virtually knew their own way back without a driver at the wheel. But it's a strange experience, driving in a totally barren, pitch black landscape. With regard to the jabs we'd received, it was now just a matter of waiting to see if there would be any reaction to the booster.

When we finally made it back to our tent, Gaz, one of our '11 EOD Regiment' neighbours informed us that he'd heard that the US had started bombing specific areas to breach Iraqi defences, although according to the later news bulletins, war had "not officially started".

In an attempt to reassure the people of Iraq, thousands of leaflets would be dropped over the populace, bearing the message that only military targets would be sought, and that all attempts would be made to avoid civilian casualties. This was no doubt, a bit of 'hearts and minds'.

As I woke to take my NAPS tablet, I could hear the news reports on a radio stating that at around 0230 hours GMT, some ninety minutes after Saddam's ultimatum had expired, our warships off the coast had launched around 40 missiles as the US launched a series of air strikes which had struck military targets in and around Baghdad. Although as yet, a full scale bombardment had not taken place. As we listened intently, there were uncorroborated reports that the Iraqi Prime Minister – Tariq Aziz, wanted to defect, along with some of the Iraqi military, who were interested in becoming part of a force to help remove Saddam, and that Saddam now wanted Tariq executed.

Everyone now had something tangible to talk about over breakfast. There was no pondering, no ifs, no buts, no maybes. The clock had counted down to zero and could not now be turned back.

Her Majesty the Queen later issued a message for everyone serving out here, which read:

> "At this difficult moment in our nation's history, I would like to express my pride in you, the British Service and civilian personnel deployed in the Gulf, and in vital supporting roles in this country and further afield. I have every confidence in your professionalism and commitment as you face the challenges before you. Especially for those of you now waiting to go into action, may your mission be swift and decisive, your courage steady and true, and your conduct in the highest traditions of your Service both in waging war and bringing peace. My thoughts are with you all and with your families and friends who wait at home for news and pray for your safe return".

It was impossible not to feel a sense of pride after hearing the Sovereign deliver that short but uplifting message. Chests were fit to bust like pigeons puffing themselves up to show off to their potential mating partners, which is probably how the men of the '1st Royal Irish Regiment' (a major component of '12 Armoured Brigade') felt when their Commanding Officer, Lieutenant Colonel Tim Collins addressed his men just hours before they pushed their way through the sand ramparts and on into Iraq. I also thought it was a damned inspiring address, made all the more impressive because he'd given it from the heart.

The following is most, if not all of that very speech:

> "We are going to Iraq to liberate not to conquer. We will not fly our flags in their country. We are entering Iraq to free a people – and the only flag which will be flown in that ancient land is their own. Show respect for them.
>
> The enemy knows this moment is coming too. Some have resolved to fight and others wish to survive. Be sure to distinguish between them.
>
> There are some who are alive at this moment who will not be alive shortly. Those who do not wish to go on that journey, we will not send; as for the others, I expect you to rock their world. Wipe them out if that is what they choose. But if you are ferocious in battle, remember to be magnanimous in victory. Iraq is steeped in history; it is the site of the Garden of Eden, of the Great Flood and the birthplace of Abraham. Tread lightly there.
>
> In the near future you will see things that no man could pay to see, and you will have to go a long way to meet a more decent, generous and upright people than the Iraqis. You will be embarrassed by the hospitality they will offer you, even though they have nothing. Don't treat them as refugees in their own country. Their children will be poor. In years to come they will know that the light of liberation in their lives was brought by you. If there are casualties of war, then remember that when they got up this morning and got dressed they did not plan to die this day. Allow them dignity in death. Bury them with due reverence and properly mark their graves.
>
> It remains my foremost intention to bring every single one of you out alive. But there may be those among us who will not see the end of this campaign. We will put them in their sleeping bags and send them back. There will be no time for sorrow.
>
> The enemy should be in no doubt that we are his nemesis and that we are bringing about his rightful destruction. There are many

regional commanders who have stains on their souls and they are stoking the fires of Hell for Saddam. He and his forces will be destroyed for what they have done to their people. As they die, they will know that it is their deeds have brought them to this place. Show them no pity.

It is a big step to take another human life. It is not to be done lightly.

I know of men who have taken life needlessly in other conflicts. I can assure you that they live with the mark of Cain upon them.

If someone surrenders to you, remember that they have that right in international law, and ensure that one day they go home to their family.

The ones who wish to fight ... .well, we aim to please. Remember, however that if you harm your regiment or its history by over-enthusiasm in killing, or cowardice, know it is your family who will suffer. You will be shunned unless your conduct is of the highest order, for your deeds will follow you down through history. We will bring shame on neither our uniform nor our nation.

As for chemical and biological weapons, I believe the threat is very real.

We know that the order to use these weapons has been delegated down to regional commanders. That means he has already taken the decision to use them. Therefore it is not a question of if, it is a question of when they attempt this. If we survive the first strike, we will survive the attack.

As for ourselves, let's bring everyone home safely and leave Iraq a better place for us having been there. Our business now is north. Good luck".

Some fine words that will, no doubt be long remembered in the annals of military history, that have since found a place on one of the walls of the White House. This battlefield speech will stand alongside Lincoln's Gettysburg address and Churchill's wartime rhetoric. (Abraham Lincoln actually thought that few would remember his speech). But, Collins had now written a simple and stirring piece that the 21st-century soldier could identify with.

It was around this time that I happened on a rather good newsletter that was doing the rounds – 'The Sandy Times'. It gave brief reports on all Gulf related happenings which reflected all three services, along with published letters and news from home, cartoons, jokes and other bits and pieces.

I found it was a great little read, although some of the published messages tugged at the heart strings a little. But, the other interesting thing about it, was that the first issue was numbered '26', This was because it had last been circulated to my predecessors who had been deployed out here in 1991 on 'Op Granby' – the British phase of the Gulf War, with the last issue of the campaign finishing on issue '25' … obviously. So, for however long that the current war would last, then this publication would continue each week until the end of the conflict. Therefore, it was generally hoped that there wouldn't be too many successive issues. (As it would turn out, issue '33' would be the final one) This was the 'ST' front page at the start of the war;

This particular day, we were heading out to '23 Engineer's location where we had cleared our task in rapid fashion, despite the numerous incoming missile warnings that 'stopped play' every so often. 'Gasperators' were on and off several times over a period of a couple of hours. Intermittent news bulletins had informed us that a couple of missiles had landed north of Kuwait City, and so the alert state was heightened even more. Still, everyone went about their business with as much normality as possible. Shortly after, we heard the unmistake-able sound of a missile impacting somewhere in the desert, and not that far by all accounts – within a 'K' or two of our position.

Where the incoming had hit, it was believed that around a dozen people had been injured, within the vicinity of 'Camp Rhino'. We'd been told to stay put and wait for further orders. Along with a fair number of others, we were in the mess tent at the time, so in between each alert, we brewed and followed events on satellite TV. Most people were in pretty good spirits and reasonably chilled out, all things considered. Although many individuals were concerned that until confirmed otherwise, that the incoming ballistics may be carrying chemical or biological 'nasties' – which did give people something to think about. But I don't recall anyone mentioning it or getting into any kind of in-depth discussion about it at the time.

The bulletin being relayed on the screen made events seem even more surreal. A female news reporter was doing her best to give a live report whilst wearing a respirator. The reporter and the TV crew were probably no more than a few K's away and were reporting on the very missile that had just hit. It did make for a bizarre moment, and the irony of the whole situation was not lost on us … sitting here in 'rezzies', watching someone trying to give a news report whilst wearing one as there was 'incoming' somewhere in-between … a very strange situation indeed.

I remember declaring to one of the other 'Tigers' that I wouldn't have wanted to have been anywhere else at that particular time. In retrospect, it probably comes across as being a very odd thing to have said, but I suppose it was a case of 'you had to have been there at the time'. It later brought to mind an incident as told to me by one of the other 'Tigers' back at Arafjan. Once the threat of 'real' incoming became apparent, the subsequent alerts had a few of our US coalition Cousins back in 'Hanger 10' getting rather jittery to say the least – but then again, they didn't have the world renowned 'stiff-upper lip' to bring to the fore in a crisis, did they!

Anyway, when we finally got the ok to move out, we headed back to base. We'd only just got back in and parked up, and just as I was releasing my weapon from the weapon rack, the alert was given for further 'incoming'.

I, along with the rest of the 'Tigers, just grabbed our NBC kit and basically dived into the scud trench, just a matter of a few yards away. Our 'rezzie's were already on, as people came scurrying from all directions, making a bee-line for the same trench. Within a minute it was 'sardine city', which made it even harder to get on the over-trousers, boots and smock. With the close proximity of bodies, I'm surprised that I managed to actually get any of my gear on at all. The amount of dust that had been kicked up by people jumping in beside us didn't help either. We were now also having to wear body armour and helmets until told otherwise. So, bit by bit, virtually all of our protective kit was being worn (the level of threat dictated the protective dress state). But everyone did the 'buddy-buddy' bit by making sure that 'rezzies' and hoods were sealed correctly. Twenty minutes later, with no 'bangy' things having landed within our immediate vicinity, we were given the all clear. It was then, back to business as usual.

Reports were coming in that "the main use of force would be unleashed" within 48hours. A lot of people were thinking, "Let's get this sorted, so that we can get on and do what we need to do, then go home!"

The US had intensified their barrage on Iraq as our boys, a little further north of us, headed through the border.

Later in the evening, as things started to escalate, further scud attack warnings had us diving for our trench, just to the rear of our tent (whatever the 'incoming' was, most referred to them as 'scuds'). We again ran and scrambled like lemmings for the edge of the trench, hopped on the sand-step and touched bottom. In no time at all we were standing room only again. "I'm sure we've been here before?" I remarked to no one in particular.

Once the dust cleared and everyone had started to regulate their breathing inside their 'rezzies', things calmed down again and we watched and waited. People were looking at their neighbour and asking their compadrés in muffled tones, "(so and so) is that you?". In the dark and fully suited up it wasn't the easiest thing to recognise a buddy – unless, of course, you knew for sure who was next to you, or knew their build, height, or could see their name on their suit. Despite the fact that things were happening for real, as with our earlier encounter with 'incoming' over at '23 Engineer's location, nobody seemed to get into a blind panic, and if anything the whole situation was handled with a sense of fatalistic humour. That's not to say that people were blasé about what was happening around us, but things were treated with the usual sense of typical 'Britishness'.

To be honest, if something had impacted somewhere in the vicinity, then we would more than likely have been quite safe from the blast. But, we had no means of protection from a lucky (or very unlucky for us) direct hit, which would have finished us all off. After all, we were crammed into a reasonably small space so it would have been "Goodnight Vienna!" but *ce'st la guerre*.

We had a military photographer in with us, who was snapping away trying to capture the moment, but in typical fashion, as he aimed his camera for the 'money-shot', guys were doing their best to pull faces inside their respirators – which is not an easy thing to achieve. Probably crossed eyes were all he would see through the viewfinder with, no doubt, a fair few exposures of people giving the camera 'the finger' or other self-explanatory hand gestures.

After, I don't know how long, a lone figure came out of the darkness and approached our trench to announce, "OK GUYS, ALL CLEAR!" which was followed instantly by a muffled cheer from inside a dozen or so respirators. It was a most gratifying feeling, is all I can say, but the common sentiment amongst us all was that this was going to be one hell of a long night … and we were not wrong.

Back in the land of 'Snoozeville', most of us had only been asleep for an hour or two when the next alert came, at around midnight, followed by another at 2am. In the end we all decided to keep most of our kit on whilst trying to get the remaining few hours of sleep. I did, however, remove my boots, as I needed to let my poor feet breathe for a few hours. However, some while later, I awoke with a start as I thought I heard what sounded like the 'crump' or 'thud' of two impacts, somewhere out in the desert. And, I wasn't alone in this thought either. Herbie also reckoned he'd heard the same thing. But to this day we don't know for sure what it was. We did find out however, that the Patriot missile batteries had been successful in knocking out about 99% of all the incoming ballistics that were headed in the general direction of Kuwait City and its surrounding areas. There left, of course, the other 1% (give or take) that made it through. Most of the Iraqi missiles were taken out at extremely high altitude and at transonic speed by any one of the 27 PAC-3 Patriot batteries stationed in Kuwait, Bahrain, Qatar, Saudi Arabia and Jordan, so there was a considerable amount of aerial protection for the numerous troop bases dotted around Theatre.

Perhaps the sounds we heard in the small hours were the Patriot batteries south of us at Kuwait International letting loose on some of Saddam's incoming, although I did learn later that a few missiles had impacted in empty areas of the desert.

My southern-based Tiger buddy Tony (not the animated character on the front of a packet of Frosties) informed me much later that he and some of the other guys had ended up spending three "hellish" days in 'Noddy Suits' because of the alert state down there. In the end they were all for taking their chances without their suits, such was their level of discomfort. This was no doubt one of those experiences that remain long in the memory, hopefully never to be repeated.

It was strange that despite being that much nearer the border and within easier range of any possible missiles that could be launched from within Iraq, we never had to wear our suits for anything like that amount of time and, fortunately for us, we wouldn't be required to for the rest of the campaign, either.

Six a.m. came all too soon. I yawned like crazy as I swung my feet out and over the edge of my camp cot and carried out my morning ritual of upending my boots (as I would do for the rest of the tour, especially when out in the 'boonies') just in case some nasty little desert critter had decided to find itself a home for the night. I didn't fancy the thought of my foot contacting the sole of my boot with the sickening crunch of something in between, or indeed the new tenant trying to repel my size-9 with its own weapon system – i.e. a sharp tail, fangs or otherwise. This was something else that I remember my father telling me of his time in the deserts of North Africa during World War II: "You always up-ended and tapped your boots first thing before putting them on again."

This was the morning that the remaining six of us were to head out for Arafjan to RV with the rest of the team and, despite the much disrupted night's sleep, we packed up all our gear in no time and left an empty space as though we'd simply never been there. It was hard in a way, having to leave our corner of the tent that we'd called home for a little while. We'd all got used to being up here in the desert and were getting rather settled. But then again, this wasn't Butlins. I had already started to lose count of the times we had 'bugged out' from different locations. And this was just the start. We were like wandering nomads, akin to the Bedouin. I complained that we'd moved ourselves and our kit "more times than Pickfords have moved bloody houses!"

Anyway, after a quick breakfast we made for the highway and pointed the vehicles south for Arafjan.

Unlike one of our earlier trips, there was hardly any traffic on the highways. We passed maybe one or two US vehicle convoys, heading in the opposite direction, but certainly nothing on the scale of what we'd seen during the previous two weeks. The only thing missing here was some tumbleweed blowing across our route, just like a scene from a 'Spaghetti Western'.

An hour or so later we were back in 'Hangerville' but this time there were a lot less bods around. Arafjan appeared a different place and, to add insult to injury, all the 'munchies' outlets were closed until further notice. When we'd been informed earlier that we would most likely end up back there for a spell, most of us had drooled at the thought of a juicy cheeseburger and the hospitality of the American cookhouse. Boy were we ever wrong! Due to restrictions on food for a while, everyone had to rely on MREs again. Even the thought of a salad had kept me going, which until now, hadn't been a problem. But now what with our current state of affairs and the constant missile alerts we were getting, we all wished that we were back up at good old 'Hammersmith', even though we were considerably nearer the danger of 'incoming'.

With the exception of a few of the team, the whole of Tiger had converged on Arafjan and, although it wasn't a patch on the last time that we'd RV'd here, it was good to see the rest of the guys for a while and catch up and compare notes, as it were. Tony and I had talked about keeping an eye open for our third 'Musketeer', Gordon, who, around this time and unbeknown to us was a good way north. We wondered what tales we'd have to discuss over a 'cool one' when this was all over, providing, of course, that we all got back home safely and in one piece.

'A' Day had started with a full-on sea and air attack – said to be one of "shock and awe," to quote George 'W', although how much shock and awe the Iraqi armed forces were experiencing, I'm not sure. However, the initial aim of the onslaught was to achieve "rapid dominance" both psychologically and militarily. In essence, 'Shock and Awe' is the modern day equivalent of the highly effective Blitzkrieg strategy used by the Germans during World War Two, but obviously featuring today's much more lethal and high-tech weapons.

By this point, the coalition had now pushed a hundred miles into Iraq.

News came through to us that 9 of the 500 oil wells had been sabotaged with others said to be booby-trapped. Our British Marines of '3 Commando Brigade', with U.S. Marines under its command had now taken the Al-Faw Peninsula and pushed inland. (where we '1 Div Tigers' would end up) was not yet clear of resistance, although it was believed that what resistance remained, it was only minor. The effect of the previous leaflet drops with the message of fair treatment for those who surrendered looked like they had started to pay dividends, as there were groups of Iraqi soldiers throwing down their weapons and giving up the fight, but that didn't mean to say that it was a total 'cake walk' – there were still some very determined Saddam loyalists who would not give ground easily. But on the other side of the coin, we also heard that Iraqi Officers were threatening their subordinates with death, should they attempt to flee or simply surrender. So, despite the advances being made by the coalition, Saddam's regime showed no immediate sign of quitting.

In between our routine and other activities, I grabbed brews and took them over to the welfare TV tent in order to keep abreast of events as they unfolded.

The UN had warehouses full of food supplies for an expected wave of refugees. The bombing and missile raids had been successful in knocking out several key sites. The Republican Guard HQ, Saddam's Presidential Palace, The Ba'ath Party HQ, Air Force HQ and Muthena and Rasheed Air Bases had all been hit. We '1 Div' Tiger's had been told that we were heading back north pretty soon and that we were to make ready to move out, but that quickly changed. We were to be here a further several days as it would turn out, so we'd just have to "hang tough".

It was speculated that when we did move, we would be heading through the Kuwait-Iraq border. This was something that I don't think many of us had really thought about too deeply up until this point in time, but now it looked like 'Tiger' was, or soon would be Iraq bound.

When several of us had completed our given task over at 'Kohima Camp' (which, unknown to us at the time would, in a week or two be our 'new' home … again) we were glad to have finished a little earlier, as the heat had been uncomfortable, making even me a little irritable. However, our luck did change for the better in one respect … fresh foodstuffs were back on the menu, thank goodness!

After a much improved evening meal, a bunch of us headed for the TV tent where we sat glued to the large TV screen for just short of two hours, piecing together the events of the last couple of days. Most times in here, it was standing room only, and as one posterior vacated a seat, another filled it.

Our 'Country Cousins' who vastly outnumbered us, let out the occasional 'whoop' and 'holler' or 'Get Some!' as the news bulletins focussed on the latest military achievements that their counterparts had made up and over the border.

It was around this point in time, that for reasons of 'opsec', we Brit's had surrendered our mobile phones, for the old saying was true, "Loose lips sink ships". Plus, we knew that all telecommunications were being monitored anyway. So, that was one less means of communication with home. Although I must admit to not having used mine since having landed in Kuwait. But, on the other side of the coin, I could still see many Spam's walking around with theirs, unless I was much mistaken, and it was only key personnel who got to keep them?

Anyway, next morning a lie-in had been granted. That is, after waking up to take the NAPS at 0600. I reasoned that we had to be grateful for small mercies and pulled the hood of my 'maggot' over my head to try and block out the world around me, which was no easy thing to do with several hundred Spams around you. There was one occasion however, when after having wakened a little earlier, I took my pill then stuck a previously prepared note to the outside of my 'scratcher' which read, "NAPS taken 0600". That was because our team Sgt liked to wake everyone and remind them, just in case.

Anyway, it did the trick, which left me a little longer undisturbed in 'Snoozeville'. This was an admin day and my most important task was to get my 'scratcher' dobied. With a slightly more relaxing start to the day, I managed to shower, grab some breakfast without the 'incoming' alert going off, followed by a spot of queuing for the PX which had now re-opened.

My main aim was to buy a pair of desert style boots, to replace my own boots, which were rapidly starting to disintegrate. They were a pair of 'All Terrain' jobs, and although they were nothing special, they had got me through my previous UN tour with feet intact. But alas, they weren't designed for the rigours or indeed temperatures of desert life. Anyway, as I scanned the shelves in the PX, I guess it wasn't my lucky day, as along with everything else, the stock had already begun to run out. There were some small sized pairs left on the shelf, which was fine if you were a 'Hobbit' or a 'Munchkin'. Well, if nothing else, my flip-flops were still serviceable … .just about. I wondered whether the OC would notice!?

The coalition was making good progress on their move towards Baghdad, employing 'bump and run' manoeuvres, but there were pockets of resistance that were hanging in there, and needing to be dealt with. Several Americans had been captured and paraded on Iraqi TV along with some unsavoury images of the dead. It was obvious that Geneva Convention protocol meant nothing to the Iraqi forces, and no doubt, this would inflame things even further. Sadly, 8 Royal Marines and 4 US Marines had been killed when a 'Sea Knight' and 'CH-46' helicopter had collided.

When we caught up with the later bulletins, the northern cities of Mosul, Kirkuk and Saddam's (cited) hometown of Tikrit had been attacked by B2 Stealth, and B52 Bomber's, along with around 300 cruise missiles.

Basically, Baghdad was getting a good ole' fashioned ass-whoopin'!

Back over at 'Hangerville', the opportunity arose for us to move our 'parrots and monkeys', and so we re-located. This time we 'Tigers' positioned our cots against one of the hanger walls and stowed our gear. It was so much better than camping out in the middle of the floor, plus the fact that when the wind got up, dust would blow in and coat those who were opposite or nearer the doors, first. What's more, this was our little corner of British Sovereignty, and we even had our Union flag (and Taf with his Welsh dragon) tied to a girder above our bed spaces. Out-numbered and out-talked, we flew the colours defiantly.

We also had the advantage of a little solid cover being next to a wall, seeing as most of the American's were spread across the whole of the floor area.

This turned out to be the best thing we could have done when further missile alerts were called. All that we had to do was pull on 'rezzies', body armour and helmets and watch our American cousins perform as we lay in our pits, not needing to move. There was always the chance that a stray missile could make a direct hit and bring the wall down upon us, but again, c'est la vie.

The only disadvantage of being positioned where we were, was that the Brit 'Postie' Unit had their sorting area right next to us, and they worked through the night – something that we just had to try and get used to until they or we 'bugged out' again. I, like most people, just pulled the 'maggot' hood over my head to try to keep out any noise. And as if for good measure, this particular night we had a number of "Lightning! Lightning! Lightning!" alerts, and I got to thinking how nice it was to be back … NOT.

My only comfort was that I'd had the simple luxury of sliding into a clean 'scratcher' – a most gratifying feeling. I'd almost forgotten how the surrounding Spam's liked to debate every detail of the previous alert, and how bloody long it took them to settle down … Noisy Bunch!

Tony Blair had addressed the nation regarding the start of war. As with the Queen's message to the troops, you couldn't help but feel a little impassioned by the following address, (whether you liked or disliked what the Prime Minister stood for, or believed in the reasons that we were all out here);

> "On Tuesday night I gave the order for British forces to take part in military action in Iraq. Tonight, British servicemen and women are engaged from air, land and sea. Their mission: to remove Saddam Hussein from power, and disarm Iraq of its weapons of mass destruction. I know this course of action has produced deep divisions of opinion in our country. But I know also the British people will now be united in sending our armed forces our thoughts and prayers. They are the finest in the world and their families and all of Britain can have great pride in them. The threat to Britain today is not that of my father's generation. War between the big powers is unlikely. Europe is at peace. The Cold War already a memory.
>
> But this new world faces a new threat: of disorder and chaos born either of brutal states like Iraq, armed with weapons of mass destruction; or of extreme terrorist groups. Both hate our way of life, our freedom, our democracy.

My fear, deeply held, based in part on the intelligence that I see, is that these threats come together and deliver catastrophe to our country and world. These tyrannical states do not care for the sanctity of human life. The terrorists delight in destroying it. Some say if we act, we become a target. The truth is, all nations are targets. Bali was never in the front line of action against terrorism. America -didn't attack Al Qaida. They attacked America. Britain has never been a nation to hide at the back. But even if we were, it wouldn't avail us. Should terrorists obtain these weapons now being manufactured and traded round the world, the carnage they could inflict to our economies, our security, to world peace, would be beyond our most vivid imagination. My judgement, as Prime Minister, is that this threat is real, growing and of an entirely different nature to any conventional threat to our security that Britain has faced before. For twelve years, the world tried to disarm Saddam; after his wars in which hundreds of thousands died. UN weapons inspectors say vast amounts of chemical and biological poisons, such as anthrax, VX nerve agent, and mustard gas remain unaccounted for in Iraq.

So our choice is clear: back down and leave Saddam hugely strengthened; or proceed to disarm him by force. Retreat might give us a moment of respite but years of repentance at our weakness would I believe follow.

It is true Saddam is not the only threat. But it is true also – as we British know – that the best way to deal with future threats peacefully, is to deal with present threats with resolve. Removing Saddam will be a blessing to the Iraqi people. Four million Iraqis are in exile, sixty percent of the population dependent on food aid. Thousands of children die every year through malnutrition and disease. Hundreds of thousands have been driven from their homes or murdered. I hope the Iraqi people hear this message. We are with you. Our enemy is not you, but your barbarous rulers. Our commitment to the post-Saddam humanitarian effort will be total. We shall help Iraq move towards democracy. And put the money from Iraqi oil in a UN trust fund so that it benefits Iraq and no-one else. Neither should Iraq be our only concern. President Bush and I have committed ourselves to peace in the Middle East based on a secure state of Israel and a viable Palestinian state.

We will strive to see it done. But these challenges and others that confront us – poverty, the environment, the ravages of disease – require a world of order and stability. Dictators like Saddam, terrorist groups like 'Al Qaida' threaten the very existence of such a world. That is why I have asked our troops to go into action tonight. As so often before, on the courage and determination of British men and women, serving our country, the fate of many nations rests. Thank you".

24th March – 1st April

After laying there, doing my best to blot out the morning 'hub-bub', and grab that extra few minutes, I quickly realized that it was a complete waste of time. So, I got up, cursing the Americans for their infernal noise as I slid on my sandals, grabbed my washing gear, towel and rezzie and dragged myself over to the showers, but still managing a few polite replies of, "G'mornin" on the way. I just hoped that another 'incoming' warning would wait until I was actually in the shower unit. I didn't really fancy spending time caught out between the hanger and showers, sitting in a concrete scud shelter dressed in nothing more than a pair of shorts and a towel. But as was usually the way, unless you were up seriously early before 'sparrows fart', there was always a queue for the basins or the showers. (Mind you, Rob, one of my Artillery cohorts, always seemed to rise before anyone, and I mean, absolutely anyone). In fact he was up so early that he'd grown a beard again and needed another shave before anyone else had dragged themselves from their pit!) As each individual was squared away with a wash basin, their 'IPE' was never more than a few feet away. Sometimes, whilst having a wash and shave, my gear would still be hanging round my waist … .just in case.

I didn't really fancy having to don a respirator with a face full of shaving foam, although I would imagine that it would make it a lot easier when attempting to slide it on over my mug.

Although I must admit to a 'faux-pas' on one occasion however, when in half-dazed mode, I'd just made it to the ablutions and realised that I didn't have my kit with me, and rapidly returned the hundred yards or so to 'Hanger 10', whilst doing my best not to lose a sandal on the way or indeed, stub my toe.

I berated myself severely for my slack drills as I made the return journey, (and the fact that I didn't want a kicking for not having it with me).

The queue for the ablutions had got a little longer in my absence.

Well, it was my own fault. Needless to say, it was a lesson learned.

But fortunately, on this particular morning, we'd all managed to get through to breakfast and beyond without the need to take immediate cover. I guess we had to be thankful for small mercies.

Whilst we waited to be briefed regarding our next move further north again, we had one important task to do involving our vehicles. Apart from the usual 'first-parade' checks that all personnel carry out, we needed to get chevrons painted on the roofs and sides of the rovers. This was something that the Brit's had displayed on all vehicles in a time of conflict since the '91' Gulf War. The chevron, or '< less than' sign basically identified us as 'friendlies' to anyone who fought on the side of the coalition (not least American pilots). It was quite an unnerving thought to consider that it was possible to be targeted by one of our own, as it were. So, we set to with paint and templates trying to get the signs done as the day-time heat virtually dried the paint as it was being applied – we had to be extremely quick.

But the thing that we really needed for our vehicle roofs were, day-glo orange panels. That way, there could be no mistaking a friendly vehicle, or could there? Stories of 'blue on blue' incidents were not funny, and I certainly didn't want to end up as a combat statistic, brought about by a case of mistaken identity by anything that had the potential to 'take a vehicle out' with me in it.

The term 'blue on blue' came from war games, where 'blue's were known to be friendly and 'red's, the enemy. But, it would only be a matter of a week later that US General Richard Myers would end up having to apologise for the deaths of 5 British soldiers killed under 'friendly fire' – strange term really, as there was nothing friendly about it, if you ask me. And, whilst on that particular subject, the crew of an RAF Tornado were killed when they were apparently shot down by an American Patriot missile. So, it just goes to show you, that you could never be 100% sure (or safe) in this kind of environment.

But sadly, we learned of our very first British War casualty (not killed through 'blue on blue' or other accident) – Tank Commander Sergeant Steve Roberts had been shot and killed whilst allegedly trying to quell a disturbance near Al Zubayr, a suburb of Basrah. Another reason for mentioning this particular soldier was because he gave up his body armour★ to someone else. This gave us all an instant 'spooky' moment because we also had a Steve Roberts in our team. Armed with this news, he informed his next of kin as soon as he could to let them know that he was ok, just in case a news bulletin had been misinterpreted – anything is possible, especially when you're 3,500 miles away from home. He certainly didn't want his family getting a fright. That much, we could understand.

Saddam had decided to give an address on National TV, and this is the abbreviated version:

"O brave fighters, hit your enemy with all your strength. O Iraqis, fight with the strength of the spirit of jihad which you carry in you and push them to the point where they cannot go on. Hit them so that good and its people may reign and evil evicted back to its place. O Arabs, o faithful of the world, o those who support justice and oppose evil, we will herald the victory that God has promised us in the conflict against the lowlifes and enemies of humanity."

Yeah, Right! All that I can say is that I think he'd got a few wires crossed somewhere, and he'd definitely had too many hits on the old bubble-pipe. 'Lowlife's and enemies of humanity? … .I mean, come on?!

He was another one who was definitely off the Christmas card list!

The circumstances surrounding the shortages of kit and equipment, mentioned near the beginning of this book were later borne out in an Audit office report which related to the discovery that thousands of body armour sets went missing. Since the 1999 Kosovo war, up to 200,000 sets costing £170 apiece 'seem to have disappeared', the Audit Office commented.[4]

Author's note: And, whilst (as I also said earlier) this did not affect combat effectiveness, most of us out in the Gulf were of the opinion that, 'We're out here fighting and they can't even supply the proper clothing, never mind the rest of the kit'. And as I'd heard a number of people say, 'Black boots and green uniforms don't exactly help you to blend in with your desert environment!' This was another reason why a lot of Americans were so incredulous with regard to the fact that (we) the Brit's should be sent to war with anything less than a full complement of decent equipment.

In the afternoon we loosened up the muscles by having a spot of volleyball, which also helped to colour in the white bits of flesh not seen by the sun in a while. At least for the moment, the tannoy system was 'alert-free' as we'd not been sent scurrying for cover in quite a while (maybe someone had just simply got fed up and had covertly sabotaged it with a pair of cable cutters!) But just in case, we had our route plotted to the nearest hard shelter, should the unsporting Iraqi's decide to ruin our game.

---

[4] 'The Desert Rats' – John Parker *p.346-347*

Later, after pulling on clean kit, I made my ritual visit to the welfare tent to find that the Iraqi 51st Division, of about 8,000 soldiers were now POW's and that Saddam had now disappeared – whereabouts unknown.

Evening meal was finger-lickin' good. It was a favourite choice that I'd had once or twice since we first arrived: surf'n'turf … crabs legs and steak. For the crabs legs, a 'leatherman' was a must, in order to be able crack them and get the flesh out. Despite the considerable amount of fiddling about with them, they were 'droolicious'. Well, I made a fuss of them anyhow, and appreciated the fact that we were not on 'compo' rations or MRE's full time. My simple motto was, to enjoy it while you could get it.

The night rolled on with one or two alerts of incoming (the saboteur must have been caught), so it was possible to get a reasonable night's kip, all things considered. I later learned that it was mobile 'Abadil-100' and 'Al Samoud' Theatre Ballistic Missile launchers, situated a little way north of Basra that constantly harassed us here in this sector of Kuwait for the best part of a week.

As I lay in my 'scratcher' listening to the radio reports, two brigades of 3 (US) Division were somewhere in the region of 50 miles from Iraq's capital city, and the number of Iraqi combat dead believed to have been around 500 since day one of the conflict (mostly around Najaf and Nasyriah).

Brit forces had encountered numbers of Iraqis in and around Basrah who were rearing up against the regime, and this was something that the Brit's wanted to capitalize on, and therefore gave the promise of support to all those who were willing to assist with the ousting of Saddam – if indeed he could be found.

On the slightly brighter subject of troop welfare, the PM had announced that he would look into free parcel post for families of those serving out here. This was a gesture which would really make a difference, not least where morale was concerned.

We were briefed that 6 of us would heading over to Ali Al Salem Air Base to complete a couple of days work in and around the base. One of the guys had already been over there to do a 'recce' and returned with the news that the RAF accommodation had air conditioning, real beds with thick mattresses, and although it was a little cramped, who cared. Not only that, but the food was really good. Well, I've never heard of those RAF 'chappies' having anything less than decent board and grub. It was a case of, "When do we leave?!"

In the meantime, I had to somehow get myself some suitable footwear as the soles of my boots were starting to split. Like a lot of my countrymen (or 'Borrowers' as may be recalled), deals were being struck for items of desert kit that we Brits were 'diffy' in. Nobody was particularly looking for 'bukshee' kit unless that is, we could actually sign out desert wearable stuff from our own QM's. But with so many Americans about, there must have been someone willing to trade for a pair of boots? Coincidently, I'd struck up a conversation with this one particular US soldier, who had set up home not too far away from where I was, and we'd exchanged the usual 'hello's in passing etc. It just so happened that he had a spare pair of boots that he'd bought himself. What's more, they were my size too! Although this left him with just his general issue pair, he was more than willing to trade. But what did he want in exchange, I wondered?

My luck was in, because he was after the very item of kit that I had in my hold-all … a British Army Field Jacket. It too was my own spare. So, we handed our trades over. I was minus one jacket, but now had a pair of desert boots on my feet. After doing a little 'victory dance' and a very bad 'moon-walk', I was a much happier bunny. Now all I had to do was kit out the remaining 90% of me somehow.

This was the only night that I can remember, where we didn't have any missile alerts at all. But we did have some heavy rain – one of only two nights in the whole of my time out in the Middle-East.

Back home, anti-war demonstrations had taken place but the Sunday papers noted a massive swing towards support for the war. "Fine, it's a free country," I thought, but people taking to the streets and demonstrating didn't really help the mood of those of us who were out here at the 'invitation' of the Government. Everyone was out here to do a job and we didn't want to have to think about what Joe public's perception of us was. We were here, they weren't.

It was over a 100 K's to 'Ali'. We'd been up and beyond there a few times now, when we were heading to and from 'Hammersmith'. Travelling in day-time temperatures was starting to become a little more uncomfortable in the rovers. Basically, this is because they are nothing more than an aluminium box on wheels, and every panel absorbs the heat. Every surface had now become extremely hot.

When driving past the open areas of the desert, the heat reflected off the sand blew in through the windows as though somebody had a hair dryer pointed directly at you, raising the temperature by several more degrees.

Believe it or not, it was sometimes cooler to simply keep the windows shut and persevere with it until you reached your destination. My feet felt as though they were on fire, and it wouldn't be too much of an exaggeration if I said that you probably could have boiled water on the floor pan of the vehicle.

After showing our ID's at the first of three checkpoints, the Kuwaiti guards waved our vehicles through. It was then just a case of following the semi-circular road that wound around to the base. On the descending approach to the main entrance, there was a commanding view out over the desert as we passed a sign, which read, "Welcome to Ali Al Salem Air Base".

When we were finally through the last two checkpoints, we headed for the mess hall and parked up. It appeared that once again we'd timed it just right for grub.

The plan of action was to grab lunch then crack on with a couple of hours work in the p.m. As we walked into the 'air-conned' atmosphere, I'll never forget looking at the mouth-watering selection of food on offer and not being able to make up my mind about what to have. The BBQ'd half chicken and chips won out in the end. Then, with belly's sufficiently stuffed, we headed out of the parking area to find our temporary accommodation, passing a couple of cammed-up WMIKS with their twin mounted 'gimpys' as we went. The WMIK teams had been out on patrol around the air base perimeter and were no doubt coming back in to grab a spot of lunch. After all, it was worth travelling back in for and no mistake.

Once we had located our accommodation, we quickly dumped our kit in the well chilled portakabin, courtesy of the wonderful air-conditioning, we headed back out again to try and get an appreciation of the base and the remainder of the task ahead.

This place was an aviation spotter's dream. Well, it was an air-base, so I suppose it was only natural that there would be all manner of 'Big Boy's Toys' flying around, with anything from GR4 Tornado's, USAF heavily armed AC130 Spectre gunships (aka 'Puff the Magic Dragon'), and various types of Helo's.

During the course of the afternoon, our 'mini-team' had RV'd at a designated smoking area for those requiring a nicotine fix, whilst I went and acquired some cold bottled water to quench our thirsts.

I just happened to bump into a Flight Officer who was interested to know what we army bods had been tasked to do whilst on 'his turf'. After a brief, though friendly chat, he said that if there was anything we needed, then we only had to ask.

"Many thanks Sir," I replied, and just as I was about to head back to the rest of the team, a thought came to me, and I spun round on my heel. "Well Sir, there is something that you may be able to assist us with. We're due to be heading over the border at any time, and the one thing that we need for added vehicle protection, are luminous panels for the roofs of our vehicles".

He rubbed his chin and said, "Just give me a few minutes. I think I may be able to help you out…" Ten minutes later he returned and promptly handed me a 12-metre roll of self-adhesive orange 'day-glo'. I think he was quite pleased with himself, knowing he'd been able to assist a bunch of Her Majesty's 'Tommies'. I was mightily pleased too; it made me feel a lot happier knowing that we could now ensure that our rovers would be a little more visible (from the air).

Later, back at the vehicles, I cut one-metre panels for each of the three rovers we had with us, clambered up onto each bonnet and set about positioning the panels. Once they were stuck in place, I then used 'black nasty' (or Gaffer tape – a million uses!) to create the chevrons set against the orange. Job done and dusted.

As far as I was concerned, it was a very valuable half hour spent. There was now enough panelling for each of the remaining team vehicles as well. So, it just goes to show that the old saying, "If you don't ask, you don't get," is true.

Later, when we'd done all that we could for the day, it was wonderful just to be able to forget about the exterior heat for a short while. That was until it came to having a 'skin-peelingly' hot shower, due to the fact that the sun had been baking the water tank all day. Anyway, we all made a bee-line for the canteen again to sample the delights of RAF cuisine. And again, the food was superb, with puddings and 'stickies' to follow. And, there was even a cheese-board on offer! The only thing missing here was a nice glass of red wine. That was just something I'd have to dream about.

After evening meal, I headed across to the welfare-cum chill-out room (minus air conditioning this time) known as 'The Oasis Club' to catch up on the latest TV news.

The other bonus of being at 'Ali', even for a short duration was that the Paradigm welfare phones were still in use. The fact that I hadn't been able to phone home in about a fortnight, made it a priority. I tried Linda's work number to find that she was out on a training course, so I dialled our home number to leave a quick "I'm alright and hope you're okay" kind of message on the answering machine, to find my own recorded voice. She obviously didn't want to change the message.

"Try later on," I thought. Allowing for the time difference, my intention was to phone around 10pm Kuwait time, but when I got near the phone shacks, the queue was horrendous. So, I endeavoured to phone next day, and finally got hold of her. As can be imagined, she was more than relieved at being able to hear my voice after what was a considerable length of time.

That fortnight without husbandly contact no doubt felt longer from her side of the world. But, it was nice to be wanted.

As 1000 paratroops of US 173 Airborne Brigade jumped into Iraq to seize control of an airfield, good old '1 (UK) Armoured Div' captured an important bridge at Basrah, along with the airport too. The Challenger 2s and Warrior armoured vehicles of the Black Watch battle group fought their way through a barrage of mortar fire and rocket propelled grenades, pushing 4kms inside the city limits. With the approaches to the city now controlled by the Brits and the Ba'ath Party HQ now destroyed, the 'Chally 2s' of the Royal Scots Dragoon Guards intercepted 14 Russian-made T55 tanks that were heading south towards the lightly-armed Royal Marines. The biggest tank battle since the Second World War ensued – and was over in minutes.

The 14 Chally 2s (part of '7th Armoured Brigade – The Desert Rats) opened up with their 120mm guns until all 14 of the enemy tanks were just smouldering hulks. Four companies of infantry were also taken out, leaving around 100 Iraqi soldiers dead.

Although the following quote would be considered rather grim humour to some, I particularly liked what Central Command in Qatar had to say about the tank action: "There were 14 of ours and 14 of theirs. The final score was 14-nil. It was an away fixture and the away team won".

I realized that I had been in-country just on a month and in some ways it was hard to believe. Maybe because we'd been up and down, backwards and forwards like 'blue-arsed flies' that we just didn't notice the passage of time. Mind you, that would figure, because most of us had to ask someone else what day it was most of the time.

Anyway, this particular day we'd zipped through a good proportion of the task we were set and took a mid-morning break, where I managed to catch up a little on the war. The only problem was that the lounge chairs in the 'Oasis' were a little too comfy, and with the building heat of the day, I could feel my eyes starting to close. We were certainly going to miss the level of comfort here, once we were back in 'Hangerville', that was for sure.

We had to wait for the 'Staffy' to arrive so that we could hand over all of the current data we'd gathered, which meant that he could then in turn fire it back to HQ Land Command. We were in no hurry, as I started to become one with the chair, glad to be out of the heat. Before we knew it, it was lunchtime, and it was after all, such a chore having to force that wonderful RAF grub down. Oh dear! How sad! Never Mind!

Shortly after lunch, a missile alert was called. "Damn and blast it!" But this time, we didn't have to dive into a dusty slit trench. Everyone in the vicinity headed for the steps which led to one of the underground reinforced bunkers.

So, with us all 'rezzied up', everyone sat there in the relative cool waiting for further instructions. What with the current alert state and with such protective cover, it meant that we didn't have to don full NBC gear, which was a bonus. And, fortunately we didn't have to wait too long before the all- clear was given. We could then get on with the day.

I supposed that this was what it must have been like back in Blighty from 1939-45, with the prospect of air raids disrupting all manner of everyday goings-on and the population having to hastily don gas masks and get under cover, then afterwards, carry on regardless.

A little while later, four of us set out onto the base perimeter road. We were headed for the Ordnance and Ammunition bunkers a good way around the air base. These massive concrete bunkers that stood out against the skyline, had apparently housed Iraqi hardware back in '91'. There were several dotted about, and a few of them had very visible impact damage inflicted upon them from coalition bombs that had found their mark. As we were security checked through the main compound, I could see some of the bomb damage. On closer inspection to one of them, the 20 feet of solid reinforced concrete had been breached, leaving a circular hole right the way through. I was suitably impressed, anyhow.

But, more amazing to me, was the amount of stuff that I was surrounded by that had the potential to go "Bang!" You name it, it was all here. There were racks, cradles and crates with a vast array of ordnance … 500lb bombs, 'Sidewinder' air-to-air missiles, 'Paveway' bombs, and last, but not least, probably the RAF's most advanced weapon, 'Stormshadow'. This was a turbojet-powered missile, which was designed and developed for taking out high value targets whilst minimizing collateral damage. That said, I certainly wouldn't have liked being on the receiving end of any of this lot! (Part of our job on this afternoon was to capture some of the data on the rolling stock that carried this deadly cargo).

Whilst cracking on with the task in hand, I managed to have a word with a few of the guys who were busily readying a lot of the ordnance (fitting and setting timed fuses) for loading aboard the GR4 Tornado's that were parked under their curved-roof shelters just across the base. I couldn't help wondering as I looked at all of this explosive weaponry, where some of the individually marked pieces might be dropped.

One of the still intact bunkers that was being used to house some of the armaments, had a couple of small anti-rooms, which I was told, might be of interest. Upon looking inside the solid, sparse rooms, I noticed a number of drawings and sketches adorning the walls. Some were rather crude, whilst others were quite detailed. One or two of them had some religious significance by the look of them. One of the ordnance 'techies', informed me that back during the '91' Gulf conflict, the Iraqi military had held and interrogated Kuwaiti Nationals in these very 'cells', then later took them out and executed them.

Whether this story was verbatim or not, I would deduce from the images on the walls that these poor unfortunates did indeed meet their end at the hands of the same tyrannical regime that we were now here to 'sort out', some twelve years on.

When the desert heat had got the best of us and with tasks completed for the day, we headed back for the cool haven that was our temporary accommodation. It was a relief to cool down a little prior to scrub-up for evening meal. Later on, I managed to catch George 'W' and Tony Blair's speech from Camp David. Each leader gave an impassioned address, and whether you believed in the war or not, it was stirring stuff.

The PM's speech reminded me a little of Mrs 'Thatch' in her glory days during the build up to the defence of the Falkland Islands.

One of my compadrés added that it was rather 'Churchillian'.

On the war-front, most of the southern oil fields were now in safe hands, although there were several, further north, that had been sabotaged and were now on fire. It would cost millions of dollars to put them out.

Our Government were in a state of absolute outrage over the Iraqi TV station 'Al Jazeera's screening of the images of two of our serving countrymen who'd been captured and killed. But, it just hardened people's resolve to win through and bring all "war criminals" to justice.

As an interesting aside to what was happening on land, the Australian Navy clearance diving team had been working with the British Naval forces to clear the approaches to the port of (and soon to become our operating base), locating and disposing of mines. But they also had some help from two of our mammalian flippered friends … ..Dolphins.

They had been trained by the US Navy, and had been taught to mark any mines they found with floats. Their natural built-in sonar allow them to locate objects underwater, so with their flipper mounted cameras, it made it possible for them to "eyeball" anything perceived as a danger, with the obvious images relayed to the vessel. These were the "sniffer dogs" of the ocean.

I remember there was one very funny moment during a short TV news report that had me absolutely crying with laughter. The Iraqi regime had told the local populace to take up arms against the coalition. The news camera was panning around, the scene was; non-regular anti-coalition fighters brandishing AK's. This one Iraqi is fiddling with his weapon as though he is about to clean it when he mistakenly squeezes the trigger, sending an automatic burst of rounds skyward. Well, the expression on his face was one of "Oh ⋆@#~⋆#!" and it was captured on film for all the world to see.

But that was it for me – too late, the damage was done. And with that I just collapsed into a heap. I laughed so hard that it hurt. Herb, sitting next to me was in no better condition. Later that same evening, we waited for a repeat of the same news report, which still had the same effect. When I finally settled down, I commented that this little snippet of footage should be shown and used as a visual aid in weapon training, as an example of how not to handle a weapon.

Well, before long, (but making sure it was after lunch) we were Arafjan bound again … .. and home to 'Hangerville', but not before we had the compulsory visit to the American PX. There was always something in there to take your fancy. Even if it was just a bag of 'beef jerky'. The stuff was habit forming, and although it looked none too appetizing, it was pretty tasty. It always sold out quickly back at Arafjan, so it was worth buying a bag just in case. It was good to have on standby when you were hit by a case of the late evening 'munchies'- even though it was like chewing raw-hide to begin with.

The reports coming in were saying that Baghdad was seeing some of the most violent bombing since the war had begun. In an attempt to impede the B52's from visibly sighting their intended targets, not least the Republican Guard, the Iraqis had lit oil fires to create plumes of smoke.

In Kuwait, which was some considerable distance from Baghdad, a shopping centre had been hit by an Iraqi missile killing a number of civilians. This just reinforced the fact that nobody even within a reasonably large radius was safe from Saddam's arsenal, not least because we'd heard reports that his missiles couldn't target anything with any degree of accuracy.

The Iraqi military had made a statement that should our troops reach the capital then, the streets of Baghdad would become "a graveyard". At this point, there were around 125,000 coalition troops fighting in Iraq and although sandstorms had been hampering some advances, there were further successes in the respect that the Kurds and US Para's in the North (Mosul), had attacked and captured a key bridge over the Euphrates river.

Whilst in Nasyriah, the US Marines had captured an Iraqi General, who may have been of some use with regard to critical information (if of course he was willing to 'spill the beans'). So, while the Americans were making good progress in the north of Iraq, the Brit's were securing the strategic areas in the south. There was now, however, an additional threat … suicide bombers.

Near the city of Najaf, an Iraqi officer had driven up to US checkpoint and detonated a device which killed five soldiers. Apparently, the Iraqi officer received two posthumous medals for his bravery from Saddam.

Aw! ain't that nice of him!

And in typical tyrannical form, the Iraqi regime was still threatening those men with execution who wouldn't fight against the coalition. But one of the best (and darkly funny) reports to come through was, that Baghdad's Commander of Air Defences had allegedly been sacked because his missiles had fell short … on Baghdad. Now that was an 'own goal' if ever there was one, and no mistake!

In a continuing line of mirth, one Mohammed Saeed al-Sahhaf, the Iraqi Information Minister, better known as 'Comical Ali' to us, and 'Baghdad Bob' to the Americans, claimed that, "The infidels are committing suicide by the hundreds on the gates of Baghdad". This may not be the literal translation, but it was something like, as it was not uncommon for his interpreter to embellish some of his statements. Anyway, 'Ali' was Saddam's master of 'spin', and was no doubt "requested" by his boss to remain in place until the very last moments, whilst doing his utmost to convince the Iraqi population that they should be under no illusions that the regime had the coalition on the run. This was the 'Diamond Geezer' who later claimed that there were no coalition tanks in Baghdad, as they're virtually rumbling past him. Another little gem was, "Lying is forbidden in Iraq. President Saddam Hussein will tolerate nothing but truthfulness as he is a man of great honour and integrity. Everyone is encouraged to speak freely of the truths evidenced in their eyes and hearts". "OK, Yeah, Right!"

This guy was a 'legend in his own lunch-time'. What's more, he had a whole catalogue of very descriptive rhetoric with which to denounce the coalition and rally the people – most of which was pure, though extremely humorous tosh, intermixed with bits of ancient texts which no doubt hailed back centuries. His broadcasts would later turn up on a best of 'Comical Ali' DVD and he would go on to become an even bigger media celebrity across the Arab nation. So, if anyone could boost morale for not only an opposing force (us) but half of the western world, it was 'Ali' – he was truly priceless.

Someone mentioned it was Saturday, not that it mattered much as we had to get squared away for a move out the next day (which just happened to be Mother's day and also my big Sis's birthday too).

We'd been informed that within the next week, a further 45,000 US soldiers would be landing 'in-country', and for a while, this base would be home for them. All that I could think about was the rise in decibels, especially when the hangers were filled with wall to wall Spams. (We also noticed that the neighbouring hanger had started to set up rows and rows of steel framed bunk beds with decent looking mattresses – it looked like they were getting mighty comfy across the way). But the new influx would also mean even longer queues for the cook-house at grub-up. So it was probably just as well that we were moving out, because I think there were one or two of our guys who's tempers were starting to fray a little, what with all the background noise especially when we were trying to get some shut-eye. And the last thing we needed was a "diplomatic incident".

Vehicle prep was the main order of the day, which included the removal of half the desert from the air filters, but just as importantly to my way of thinking, was the securing of the 'day-glo' panels to the one or two team vehicle roofs that still required them.

The chance to 'dobi' kit was always a priority, and I wasted no time in sniffing out a much desired washing machine. Two of the 'Tigers' had been tasked to go and find some 'assets' over the border. The 'fly boys' were choppering them in to the location near Safawan, which was still considered to be a bit of a dodgy area, in that the route through the place was called 'Sniper Alley'. However, they were up and gone around 4.a.m. and although they would only be away for a day or two, they were amongst the first Tigers into Iraq. When I met up with them a couple of days later, Herbie said that he'd marked this particular Mother's day as the day he flew over the Kuwait-Iraq border. And as crazy as it might seem, I had to admit that despite any possible dangers, I did envy them a little.

I'd decided that the 'Kuwaiti Cough' that had been dogging me for just on a month, had to go. I was sick of waking myself up (and anyone else who was within earshot) during the night (bladder not withstanding). And so, after a bit of a wait with a fair number of other people in the med centre, some of whom I might add, were in a much worse state than myself, I finally managed to get some Linctus. The last time I'd tried up at 'Hammersmith', there were no supplies, but finally …

Next morning, I was up and already eating breakfast by 6a.m. Today was the day we were heading out for 'Camp Fox'. It had only been a few weeks since we'd been there, but it seemed like a lifetime. Our only hope was to be able to get ourselves a little more comfortable than our last visit. Memories of 'Sardine City' came flooding back. Anyway, when we finally drove through the check-point, 'Fox' had indeed changed for the better. It didn't even look like the same camp. The old dining and welfare tents that had previously been blown away by "The Mother of All Sandstorms," had been repositioned. Shower units were up and running and the accommodation tents now had wooden flooring with bunk beds with thick mattresses and soon-to-be-working power sockets. This place was looking better all the time.

We were due to be here for about four or five days, but the eight of us all agreed that we'd need to stay a bit longer (given the chance). So, with the memories of our previously cramped confines instantly erased, we got our gear stowed, much happier in the knowledge that we could now be a tad more comfortable, and then proceeded with our task.

Our task however, was a little different this time as it was classed as "Operational Assistance" in as much as we were here to sniff out key ISO containers in which lay much needed components for vehicles and armour (amongst other stuff). We were the bods on the ground, and apparently the best people to find them. So, it was imperative that we found as much as we could in the time available. Ah! … It was so nice to be in demand! We had a hell of a grid-square in which to search out the misplaced ISO's. But, I did have one spine-chilling moment during our search, and that was when I happened upon an unlocked container. In order to verify the contents, we were to look inside (where we could), but instead of maybe key engine components for a Challenger 2 tank, my gaze was met with a rather large supply of body bags which were marked up with something like, "bag – body remains x1" or something very similar to that. It was just another one of those chilling moments.

Whilst moving around the area of 'Fox' we had to be really mindful of the enforced speed limits, as the RMP's took no prisoners as it were, and none of us particularly wanted a verbal kicking from the Master Driver for such infringements. After spending a good few hours out in the 'boonies', we all RV'd for lunch back in camp, which was pretty good – fresh salad stuffs were the order of the day, just the job. This was the pattern for the next few days, where we'd head out into the area, back for lunch, a few more hours out, then 'end ex'. Its funny how after just a day or two, a location starts to become a little 'homey'. The beds were great, the grub was good, the showers were superb … .what more could you ask? The only down side was that we would be gone again within a few more days, but there you go. However, we did get the chance to trundle our way down the track that led to the American sector to check out their PX. This was a chance to pick up those little treats or munchies, or simply to stock up on a few bits and pieces that may had previously eluded us. One of the 'Gucci' items that they did have in stock, and which a couple of the guys bought, were the Camel-Back re-hydration systems (and at a good price too).

The news came in that Baghdad's Ministry of Information had been heavily bombed. It had only been 11 days since the start of the war and up to this point, around 6,000 smart bombs and nearly 700 cruise missiles had been launched by the coalition. I wondered again as to how many of the bombs I'd seen over at 'Ali' had found their targets? Our RAF Harriers had destroyed a key fuel dump at Karbala whilst the Presidential Palace in Baghdad had been hit again. At home, eighty four percent of the Brit's were now in support of the war, which appeared to be a bit of a turn-around. And, with regard to the home front, Saddam was threatening our way of life there too. He had declared that he would unleash suicide bombers on London ('martyrs' he'd rallied to sacrifice themselves) the same way that the Iraqi officer had killed the four US soldiers at the checkpoint in Najaf.

1st – 8th April

The rest of the team had gone on ahead to our operational area, leaving me behind to drive 'JB', our '1 Div' team leader, out to them after he'd finished his 'O' group. He'd then be able to give us a heads-up regarding the latest security issues and 'hard' intelligence that had come from his morning brief, which could include things that would directly affect us, such as limited vehicle movement, threat state and so on. This gave me a little more time to re-fill my brew and catch up on overnight events. Sadly, 26 Brit's had now been killed thus far, but only 4 of those had been killed by opposing forces, whereas the remaining 22 had died as a result of heli accidents or 'Blue on Blue's.

Whilst Baghdad was still taking a pounding, there was still some resistance here and there around Basrah. 2,000 elite Aussie troops were due in theatre, bolstering coalition numbers further, whilst Geoff Hoon appeared to dismiss the likelihood of further British reinforcements being sent out, stating, " We are absolutely confident that we have sufficient forces in theatre to deliver the military objectives that we set out".

Yes, but would that remain the case?

Back in the UK, The Chancellor of the Exchequer Gordon Brown, had also announced that a further £1.2 billion had been allocated to Op Telic, which increased the special reserves for the war in Iraq to £3 billion. He'd initially announced that he was prepared to 'spend what it takes' to disarm Iraq.

Now that's a lot of dollar in your back pocket!

On a more serious and tragic note, a '4x4' vehicle that failed to stop at a check-point, had been shot at, killing several Iraqi civilians. The even more emotive thing about the whole situation was that women and children were amongst those killed. An investigation had started. But, what with the increase in suicide bombings, if somebody knowingly failed to stop at a check-point, did they not risk life and limb by 'running the gauntlet'?

In the meantime, check-point procedures were under review.

At this point, there was much speculation as to whether Saddam was actually still alive, whilst the Arabic TV channels were showing him having made three appearances, supposedly, very recently. With so many "doubles" playing the part, it wasn't so clean cut. But for those of us having watched "him" on the broadcasts, we were saying, "It's a puppet!"

In my opinion, it was a latex puppet from the 'Spitting Image' TV series.

In the meantime, US troops had finally captured Karbala, whilst another of their countrymen, or in this case, country-women: one Private Jessica Lynch made headline news after being portrayed (by US spin-doctors) as a true heroine. She was one of 33 soldiers in an 18 vehicle convoy of the US 507th Maintenance Company (largely made up of cooks and mechanics). They'd taken a wrong turn near the town of Nasiriya, and ended up heading into the centre, which was still controlled by Saddam loyalists. The convoy was ambushed, eleven soldiers killed and 6, including Private Lynch were captured. The tale surrounding the type of injuries that she supposedly sustained, the alleged mistreatment at the hands of the Iraqi hospital staff, and the subsequent rescue mission, was nothing more than fabrication (in fairness, the hype wasn't down to her, and she insisted that she couldn't remember after she had been injured). Whilst she had no doubt had a rough time of it, when the US Army enquiry concerning the incident was conducted later, it appeared that most of the story had indeed been invented.

Maybe the press needed to give the American people a hero at this time, but unfortunately, one way or another, "The truth will always out," as they say.

As the sun moved across the clear skies above the desert, we were out in the middle of nowhere at '61 Ammunition Squadron', which is really were you'd want your ammo … in the middle of nowhere! Because if this lot went up for whatever reason, it would be one of the best 'Guy Fawlks' displays imaginable, not to mention the most deadly.

With being out in the desert more and more, I had to keep an eye on my feet, even with my now bedded-in US desert boots. No matter what I did, it didn't take long before my feet became 'redders' and my single greatest pleasure these days, was sticking them in a bowl of cool water, just to revitalise them a little, and that was my intention once we'd finished out here for the day. We 'end-exed' slightly earlier than usual, which gave me the opportunity to do a bit of admin – which in my case amounted to a bit of hand washing.

We didn't have the obvious luxuries that Arafjan provided, (but then again, out here who else did), but that was ok, a bowl of water and a cup full of soap powder would replace a washing machine and a hot desert wind would dry stuff quicker than any tumble dryer could ever do, believe me.

As the '3rd US Division' attacked and virtually destroyed the Republican Guard south-west of Baghdad, near Kut, whilst at Karbala, the British '7th Armoured Brigade' discovered an arms dump with over 700 tank rounds. That meant 700 less rounds that could be fired back at coalition forces. But having said that, there probably wasn't a great deal of armour left intact that could still chuck the stuff at us!

The Brit's had by now, strengthened their hold on the Basrah area. But local hard-line irregulars, led by one Ali Hassan Al Majid (better known as 'Chemical Ali' and who just happened to be Saddam's Cousin), mortared and machine gunned a number of civilians who were attempting to assist British forces. This basically just about summed up the kind of barbaric regime we were all out here to break. Never mind about the supposed WMD. The coalition forces had seized the Haditha Dam on the Euphrates, whilst heavy bombing continued in and around Mosul, Dohuk and Kirkuk.

Next day, with our task in the area complete, we headed on out for the highway and our now well travelled route. We knew the landmarks and distances pretty much, so when we turned onto the 'King-Fahad-Bin-Abdul Aziz Road' (could a name be much longer) we knew that we were only around 20 or so K's to Camp Arafjan, home of the 'Mubarak 15th Armoured Brigade' and countless 'Spams'. As we got a little nearer, I could make out the 'spring onion' off in the distance, "Not far at all now," I thought. Looking at the fuel gauge I knew we'd need to fuel up our convoy of five vehicles and be ready to move if necessary. And so, we got in line behind a queue of Humvees, and waited as the line slowly moved toward the fuel point. We were all feeling rather jaded after the heat of the day, mind you the couple of hours spent 'cooking' in an oven on wheels didn't help matters.

Finally, when all of our worldly possessions were once again unloaded back into 'Hanger 10', I threw off my boots and breathed a sigh of relief, as did my feet.

Soon after, we were given the latest intel brief. It had been previously alleged, that Iraq still had a number of illegal 'Al-Samoud 2' missiles which had been discovered. These missiles were more than capable of reaching us … now there was a comforting thought. Saddam had originally agreed 'in principle' to destroy them, as they exceeded the maximum range of 150 Kilometres as set down in the 1991 Gulf war cease fire agreement.

However, both the US and British Government's had dismissed any notion that Saddam would comply, as they believed that he was simply game-playing – something that he was very good at.

In Northern Kuwait, a flock of sheep had been spotted, apparently lying dead, which gave cause for concern with regard to the possibility of some kind of biological or chemical airborne 'nasty' having been released over the border. In the meantime, pathological investigations would continue and updates would be shared with the rest of Group Support.

As the Irish Guards battled for ultimate control in Basrah, we learned that '40 Commando RM' had made a grim discovery in the nearby suburb of Abu Al Khasib. It was thought that they had found what appeared to have been a torture chamber. US forces were now only 20 miles from Baghdad, but further reports coming in maintained that the reminder of the Republican Guard was heading south to engage the US forces.

Another 'Blackhawk' had been shot down by small arms fire over Karbala, killing 7. I got to thinking that the title of the book and film "Blackhawk Down" would take on a different meaning. And sadly, another BBC cameraman had been killed by a mine – one of a number of British TV crew members who had been killed or were now missing since the start of the conflict.

We were tasked to head up to the area where '5 Group Support Regiment' were located, back up near our old stomping ground. After driving the 100 plus K's North on an "Operationally Urgent" task, we ended up doing no more than the usual 'hurry up and wait' whilst the senior ranks amongst us sat in on a brief to establish what was required of us.

As we waited around in the damnably hot canteen and had a brew, followed by another, the heat simply sapped us. The up-shot was, that for the moment, the 'Job' (whatever it had been), was cancelled.

So, we high-tailed it back to Arafjan, slightly more hot and bothered than when we'd set out earlier.

Still, we were back to the land of decent showers and decent grub.

Although, I couldn't help thinking that this place was like a magnet, it kept pulling us back to it.

The end of day reports had said that 'Saddam Hussein International Airport', some twelve miles from Baghdad, had been taken by the '3rd US Infantry Div', leaving three hundred and fifty Republican Guard dead, whilst heavy bombing still continued by the coalition forces.

As we settled down for another night in 'Hangerville', you could still feel the heat of the day radiating from the breeze-block walls, and despite the roller doors being open, very little breeze managed to penetrate to the interior.

This was a close one.

One of the guys had just simply picked up his camp cot and plonked it outside, next to one of the vehicles in the hope of getting a little respite from the general hub-bub, and catch whatever breeze there was to be had.

I just ended up sleeping on the top of my 'scratcher' in a pair of shorts.

Next morning, as a few of us headed for breakfast, 'Daz' was still there, fast asleep in his 'scratcher', totally oblivious to the noise of Humvees and other vehicles driving past. What a guy! I couldn't resist this 'Kodak Moment', so I grabbed my camera and immortalised him forever.

Our earlier brief regarding the "dead sheep" incident had turned out to be a mistake. Apparently, they weren't dead at all, they'd all just been having '40 winks'!

News came to light that 'Chemical Ali' had supposedly been killed in an air raid on his residence, so he was one less monster to have to worry about (or so we thought). It turned out much later that he was still at large.

US armour had made it to Baghdad – not less than a hundred tanks rolled into the city, and two of Saddam's palaces were now also under US control.

And obviously, when the Americans knocked on Saddam's door, he wasn't of course home … a bit rude of him really.

Again, there was more speculation as to whether he was still alive, despite the Iraqi Information Minister reading out a statement that had allegedly been written by Saddam himself. It was considered that he was quite possibly seriously wounded (if not dead) from all the heavy bombings that had taken place. But we reckoned amongst ourselves that he was well out of there. Probably sitting at the side of a Swiss lake and smoking big cigars.

The Iraqi Vice President, Taha Yassin Ramadan had previously stated that there were still around 6,000 Arab volunteers fighting against the coalition. The veteran BBC reporter, John Simpson, had been travelling in a convoy in northern Iraq when they were attacked by "friendlies" – a US F-14 had mistakenly targeted his convoy as enemy, and dropped a 1000lb bomb on their position (despite the orange panels on the top of their vehicle roofs identifying them as coalition). During the whole sorry episode, his translator and around 17 others that included Americans and Kurds were killed. John was 'lucky', even though he himself had been hit by 14 pieces of shrapnel, one of which lodged in his hip and would leave him with a permanent limp, plus one burst ear-drum burst courtesy of the blast.

(His own story regarding the events surrounding the disaster make for quite a dramatic read too, I might add).

As we cracked on with our vehicle checks, most of us who had driven them, reckoned that by the end of the operation, half the vehicles would only be fit for target practise out in the desert. One vehicle that we inherited a little later happened to be a left hand drive, long wheel base Land Rover. Funnily enough it was the only one within the whole of the team that was painted in desert colour. But that was its one and only attribute – it was a total pig to drive. We called it the 'Sand-Rover', but everyone avoided it where possible. But as far as vehicles were concerned, we just had to do our best with them for as long as possible.

The Sgt Major had come back from doing a recce up near Abdaly, some 15K from the border. So, we were briefed about the next couple of day's activities, which was to include our move out of 'Hanger 10' and across to 'Kohima' – the Brit enclave just to side of the main camp.

Arafjan was expecting another several thousand Americans to arrive in the very near future and every available bit of space would be needed. But it was mainly for the sake of our own sanity that we needed to be out of there.

Three quarters of Baghdad was now surrounded by US forces and the Republican Guard now ceased to exist as a cohesive fighting force

We were back on familiar roads again, heading north to catch up with a couple of the supply units before they upped-sticks and left. As we left the main route making a bee-line for the Bubyan Peninsular, the wind suddenly started to pick up. Within a matter of minutes, we were engulfed in a swirling sand storm. The signal was given for us to pull over, whilst the Sgt Major's vehicle took off to scout ahead. In order for us to get out and stretch our legs, it required the use of Shemagh's and masks. To ensure our safety whilst stopped at the side of the road, a few of us set up an all-round defence at front, rear and centre of our small convoy. It paid not to take any chances, despite being able to operate in the "relative" safety of our current host country.

After 20 minutes or so, the Sgt Major returned and gave the order for us all to turn back around and head for home. This had been a fruitless 320 Kilometre trip. But as we joined the network of criss-crossing highways as we neared Arafjan, we were greeted by a rather funny sight – a camel sitting on the back of a pick-up truck. It was a strange spectacle to behold, so just before the vehicle disappeared up a slip road, we increased our speed to catch it, with half the guys in the convoy managing to get photo's of the beast on wheels. It certainly made for a laugh and helped alleviate the rigors of our trip. Mind you, a short while later, we also saw a horse standing on the back of a pick-up with make-shift rails around it. Not that the rails would have been very effective had the driver needed to brake sharpish or carry out some kind of emergency manoeuvre. The horse would have been airborne, but unlike Pegasus, wings wouldn't have saved it. So apart from our rolling 'zoo', the only other saving grace about the whole trip was that we just about made it back in for lunch. We'd try again next day.

There was now, little to no resistance in Basrah, which highlighted the success of 'Operation Sinbad' – '1 UK Armoured Div's mission to take Basrah, utilising '3 Commando Brigade' to advance from the South, with '7 Armoured Brigade' attacking from the West and the North, and '2RTR' (Royal Tank Regiment) clearing the central areas, with US Cobra gun-ships giving air support. With 4000 troops now occupying the city, I think the point was being made rather strongly.

In a story related to me later when we were up at Basrah, as this particular assault went in, the RSDG's had to fire on each other's tanks with their chain-guns to remove the Fedayeen fighters who were climbing on the hulls in an attempt to shoot in the sight blocks and open the hatches. Even after witnessing the hopeless attempts to over-power and 'kill' a 'Chally 2' by their comrades, the fighters still kept coming – firing RPG's which simply bounced of the heavy-duty armour. But maybe it wasn't just fanatical zeal which spurred the Fedayeen on, perhaps it had something to do with the fact that $8,000 had been offered, supposedly by Saddam, to anyone who destroyed a coalition APC or Tank. This equated to about a 1000 months salary for an Iraqi teacher. So in reality, it sort of made the coalition more than fair game, I suppose.

The major ground assault for Baghdad had begun, with fierce fighting taking place over the River Tigris. As with Basrah, US planes gave air support to the armour as they headed for the centre. We'd heard that as the tanks rolled towards the Ministry Of Information, 'CentCom' (Central Command) were convinced that Senior Iraqi Officials were still holed up inside.

It was around this time that a 'B1B' Bomber dropped four 2000lb bombs on a restaurant where it was believed that Saddam and his sons, Uday and Qusay were dining. Although US intelligence was "quite confident" that Saddam was now dead, there was no way to be sure.

But there was however, a very large crater where the restaurant once stood.

We got word to pack up all of our 'Parrots and Monkeys' (as an old Sgt Major of mine used to say). We were finally getting a new address – 'Kohima Camp', a few hundred yards away. Well, for a couple of weeks anyhow. As with all the other Brit camps, vast improvements had been made here too. We had an air conditioned mess tent which saved you sweating into your dinner (and not an 'all in stew' in sight, either). The food turned out to be pretty good, if a departure from American grub. But every little helped no end. Anyway, once we'd relocated to our tent, which was a slightly smaller version of our Bedouin abode up in 'Hammersmith', gear was quickly stowed, and I was at home the minute my chair and floor mat were in place.

I'd earned the nickname of 'Kaptain Komfort' by one or two of the guys, but I didn't care. Anyone can be uncomfortable and miserable too, and my intention was to be neither.

After lunch we set off for the highways heading north again, up around Abdaly area, trying to catch '6 Supply's 64 Petrol Squadron' before it too bugged out. When we eventually got up there, we were now probably only about 10 K's to the border. Again, as with the previous day, the wind started to pick up again. Fortunately, we had enough 'Tigers' out on the ground to get all the data we needed before the sandstorm started to roll in. We had planned to hook up with another unit, but they had already upped sticks and left, so the decision was made to get back to base as soon as.

I was totally 'chin-strapped' after the three hour drive, and we trundled into 'Kohima' around 1900 hours. At least this time we hadn't driven all the way up north and back for nothing. But fortunately, we'd just made it back in time to catch a late evening meal, then I hit the showers, wrote a couple of 'Blueys', then clambered into my 'scratcher' – "End-Ex".

5. "We Seek Him Here, We Seek Him There…"

9th – 16th April

We'd been tasked to head back up North yet again. But this time in the direction of an old run-down Kuwaiti army barracks, where '3 Battalion REME' were to be found. It looked like we had a couple of day's work up here so we would stay in situ until we'd completed our task. It was better than having to do the same route repeatedly over a few days.

This rather beaten up place still had its merits though. The air conditioning had been brought on-line which improved the situation in the canteen (where a day or so earlier, we'd visited here to 'recce' the place and had sat there, gradually melting). What's more, the kitchen had only, this very day, been brought on line too. So instead of having to get foodstuffs 'imported' in, they could now start serving decent, wholesome grub.

The upstairs open-plan sleeping areas were also a little cooler at night with a little help from old 'air-con', which was just as well because the heat from the walls would have kept the night temperatures a little too much for comfortable sleeping.

This location was right on the edge of the desert, and just a little further out was 'Hammersmith', so the heat coming off the sand surface radiated around and about, heating everything up tremendously.

Bunk beds were the order of the day, "Pretty good" I thought, until I woke up next morning half crippled. There was such a drop in the springs that I may as well have been in a hammock (or maybe a hammock would have been a little more comfortable). So, I started the day in a not too-good condition and cursing the damned bed, whilst trying not to let my current predicament get the better of me.

The showers were manky but useable, but the way I looked at it was that running hot'n'cold, was running hot'n'cold, and there was no substitute for getting your hot, tired body under a stream of water, even if the colour of it was a little dubious. The original toilets were the porcelain hole-in-the floor jobs, but we'd been advised to use the portaloos dotted around the exterior of the place because the indoor plumbing systems could not really be relied upon. But the other thing with WC's like those Arab job's is that you have to have good balance when you're in squat mode or you could really "land yourself in the shit," to put it bluntly. Perhaps a little too descriptive, but maybe that was where the saying was derived from?

Each floor of the building had a balcony/landing which caught a little breeze, especially now that we were a couple of floors up. So after grabbing a brew from the kitchen and bringing it back up to our living area, we managed to sit around on whatever chairs were available and spent a little while chatting about events that had brought us to this point.

A few of the other inhabitants accommodated on our floor joined us a little later, and someone got out a deck of cards for those that wished to play. With a spot of dobying still to be done, I gave up my chair to one of the card players and set about utilising some of the running hot'n'cold to get some of my kit a little fresher. After wringing my bits and pieces out as much as was possible, I then hung my stuff out on the makeshift washing line that ran the length of the balcony, which was ideally positioned as the stuff would dry pretty quickly up here. The only problem was that with a limited number of clothes pegs, things had to be doubled up. But anything was better than nothing – just goes to show you the kind of activities that simply made the hours fly by!

Next morning (following a slightly more comfortable sleep, with the help of an extra mattress from an unused bed), I grabbed an 'egg banjo' and then headed out into the vehicle park to crack on with our job for the day.

Here, it was a little like a vehicle graveyard with written-off kit laying about the place. But, this was also one of the maintenance and repair areas where '3 Battalion REME' were doing sterling work to keep the heavy armour, amongst other stuff, in tip-top fighting condition.

Anything, requiring repair or servicing would be transported back here with a turn-around schedule of about 36 hours (more specifically armour), so the REME bods here worked extremely hard, no to mention round the clock, when the job demanded. Whilst I, and the rest of the Tigers were milling around, clambering over this and that to get the data we needed, I watched as the fitters literally threw a complete 'power pack' (engine) back into one of the AS90's (better known as 'AS Nasties'). I was always impressed by the sheer size of these beasts, and I felt suddenly dwarfed when standing next to one. They were not a tank although they looked every bit as formidable with its 155mm barrel. The reason it was still considered a 'gun' (a self-propelled one at that) was due to the fact that it had to be static when firing. However, it was thought by many, to be one of the most advanced mobile artillery systems in the world, and this was one ten year old piece of kit that the Yanks were very fond of too.

For spotters; if the calibre of the gun was changed, this thing was capable of lobbing rounds up to 40 K's, and that's a long way. I had witnessed some of the trials with the alternative calibre (Braveheart) barrel on Salisbury Plain a couple of years previously, when I was training on the 105mm Light Gun, and I'd timed the flight of a round from leaving the barrel to impact, and believe me, the shell was a airborne for a considerable amount of time. But I digress.

As I watched the fitters do their stuff, I was aware of a well tanned, if rather oily REME lass with larger biceps than me. This was enough to ensure that I kept my distance. Mind you, her tattoo's were quite colourful as well, but I reckoned an arm wrestling contest was definitely out of the question too, because I didn't want to end up requiring additional medical attention for an arm that had been wrenched from its socket!

As our small team combed the location there were a number of really banged up vehicles, ranging from Land Rover's that had been involved in 'RTA's, to vehicles with less obvious damage such as an 'APC'.

We'd heard a report that one of these had rolled in a marshy area, causing a fatality, and it had then become water-logged. Although it looked reasonably intact, the caging on its roof was a little twisted and battered.

Just by the look of some of the damage to the less armoured stuff with crushed cabs and the like, it made me wonder whether the occupants actually got out in one piece, if indeed they survived at all.

There was also a tank, minus its turret, tucked out of the way.

The aperture where the turret once sat, was covered over with a tarpaulin, for obvious reasons. That was one I didn't want to think about, never mind go and have a look at.

Two of us had been tasked to ride over to the main 'Hammer-smith' area, to hook up with one of the remaining med units and book us in for our Anthrax booster. Yes, it was that time again folks! In order to maintain the right direction in which we were headed, we had to use a line of power pylons on the horizon as a bearing point.

We were too far out as yet to be able to see the war damaged radar dishes, but as we roamed across the desert, we skirted a couple of units tucked in behind their sand berms.

It was a little more reassuring to find that there were still one or two Regiments out here in the 'boonies'. We even stopped at a Kuwaiti manned Police outpost, just to ensure we that we were on the right track. We must have looked something like a 'Dakhar Rally' contestant leaving a trail of sand dust in our wake. Lisa, who was driving, took no prisoners, particularly when we hit some kind of dip which lifted me out of my seat with just enough force for my bonce to glance off the roof of the Rover.

"Were did that come from?" she asked, as we both burst out laughing.

My reply was something along the lines that I was only booking in for a jab that I didn't really want to have, and in addition to which, I didn't want to have to be treated for crushed vertebrae or concussion on top of that.

After 15 eventful Kilometres across desert and sand track, we made it safely to our destination without getting lost. But, when we drove across to what had been '4 GS's location, where we'd previously had our jabs, half of the unit had bugged out. The only option was to head up the track to '202 Field Hospital'. At least they were still open for business. Ten Tigers were promptly booked in for an appointment with a needle the very next morning, as we were to leave the area to head back to 'Kohima'.

Jubilant scenes were now taking place in Central Baghdad as a giant statue of Saddam in al Farda square was pulled to the ground by Iraqis (with the much needed assistance of a US Armoured Recovery Vehicle). The excited crowd attacked the bronze effigy with anything they could hit it with, including the soles of their shoes, which was to be considered the ultimate insult.

The statue may well have been getting a good slapping, but the tyrant himself was still at large, and the reports now considered that he may quite possibly have attempted to get to Syria with Qusay and Uday. Now that Saddam was no longer home, his palaces were being looted by the people of Baghdad, whilst in the Iman City Mosque, Saddam loyalists were still holding out, where it was believed that key Iraqi officials were amongst them. After a four hour battle there were 2 more US dead to add to list, bringing the (Pentagon's) total of US war dead to a 101. The number of British soldiers killed, were put at around 30 up to this point in time.

A senior Shia cleric, one Abdul Majid Al-Khoei had been assassinated in Najaf. He'd been a resident of the UK for the last 12 years, and had only been back in Iraq for a fortnight when he was murdered.

On a more victorious note, 10,000 Kurds had advanced on Mosul, and with the help of US forces, they had taken the town of Kirkuk without much resistance. Eventually, the fragmented Iraqi V Corps surrendered.

Back at Kohima, after a reasonable night's kip under canvas – Bedouin style, we sorted the vehicles out, making sure that all the ration packs, water and other bits and pieces were replenished, ready for the next trip to wherever.

We'd organised a game of footy on an open area of the camp, and despite my back still giving me a bit of gip from the god-awful bunk beds, it loosened up a little, once we had a run-around. Rezzie's doubled up as goal posts, and we made sure that we were within short sprinting distance of cover, in the unlikely event of the 'incoming' alarm being sounded. The game continued without incident and gave our white bits a little exposure to UV's, and a reasonable amount of blood pumped around for an hour, we all grabbed showers and adjourned to our 'air-conned' mess tent, after which I caught up on the daily happenings on the news channel. It looked like all the major towns were now suffering from sprees of looting, and this included some of Iraq's historic buildings, where ancient artefacts had fallen prey to the mob of people who had no regard for their early history. US Military General, Tommy Franks stated that the leaders of Saddam's regime were either dead or were trying to flee.

There were now 55 Iraqi officials that had been identified by the US, who would be "pursued, killed or captured". US troops had been given packs of playing cards which illustrated the 'Fifty Five Most Wanted', to aid in their capture. However, when we tried to get hold of the cards, that was a different story. They were already fast becoming souvenirs and collectors pieces. Saddam now had a very heavy price on his head … something to the tune of $25m dollars (or £15m). Like the reward poster's of the 'Old West', he was 'Wanted, dead or alive'. Anyone that had conclusive proof that he was most definitely dead would still reap a portion of the reward. The US were also putting up the equivalent of £9m for information that would also bring about the capture of his two sons, Uday and Qusay. The both of them had allegedly been seen around Baghdad following the previous Monday's bombings, but the old tyrant himself was, and would remain, at large for some time.

There had been another blow to the Regime in that General Al-Saadi (one of Saddam's senior scientists) had given himself up to coalition forces, whilst two senior police chiefs were offering their services to the US in an attempt to curb the looting and lawlessness in the heart of the city.

A weapons cache had also been found. But this was no ordinary find. It included a number of gold-plated AK47s that Saddam apparently kept to present to loyal underlings as a reward for services rendered. I wondered how many soldiers and civilians would like one of those 'babies' as a keepsake. Not really the kind of thing you would hang over the mantelpiece; locked in a bank vault more likely. Mind you, it would certainly be a talking point at dinner parties!

In the heart of Baghdad there were pockets of militia who were still determined to hold on. During the fighting, 20 had been killed.

In the North, Kurds and Arabs had been waging a bloody battle in which two hundred had died. 'Dubya' was accusing Syria of helping Saddam's key supporters to flee Iraq and, as if by coincidence, Saddam's half-brother, Watban Ibrahim, had been arrested at the Syrian border. US planes continued to bomb what was considered to be Saddam's last stronghold in Tikrit, as the town gave itself up with little resistance. At the Port of Umm Qasr, the first aid ship had arrived, carrying upwards of two hundred tons of food and supplies for the local populace, the first time in around twenty years that a British ship had docked at the port.

It was around this time that we managed to get some desert kit. In my case, it was purely by default. I was looking to change a pair of green 'DPM' trousers before the seat went a little too threadbare – it was all but transparent now – and whilst not holding out much hope of an exchange I headed over to the QM's tent. One of the QM store guys opened an ISO container, had a look around, but no green trousers in my size. However, there were one or two boxes of desert kit and it appeared that I was in luck. The storeman must have taken pity on me, stating that he couldn't very well give me desert 'camo' trousers without the shirt. So I ended up with one official set,

"Wonders never cease," I thought. I enquired about boots, thinking I was on a roll, but I struck out. However, more stock was due in soon. With this info in mind, I let the Sergeant Major know, so that we could at least attempt to get most of the team, or those that still had no 'deserts', suited up. The upshot being that a few days later we managed to get boots, socks and a couple of the chocolate brown T-shirts (of the 'one size fits all variety' – there was only one size currently in stock!). Later on, the good old RAF ended up supplying us with more desert kit.

Someone reminded me it was a Sunday, and in particular, 'Palm Sunday'. A couple of Tigers had said that they were going to go to the evening church service and would I like to join them. After a short pause I said, "Yes, why not?" I would venture over to 'Spam Central' and attend the service with them. Although I wouldn't describe myself as a deeply religious person, somehow it seemed the appropriate thing to do, so after our evening meal three of us took a rover across to the small 'church' for the service. It was quite interesting to hear the minister adapt the various readings and texts from the Bible to our current situation, which made everything all the more relevant.

Word came to us that most of the remainder of 'Group Support' here in Kuwait would be moving over the border and into Iraq in around a week. I think that it would be right to say that most of us wanted to physically cross the border as soon as possible. However, due to the fact that my elderly mother was entering the last stages of her illness (she had terminal cancer), I would end up following the '1 Div Tigers' into Iraq a week later.

The senior ranks had known about my personal circumstances, despite my being discreet regarding the situation. They advised me that, taking into consideration that the main hostilities had all but ceased, then I was to go home, even just for a few days, to say my goodbyes to Mum. One sergeant in particular reasoned with me that he'd been in a similar situation where a close family member was concerned and had arrived home too late, never to forgive himself. So, basically, he was telling me in the strongest terms, that I WOULD go home once my sister had contacted the forces compassionate cell. Having had a talk with the boss and a phone call to my Sis (where it turned out that mum's condition had indeed taken a rapid nose-dive), the ball was put in motion.

My original intention was to have waited for the sad but inevitable phone call from my Sis to tell me that Mum had passed away, as this was something I had prepared myself for at the time I was about to deploy. All that I can say is that I was glad in the end that the senior ranks insisted I went home. Their attitude towards the whole situation was nothing short of outstanding.

So it was that, the next evening, I was on a flight back to Blighty.

Since my last visit to 'Lakeview', the residential home where Mum had lived after coming out of hospital some seven months previously, she had deteriorated and was now bedridden and reduced to eating only yoghurt-like foodstuffs.

During a week of visits I said my goodbyes, in the knowledge that she would realistically last no more than a few weeks. As I was leaving she managed a weak smile and a wave as her gaze followed me out of the room. Walking away was hard enough as it was.

She would die a little over three weeks later, but her strong constitution had enabled her to 'hang in there' a considerable number of months longer than even the doctors had anticipated. Following her diagnosis the previous September, we had barely expected her to see her 84th birthday, a week prior to Christmas.

As the Boss had given me the word regarding my rapid departure out of theatre to come home, I'd made ready with a hold-all just in case I had to move on a minute's notice. It was just as I'd got myself sorted that I heard the cries of 'Fire! Fire! Fire!' coming from outside the rear of our tent.

There were only a few of us about, and we exited in rapid fashion to find the canvas on the ridge of our neighbouring tent already ablaze. In the heat of the day and bone-dry conditions, the flames were eating the canvas away at the speed of which a rope fuse burns. A couple of us had already grabbed the extinguishers located nearby, trying to do our best to make some impact on the fire. It had been established that there wasn't anyone trapped inside, but our thoughts turned to the kit in there (and the slight possibility that there may have been ammunition amongst it – you never know). So we then attempted to concentrate our efforts on the kit, but by then, the tent itself was a 'goner'. One or two other people started doing likewise, but because Herb and I were closest in to the inferno, they just fed us with extinguishers until nothing more could be done. As the camp fire team took charge at the scene, virtually all the fire extinguishers had been discharged by then. It had taken only about 4 or 5 minutes for the whole of the tent to be destroyed – something which was aided by the hot desert winds.

Fortunately, the only victims were several Bergens and whatever other items of personal kit that had perished in the fire. Another reason why personal kit insurance was a must.

When the commotion was all over, we then had to move out of our tent whilst an investigation was launched as to the reasons for the fire.

So we set to, and lugged all of our own gear to an empty tent, which couldn't have been any further away across the camp. It required a number relays back and forth using our camp cots as stretchers on which to carry our belongings, which helped reduce the amount of trips.

The following day, our statements concerning the event, would be taken by the Fire Defence Team Officer in charge. But for the moment, that was enough excitement for one day. As darkness descended, we moved about our new abode with the aid of torchlight (as there was no power supply at this point), we were treated to another of natures awesome displays as a lightning storm rolled across the desert, some distance away. This was almost "Big Budget" film-makers, special effect lightning, the likes of which I'd not witnessed before, well, not on this scale anyhow. It was a pretty good light show and no spectator's fee!

At around mid-day, I and the rest of the '1 Div Team' would be parting ways after lunch, as they were to head up and over the border to our new area of operation – based at . My flight home wasn't until 2200 hours, which meant that once I'd said my goodbyes to the rest of the bunch, I had the afternoon to kill. So, with virtually all my worldly goods stowed in the vehicles that were to head up north, I waved the team off.

I was now left with just a small hold-all and the uniform I was standing up in. As they disappeared out of sight, trailing fine dust behind them, I was more than a little envious of them, but knew that I was going home for the best of reasons.

I headed over to 'Spam City', visited the PX , then caught up with the latest events on the news in the welfare tent. At least I could stay relatively cool for a while, in the air conditioned environment.

The big news of the day was that US President had declared that the main combat operations in Iraq were now over.

And, it appeared that for the first time in a month that the Iraq war was no longer front-page headlines back in the UK. Whilst the TV showed images of Iraqi police stations in which the cells had been previously used as torture chambers, the news bulletins scrolling across the bottom of the screen flashed up that Saddam's chief scientific advisor, Amer Hammoudi Al-Saadi had surrendered himself to US forces, claiming that he had no knowledge of weapons of mass destruction. Meanwhile, there was a really grim find at Al Zubayr – as shallow graves containing what was believed to be the remains of a number of westerners had been unearthed. There was some speculation regarding two of the bodies found, which were quite possibly those of either two British soldiers or journalists that had been missing.

The various ancient sites and buildings that had been previously looted by the mobs roaming through Baghdad, had raised some international concern, as some of the worlds oldest civilisations were to be located in modern day Iraq. This prompted the deployment of a British salvage team of conservation experts in an attempt to save the historic treasures.

After a fairly quiet evening meal, I showered, changed into my clean kit, and waited for 2100 to roll around. The OC and Sgt Major had decided they would both escort me to the airport for my flight out of Kuwait, and in the meantime they'd signed out a rather nice Pajero with 'air-con', which was considerably more comfy than a Rover. So I was quite chuffed to be heading for Kuwait International in a little style.

I'd said my goodbye's to the remainder of the 'Southern Tigers' (those based permanently in Kuwait) and headed out for the A-Pod.

Fifty minutes or so later, we weaved in and around the guarded checkpoints at Kuwait International. It was almost a shame to be giving up the cool interior of the vehicle for the rather humid night air.

So, I checked in my hold-all at the so-called departure point, which was basically a luggage x-ray machine in a tent, with a few military flight staff on duty. The 'departure lounge' was an area outside cordoned off by a hessian barrier which contained a few plastic chairs.

As the three of us had driven up, we'd noticed a number of US soldiers looking intently across the airstrip to where a C130 'Hercy-Bird' was parked up with its tail-gate opened onto the tarmac.

After having got rid of my bag, the OC, Sgt Major and myself wandered over to see what had drawn the attention of the Americans.

As we watched, one of the saddest spectacles that I think I'd ever witnessed, unfolded in front of us. There were seven Union Flag draped coffins being ceremonially loaded onto the transporter plane. As the pallbearers slow-marched each casket into the hold, I could just about hear the strains of 'The Last Post' being played on a bugle to honour the servicemen (one of which was, to date, the youngest soldier to be lost in action). It was a very solemn moment. They, like myself were headed back to Brize where their families would be waiting for their sad return.

The three of us just seemed to be naturally standing to attention, and the Sgt Major threw up a salute out of respect as the tail-gate's hydraulics slowly raised to its closed position. With no other reason for the two of them to hang around any longer, I said goodbye and shook hands with them, thanking the both of them for their grateful assistance in my compassionate situation.

I had several hours to wait as it turned out, as my flight time had been put back till 0330 … "Oh Bugger!". As I made my way over to the seating area, I spotted one tired looking guy who'd apparently been there since mid-day – poor sod! So with nothing else to do, I went off in search of a brew for the both of us. There was a US Med station not too far away, and a fresh pot of coffee had just been brewed … .just the job!

I returned with the brews, with my travelling companion wondering where I'd magic'd them from. "Well, that killed all of 10 minutes," I thought.

We'd been informed that the nearby US mess-hall would be opening at 2330, and that anyone on duty or those flying out, could avail themselves of it.

It had been a while since evening meal, so I queued with the Spam's (something that now seemed to be par for the course). I could have just had a sandwich or something light, but opted for the chicken and fries, which ordinarily, I would never have dreamt of eating around midnight, but I had hours to go, so it was a case of, "When in Rome … ."

As I was about to leave theatre, the news bulletins maintained that many of Saddam's Ministers and top Generals were scattered across the Middle-East after having fled from Baghdad – a number of which, it was alleged, were hiding out in Syria, despite the public denials from the Government in Damascus.

Finally, with tired, heavy eyes, the pair of us boarded the Tri-Star jet, which we were to share with about a dozen other passengers and cargo nets loaded with what appeared to be tracked armour wheels that were in need of repair. Apart from a dozen or so seats, the rest had been removed for the cargo skids that filled the rest of the plane. These were quite a flexible aircraft in that different seat configurations could be changed to suit the transporting task.

However, before touching down on home soil, we would have to hop over to Akrotiri Sovereign Air Base in Cyprus, drop some people off, and wait an hour or so whilst the quickest (and earliest) onward transport was sought for us. The flight staff were tremendous regarding those of us who were 'Comp B' returnees. It turned out that there were 3 spaces on a VC-10 re-fuelling tanker, piloted and crewed by the chaps of '101' and '10 Squadron' RAF. This was leaving soonest. That would do nicely.

What a treat that would turn out to be, due to the fact that an hour or two into the flight, the Pilot announced that we were to be joined by two Harriers for re-fuelling. So, as we moved into the fuselage area to look through the viewing ports that were level with the rear of the wings, we could see the two jets slowly closing on us from way off. As they began to level out at the same altitude as ourselves, they looked like they were drifting in as though being slowly pulled in by a magnet.

As the re-fuelling hoses were deployed from then Tri-Star, the Harriers positioned their fuel intake probes and eased forward into the 'funnels'.

The pilots bobbed up and down in conjunction with us, until the task was complete. The Harrier pilot on the starboard-side, gave us a wave as he disconnected himself from the hose and drifted away again … we were that close. And wouldn't you know it, that this was the one time that my bloody camera was in my bag in the hold!

It's not every day that you get a ring-side seat to something like this.

A while later after having been well fed and watered, we started to make our decent towards Blighty. Looking out of the window as we were preparing for landing, I couldn't believe how glorious the Oxfordshire countryside appeared – with the fields looking exceptionally green, interspersed with bright yellow Rapeseed. Was it because I'd seen nothing but sand for the last month or so, or did the UK look like it was in full bloom?

By the time the undercarriage glanced the tarmac at Brize, we were 'stuffed and stored' as they say. The flight crew had really looked after us, so myself and my travelling companions thanked the crew very much for their hospitality.

When I stepped off the bottom step on to native soil, my earlier thoughts about how 'summer-like' Blighty had appeared from above weren't wide of the mark. It was the middle of April and it was comparable to a warm mid-summer's day. Bizzare, is all I can say. But at least anything was an improvement on what was the norm for UK weather … rain (at this time of the year at any rate). Mind you, I hadn't seen any of the wet stuff for a while either.

Fortunately for me, a family member of a young lieutenant that I'd travelled with, had turned up to take her home and kindly offered me a lift as far as Runcorn in Cheshire, some 20 or so miles from my front door.

Well, that was a bonus as it meant that I could pick up a mainline train from there and be home in reasonably good time.

I don't really remember much about the car journey back up north, except that for most of the trip, I sat in the back with the window wound down – it was that warm.

I said my grateful goodbyes to the young officer and her relative as they dropped me at the station. And, it was just as I was approaching the ticket- counter to buy my ticket through to Liverpool, that it suddenly dawned on me that every bit of currency that I was carrying, all had the American eagle on it. Nothing but dollars. It seemed a bit daft having to use the old 'plastic' for a couple of quid's worth of train ticket, but there was no other option.

The one thing I was really stuck for however, was a coin to phone my other half in order for her to collect me from the station (my mobile phone had died on me). So, I had to ask a guy buying his ticket for the charity of a 20p piece. He took one look at me dressed in desert kit and said, "Sure, no problem. I guess you've come from afar then?" With half an hour to wait for the next train, I sat and wondered how my team-mates were doing in Iraq. Within 40 minutes of boarding the train, I stepped down onto the platform of my city station, and made my way over to the collection area to find a suitable spot to wait for the arrival of Linda.

Whilst standing there, preoccupied with the thoughts of my marathon journey from the middle-east, a vagrant came shuffling up to me, requesting the price of a cup of tea. I looked at him and then shoved my hand into my pocket, pulling out a handful of cents along with a couple of dollar coins. I couldn't help but laugh to myself, as I handed him a dollar coin and said, "There you go bud, that's all I've got. And, if you can get a cup of tea with that, then get me one too!" He mumbled something intelligible as he walked away. Well, I hadn't exactly sent him on his way without giving him something had I, and the dollar was worth about 70p. Two minutes later, another guy who appeared to be ming-monged (drunk), staggered over to me to pat me on the shoulder burbling; "Been out there to Iraq, Lad? Good on yer!"

He at least wasn't after the price of a cup of tea.

"Some home-coming," I thought.

I was beginning to wonder who or what would be next to come and invade my space. Twenty minutes later, a familiar white car pulled alongside the spot where I was standing, and a familiar voice came from the window, "D'you want a lift soldier?" it said. Within half an hour I was finally 'Home Sweet Home' behind my own front door. Thank goodness.

In the following week or so that I was home visiting my ailing mother, further controversy had been sparked off over the war in Iraq.

Claire Short had stated that "the fall of Saddam's regime did not justify the loss of a single life". Well, I suppose people were more than entitled to their opinions in this land of free speech, but I think the jury was out on that one. Whilst Tony Blair stated that "the conflict in Iraq is near the end but there will be tough times ahead in building peace". Whether the reality of just how hard it would be and how long it would take had actually registered, was another matter.

But, back over sea and sand, the Shia's who'd welcomed and supported the coalition's ever tightening noose on Baghdad were being "punished" by Fedayeen para-militaries loyal to Saddam.

It was also around this time that the Palestinian terrorist, Abu Abbas, who was wanted internationally for murder, had been captured. The cheeky bastard had been living as Saddam's guest in Baghdad, but where was his host? He was nowhere to be seen. Saddam's secret underground bunker had also been discovered whilst another of his half-brothers, Barzan Al-Tikriti had been captured. He had been one of Saddam's most senior and most feared lieutenants. Along with Barzan, a fifth senior regime figure had also been captured, which unveiled even more grim evidence relating to the sadistic torture methods of Uday Hussein ... like father, like son, I suppose. And, on the same subject matter, an Iraqi Colonel under questioning had recounted how the Shi'ites and Kurds who'd opposed Saddam, had also been brutally tortured.

On a happier note, certainly as far as troop welfare was concerned, the Prime Minister had granted that families and friends of those serving in the Gulf, were now able to send their loved ones parcels of up to two Kilogrammes in weight from the 17th April, 'FOC'. Anything was better than nothing.

In a real coup, around sixty Ba'ath Party leaders and Fedayeen fighters had been caught as they attempted to flee into Syria.

Australian SAS – 60, Ba'ath Party – nil!

It was feared that thousands of Iraqi's had lost their savings when extremist's had ransacked Baghdad's banks containing millions of dollars, and there were now no functioning banks in Iraq whatsoever, whilst the Pentagon declared that the war had now cost some $20 billion.

In a positive display of 'hearts and minds', the Black Watch and the Irish Guards had taken a less aggressive stance, by patrolling the streets of Basrah in regimental headdress rather than helmets and body armour.

If anyone knew how to project a more approachable, less threatening stance, it was the Brit's. This was something that the Spam's still had to learn.

The Defence secretary had stated that over the next few weeks, a further three and a half thousand personnel would return to Blighty, now that the decisive combat operations were complete. Those to return would include the 'Tankys' – 2nd Royal Tank Regiment, 1st Battalion The Royal Irish Regiment and 1st Battalion The Light Infantry amongst others. Naval vessels were already being deployed elsewhere along with the aircraft of the RAF.

And so, the levels of troops and other personnel were to be adjusted to meet the requirements of the task in Iraq, from a war footing to stabilisation.

25th April – 3rd May

On this very day, 88 years earlier, volunteers of the Australia and New Zealand Army Corps (ANZACs), landed on the Gallipoli Peninsular in the pre-dawn darkness. By the end of the war, Australia had suffered over 60,000 casualties, leaving few families untouched by it. No other nation had suffered as many war dead as a proportion of the total population. The Gallipoli landings were Australian's first large scale involvement in the First World War.

As the sun started its climb over the desert in the Middle-East (and as I prepared to make my return journey), the Aussie contingent in Iraq paid tribute to their fallen forebears as the 'Last Post' was sounded. It had been exactly a year ago to the day whilst on my UN Peace-keeping tour that myself and an Artillery buddy of mine had played pipe and drum at the same ceremony for those Aussies serving in Cyprus.

Now they were serving with us again in the Gulf.

With travel warrant in hand I was headed back for Brize again. But as I left home, I knew that I'd most probably be returning in a matter of weeks for an inevitable funeral. Three train changes, a taxi ride and some six hours later, I finally arrived at the gates of Brize Norton, and checked in at the flight desk.

Fortunately for me, I only had a few hours to wait for the out-bound Kuwait flight, so with what time that I did have, I checked in at 'Gateway' and managed to grab a spare room in order to freshen up and put on a clean set of desert kit. After a bite to eat, the bus came around to transport everyone over to the departure lounge to wait for the flight. Most of the service personnel were heading out to the Gulf too, except a lot these people were new 'in country'.

An announcement was made that the flight was bang on time, but with the down-side that we would need to 'bunny hop' over to Hanover to refuel, then to Cyprus (wait a couple of hours) then continue on to Kuwait. It doubled the travelling time of what originally should have been a standard one-stop journey of about six hours, but then again, what can you do 'when your boots let in'?

Stepping out into 'blast furnace' heat told me I was back. It had been surprisingly warm at home (seeing as it was still only spring) but nothing could compare to this. Although in one way I was sad to be leaving home again, in another, I was really chuffed to be back. And once I knew I was on my way, I was itching to get over the border with the rest of the team.

I wouldn't have to wait too long for that.

As I queued to re-register back into Theatre, I was greeted by a few familiar faces. The Sergeant Major, JB, Geordie and Jacko had come to collect me. So, after a round of quick handshakes, I threw my hold-all in the back of the rover, climbed in after it, then we were off. We had a fair old drive up and over the border to Umm Qasr, home of the '1 Div Tigers', so we needed to get moving pronto.

From the rover I had a rear view of the desert that was severed in two by the highway we were on. I did my best to prevent myself from cramping up in the back, and it was useless trying to have any meaningful conversation with Geordie and the Sergeant Major in the front, as the whine from the engine and the road noise from the tyres made it hard work. So, whilst admiring the golden expanse of the northern Kuwaiti desert, with its relatively flat and almost featureless landscape, apart that is from the raised escarpment that ran parallel a number of kilometres to the south – oh! and a few camels dotted about here and there too – as the hot air buffeted around me I attempted to scribble a few of my notes, although each successive jolt sent my pencil up and down the page of my notepad like a wild cardiograph reading.

I'd forgotten what a painfully uncomfortable experience it could be when travelling as 'human baggage' in the rear of a rover, due to the fact that 90% of the time I was driving, and the comfier front seats made bad roads less noticeable. Even then, some of the bumps and cracks in the roads further north could be really unforgiving on the human spine. To say that I was glad to get out of the vehicle at the end of this journey could be considered something of an understatement.

Way off to the east, through the late afternoon heat haze, I could make out a broad, dark shadow beyond the desert … the waters of the Arabian Gulf.

As we took a fork to the left, we approached what was to become a familiar landmark – a rose-coloured mosque with quite a distinguishable minaret tower, which seemed to stand alone against an empty skyline. On future trips, we knew that when we reached this point from a southerly direction, we only had around 40 minutes travelling time back to base.

We'd passed through what was a 'no man's land' of desert scrub, which was the UN Demilitarised Zone, then after a few kilometres, checked through the last checkpoint before entering which was controlled by Brit RMPs. It was at this point that we were told to put on body armour.

'Welcome to Iraq!' I thought.

We hit an undulating sand track that wound past an old army base, then on through a small village which looked like a real shanty-town. There were children milling around, just waiting for any vehicle (particularly a military one) to wave at, or hold their hands out expectantly, but in most cases, miming drinking gestures, which basically meant "give me something to drink". Some of these cheeky faced urchins were holding up the now obsolete bank notes with Saddam's face on them, whilst others had a variety of bits and pieces to try to tempt us with. As we passed them, we left a wake of dust that was thrown up by the wheels. Geordie had to be careful as the kids had a tendency to get a little too close to the vehicles as we passed. And the last thing we needed was to run over one of them.

After a few minutes humping and bumping over uneven ground we hit tarmac again. It was then that I could see the giant blue cranes at the port of Umm Qasr. This was where 'JFLogC' was to be found.

It was also to be our home for several weeks. We slowed as we bumped across the railway track that, if you followed it, would take you all the way to Baghdad. We then continued on towards the decorative arch at the entrance to the port.

With ID's cleared at the checkpoint and weapons unloaded, we headed across the open area to the large hangers that lined the harbour. As we passed the giant cargo cranes, I could see the green-blue waters of the Khwar abd Allah (or 'God's Waterway') that flowed in and out of the port. It was a sight that made me want to stop the vehicle and dive off the quayside. This was Iraq's only deep water port, which was being dredged to allow larger vessels to dock and depart without problems. This was all the more remarkable considering that only a matter of weeks previously the surrounding waters and entrance to the port were still being cleared of mines.

Once past the 'JFLogC' checkpoint we could finally park up and I could get out and stretch my aching legs and let the afternoon breeze dry my saturated shirt. On the way in, we passed a warning sign alerting all visitors to the problem of 'D and V' (diarrhoea and vomiting) … how nice!

What with the combination of heat, flies and porta-loos, it was paramount that everyone maintained good hygiene standards. It was certainly no fun having to use the 'thunder-boxes' in the sweltering heat, with a swarm of flies for company, whilst your olfactory senses were being sent into overload! Up here, the problem of cross-contamination was even more serious, as a whole battle-group could be brought to its knees and rendered ineffective if something like 'D and V' caught hold.

The heat at mid-afternoon was quite intense, although we still had the really hot months to come, and this particular region (of Basrah) happened to be the hottest of anywhere in Iraq. But when I stepped inside the hanger, the temperature rose even further. This was because the hangers seemed to retain the heat. But what exacerbated the problem was that our accommodation turned out to be '18 x 18' tents, set in rows, the interiors of which were hotter again. Tentage was also used because of the pigeon problem. Without a layer of canvas between us and the roof space, everyone would have been covered in droppings. To add to this, the kitchens were set up no more than about 15-20 metres away. So, radiated heat from the cook-house just simply compounded the problem.

I found the tent allocated to 'Tiger' and proceeded to unload my kit from the vehicle into the space that my compadrés had left me. As

I attempted to put together my camp-cot I was a lather of sweat in no time. The damned thing just wouldn't cooperate! Finally, I had everything squared away – 'mozzie net' draped from the roof poles overhanging my bed, mat unfurled and chair in position – as homelike as I was ever going to get it. Here inside, the lighting was quite dim, but we did have a single bare bulb hanging from the centre pole that was waiting to be hooked up to the generators outside. That looked promising, anyhow. Several yards away, a TV tent was set up, so at least I could catch up on daily events through means other than my radio.

Now all that we needed was room service!

A little while later, my '1 Div' team mates rolled in after a sticky day out under the Iraqi sun. It was like a meeting of old friends and it felt really good to be back again. It didn't take long to catch up on events, due to the fact that I'd only been away for just over a week.

We also had a new 'Tiger' in town. A Geordie 'full-screw' called 'Hooch', whom I was to partner up with, came in a little later. After an, "Alreet Bud, how'ya doin?" I knew that 'Hooch' and I would get along just fine. Sometimes you instantly have a sense for these things I suppose. Mind you, he liked a brew as much, if not more than me, so that was him and me sorted.

He seemed a decent guy, and as it would turn out, he had a very good sense of humour, which was one of the most important things to have in this team, as everyone ribbed everyone else mercilessly (which is the way of things throughout the whole of the British Army, and has been so for decades).

Later, whilst pouring over a map of the areas that we were to operate in and around, I realised that the Iranian border was only about 45K's away, so really not that far in the whole scheme of things, and I wondered whether there was anything that could still happen that would end up 'rattling the Iranian's cage', so to speak, which in turn could also set them off, what with the Middle-East being such a volatile place.

It was only a couple of weeks ago that the battle-group had pushed through here, fighting on and up to Al-Zubayr, just a few K's away up the road, then clearing the way to Basrah itself. Umm Qasr had already had a visit from a small group of the 'Tigers' whilst the smoke of battle was still visible in the distance, which must have been quite an intense experience for those involved. Umm Qasr had been taken and controlled by US Soldiers and British Marines in the first few days of the fighting once they had secured the Al Faw Peninsular.

And now, even the dilapidated railway line that had once run between the port and Basrah had been repaired by '17 Port and Maritime Regiment RLC', with the help of local rail workers.

One of the key projects was to bring the port back to life as this was an extremely important sea port, geographically speaking. This would also give the local populace the added stability that came with employment, which, in turn, would provide a more positive outlook for their future.

My first night's sleep in Iraq was a disturbed one due to the uncomfortable night temperatures, and the local hounds giving it all they'd got. Although there was a pleasant breeze blowing in across the port, it never managed to filter through to the maze of tents. So, what with the return journey that had already disrupted one nights sleep, and the heat keeping me awake the next, I was really 'cream crackered' when it was time drag myself from my pit. Even the local mozzie's had managed to covertly slip in under the net and steal my blood too. These beasties were more than likely 'Saddam's Special Forces Anti-Coalition Mosquito' or SSFACM's, specially bred for that very purpose, which was another reason for continuing with the Paludrine and Nivaquine tablets. The problem was, once they'd sampled and got a taste for my 'O Pos', they'd be back, and what's more, they'd bring their friends along for lunch too. If there was only one mosquito in the whole of the country, the bugger would find me!

Fortunately, my arrival up here coincided with the porta-kabin showers coming on line, so I could at least get myself a refreshing wash down. However, I quickly found out that if you showered anywhere in between mid- morning or very late evening, the sun boiled the water in the storage tanks, making it nigh on impossible to take even a remotely cool shower.

Even the cold water was virtually scalding hot – shades of 'Ali'.

We had been given an admin day, as we weren't due to head out to a previously 'reccied' location until next day, so I decided I'd 'dobi' my few bits and pieces over at the 'open plan laundrette' which was basically a canvas covered area with a few trestle tables, a supply of bowls, and a massive aluminium water pot which sat on a large butane gas burner which kept the water heated. The pot itself was big enough for two people to get in and have a bath (the thought did cross my mind on a number of occasions, believe me), but it was no doubt the biggest circular 'mess tin' that I'd ever seen.

Adjacent to this were, a number of washing lines. So, it was just a matter of finding enough hanging space and supplying your own pegs

(I knew that my purchase of a couple of packs back at 'Ali' would prove invaluable). And Boy, stuff dried bone-dry in no time up here.

Was an Iraqi breeze slightly better than a Kuwaiti breeze for drying your washing, I wondered?

This kind of thinking was really sad I know, but there was an obvious deterioration in my mental state by this point.

A little later, a couple of us wandered the couple of hundred yards around the port to the EFI shack that just happened to be doing a roaring trade in tins of Fanta. What's more, a new stock had just come in and had been chilled nicely – 4 for a dollar, extremely good value for money, mind you, not that there was a great deal else round here that you could spend your dosh on.

I found out rather quickly that meals, were usually accompanied by flies (not an optional side-order), and even more so up here than in the Kuwaiti desert, so half the meal time was spent swatting whilst eating. If I'd played tennis, my back-hand would have improved no end. These little carriers of all things nasty were so persistent. In fact, I thought that perhaps Saddam had bred a particularly annoying strain of anti-coalition fly. It certainly wouldn't have surprised me.

I've got to say that the grub was extremely good considering the conditions, so there was no problem in eating reasonably well, and although a Chef's job involves spending a fair amount of his or her working day in a hot environment, I could certainly appreciate the doubly hot conditions they were working under. My only problem was trying not to melt into my meal whilst doing aerial combat with the 'SACF's – Saddam's Anti-Coalition Flies.

At least there was a hot water urn (well, a vat with a tap) to hand most of the time, so that even when it got to late evening, it was possible to continue make a brew unless it had been drained dry or the milk had run out, which could be most frustrating. The dispenser required to be filled with pans of hot water, as it didn't boil or keep the water hot continually. So, it was obviously at its hottest when it was first filled.

However, my faithful, well travelled auto-jug would again come to the rescue and prove itself later, when we eventually had access to generated 240volt.

I was considering putting this little piece of electrical hardware in for an 'MID' or mention in dispatches, "for service above and beyond the call of duty".

Life In 'Hangerville' – (A2 within easy reach to the left).

'Snack Central'.

Tigers x4 - Jacko, Herbie, Billy and Me complete with non-issue shades.

The 20k route into 'Fox' - pure desert.

Cosy conditions, but still smiling!

US armour rolling north.

Home Sweet Home (out in the Boonies).

Lisa and I are invited in for a brew.

MRE lunch – with a storm about to roll in.

'The Patio' – a hive of activity.

Getting amongst some of 16 AA's armour as it prepares to head north.

The flyer reads: 'British Forces are working in your area', with the flipside reading: 'Stay in your homes, you will be safe. Stay away from military forces'.

14TH MARCH

DEAR LIN, HOPE YOU'RE DOING OK.
WHILST WE WAIT FOR 'THINGS' TO HAPPEN, SECURITY IS
TIGHT, HENCE NO USE OF SAT PHONES (AS COMMS ARE MONITORED)
WE'VE BEEN INFORMED THAT POST & MAIL WILL BE SLOWER DUE
TO FLIGHTS IN & OUT OF 'Q8' BEING RESTRICTED.
HOWEVER, I HOPE THAT SOME MAIL REACHES ME, AS I'VE STILL
ONLY HAD ONE LETTER - WHICH IS A LITTLE FRUSTRATING.
    DON'T BELIEVE ALL THAT YOU SEE IN THE TABLOIDS, ALTHOUGH
THE PROMISE OF DESERT KIT ANY TIME SOON SEEMS TO BE AN EMPTY
ONE, SO UNLESS PEOPLE PULL THEIR COLLECTIVE FINGERS OUT,
HALF THE FORCES WILL BE FIGHTING A WAR IN WHAT THEY STAND
UP IN - BUT THERE ARE OTHERS THAT NEED THE KIT EVEN MORE
THAN US. THE 'OC' HAS RECOMMENDED THAT AS MANY AS POSS SHOULD
WRITE TO OUR MP's TO HIGHLIGHT THE PROBLEM - NOT A BAD IDEA!
ONE OR TWO OF THE GUY'S HAVE TRADED BITS & PIECES WITH THE
'SEPTICS', BUT MY OWN BOOTS ARE NEARLY READY TO FALL OFF MY
FEET. IN THE MEANTIME, I MAY BE ABLE TO BUY A PAIR OF DESERT
BOOTS FROM SOMEONE FOR ABOUT HALF THE PRICE (NEW BOOTS ARE
ABOUT £80) AND PRINCIPLE DICTATES THAT I WILL NOT PAY THAT
MUCH, BESIDES WHICH, SOME OF THE MILITARY KIT SUPPLIERS IN
THE UK HAVE EITHER SOLD-OUT OR ARE PUTTING THEIR PRICES UP
BECAUSE OF DEMAND. (IF I DO BUY ANY, I'LL SEND G-HOON THE BILL!)
ANYWAY, ENOUGH OF MY 'SOAP BOX' STUFF.
DID YOU MENTION TO AUNTIE THAT I WAS SOMEWHERE 'SANDY' -
DON'T WANT HER TO WORRY, AND I HOPE YOUR MUM'S DOING OK....
TELL HER I'M ALRIGHT.... COUGHING UP THE DESERT, BUT I'M ALRIGHT.
AS FOR MY MUM, GIVE HER MY LOVE NEXT TIME YOU VISIT - NO DOUBT
SHE'S DETERIORATED FURTHER - WE'LL JUST HAVE TO SEE HOW
THINGS GO. WE'RE DUE TO GET 2 NIGHTS RESPITE AT OUR PREVIOUS
LOCATION (IF PLANS DON'T GET SCUPPERED) SO IT'LL BE 'BURGER KING',
'SUBWAY' OR MAYBE BOTH.
WILL SEND YOU A SMALL "WANTS" LIST AND I'M WRITE TO YOUR MUM B4
I GET INTO MY DUST-LADEN SLEEPING BAG. ANYWAY, GOODNIGHT FOR NOW.
              LOVE & MISS YOU, E XX

My last 'bluey' home just as the war is about to kick-off

Forces into Action

"The lights stayed on in Baghdad but the instruments of tyranny are collapsing."
Defence Secretary, Geoff Hoon

BRITISH soldiers and Royal Marines surged into Iraq; Royal Navy ships deployed their helicopters, missiles and heavy guns, and RAF aircraft dropped their bombs in targeted attacks. On 20 March 2003, the struggle for Iraq's liberation began.

Picture: Paul Jarvis

Moment of truth

20 March 2003: This picture by a Forces photographer, shows troops of 1st Battalion The Royal Regiment of Fusiliers defending members of 39 Armoured Engineer Squadron, 32 Regiment Engineer as they break through an obstacle allowing British toops to enter Iraq

(Left) A RAF Chinook and Sea King helicopters begin lifting men and equipment ashore.   *Picture: Angie Pearce*

The 'ST' newspaper, which helped kept everyone's spirits up.

A grimace for the camera … .getting a bit hot and bothered.

The message on this 'Baby' reads: "To Saddam with love from 'H'
(another title by which I am known in some circles).

Bomb damage.

Bomb damage seen from inside.

A captive's wall art.

'Ships of the desert' crossing our path.

61 Ammunition Squadron – way out in the 'boonies'
The flying 'tadpole' is a US Marines helicopter.

Daz proving that you can sleep through anything if you're determined enough.

Carry on 'Mind That Camel!'

Heading back from the border as the sun starts to rapidly set.

Don't mess with me 'n' my buddy!

The middle of nowhere (really just a stage backdrop of the Kuwait desert!).

SADDAM HUSAYN AL-TIKRITI
President

UDAY SADDAM HUSAYN
National Assembly Member/
Olympic Chairman/Saddam
Feyadeen Chief

QUSAY SADDAM HUSAYN AL-TIKRITI
Special Security Organization (SSO)
Supervisor/Ba'th Party
Military Bureau
Deputy Chairman

The three most wanted Aces.

Receiving a brief from the Sergeant Major
(easy to identify the 'tree frogs' from the 'sand lizards').

And on today's menu … Man Soup! (OK, I'm behind it, not actually *in* it!).

Could this be the return of Rommel? Or is it Alex doing a rather good, if unintentional, impersonation?

Americans at play.

Probably the best moment of the day for me – a soak, a brew and a bit o' music.

Prior to the gig – Alex, Hooch, Lisa and myself.

The location begins to fill up.

Nell with Gaz and Hooch.

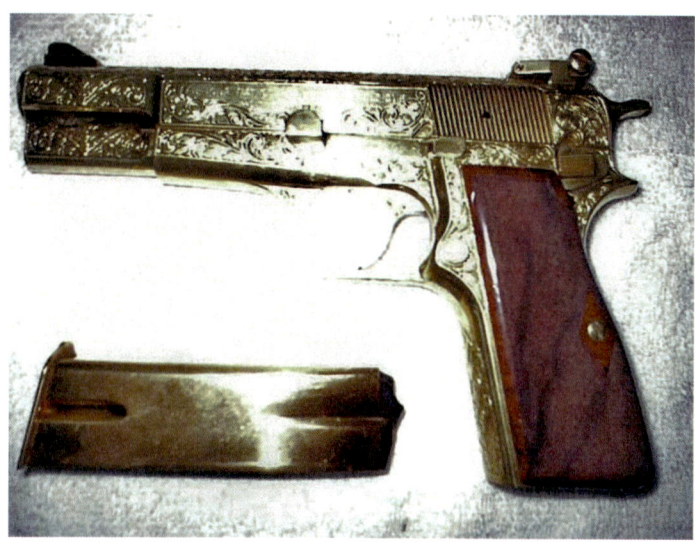

The 9mm.

Jim Davidson 'doing his bit'.

Herb & I outside the Shatt Al Arab Hotel.

Destroyed Ba a'th Party HQ.

'Tiger' heading out from the ruins.

The Palace (above) with Hooch in one of the main doorways.

The palace gardens.

Heading along Gulf Street towards the Kuwait Towers.

The view from one of the towers.

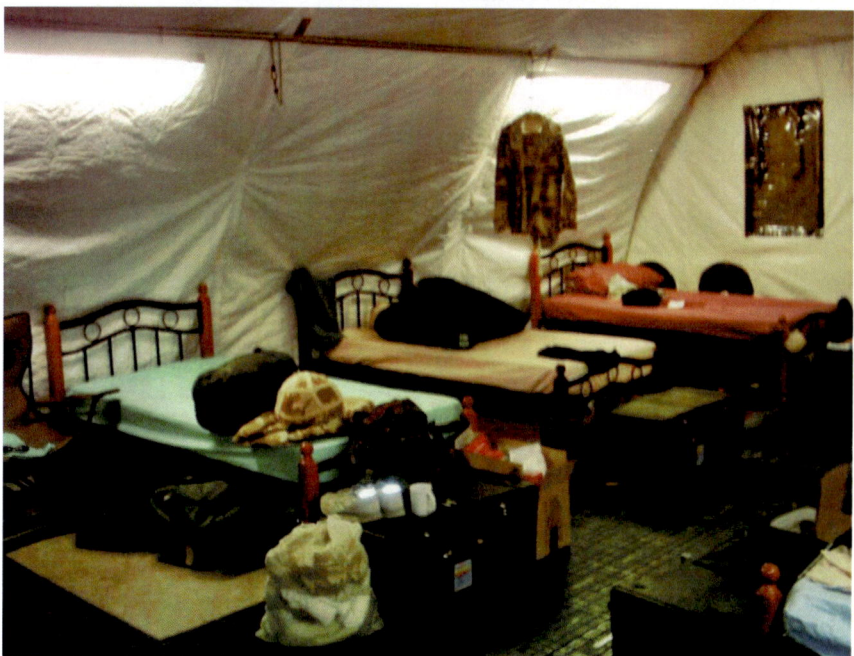

Now you're talking comfort!

Nimrods simmering in the Omani heat.

Vessels ancient and modern at Muscat port.

Mutrah.

X3 Tigers heading for our 'Herc'.

"This is Ian Williams in Oman … signing off".

A beautiful sunset to greet us as we landed at BIA.

One of the last remaining un-defaced image of SH in the Basra region.

A discarded piece of Iraqi armour.

This is one of the two Scimitars of the Household Cavalry that was mistakenly attacked by 'A10's from which Trooper Christopher Finney (a young armoured vehicle driver) rescued his gunner, amongst other actions, whilst disregarding his own injuries and personal safety. He would later be awarded the George Cross.

Two of the founding members of the 'AASAB Tea Club'
'The Grand Tea Master' – Damian (left) and the Author.

قاعدة على السالم الجوية رافقتكم السلامة
GOOD BYE ALI AL SALEM AIR BASE

Tigers pose for one last photo before heading home.

Author with jet left behind after Gulf War 1 in 1991.

It was worth a try but, despite the heat, the aluminium of a rover bonnet is not quite hot enough to fry an egg. What we really need here is armour plate!

Tiger Team at Arafjan. The author, back row, second from left. The remainder ... you know who you are!

Once people knew that my very own 'water hotter' was up and running, it soon became very popular, and it's amazing how quickly you can make new friends – especially when a brew is in the offing.

Anyhow, it appeared that we were stuck here for next few weeks until the engineers had completed the construction of the new 'Temporary Deployable Accommodation' or 'TDA', across the other side of the port. This modular tented living quarters came complete with 'air-con', which was apparently climatically controlled to keep indoor temperatures 20°C lower than outside, and real full size beds, foot lockers, decent lighting and more importantly … en suite washing facilities where the water temperature was also controlled, which meant no more scalding showers.

The Americans had been using this type of modular living quarters for more than 25 years, but that aside, they were absolute quality! Now all that we needed to do now was to bloody well get in there, because we were beginning to turn into a mass of hot, sticky, sweaty things.

From a distance the structures looked like sand-coloured tented versions of the good old Nissen hut, linked by plastic walkways. 'Moonbase Alpha' might have been an appropriate name for it. However, our re-location date over to what was to be called 'Sultan Lines', (which was quite apt I suppose) would be put back further, so we'd have to resort to drastic measures when it remained too hot at night … .we'd sleep outside.

When the port had initially come under coalition control, there'd been a problem with packs of wild dogs roaming around, and whilst the US and Brit's had made attempts to dealt with the situation, there were still a few mutts wandering about, especially at night. So, that was something that we'd need to watch out for if and when the heated confines of the tent forced us outside. But one by one, over a period of a few nights, individuals could be seen heading out with camp cot in hand.

One particular night, after most of the team had got their heads down, I lay awake listening to my walkman in an attempt to take my mind off just how hot it was. As I lay on top of my 'scratcher' in just a pair of shorts, I could see the pools of sweat starting to form on my body. In the end, I just had to get up and go and sit outside for a while. Although it was still very warm out there, it certainly wasn't as bad as the interior of 'Tent City', and I could at least feel a slight breeze blowing.

One of the locations that we were to visit had previously been 'reccied'- this was Shaibah Airfield, about an hour or so's drive. It was probably nearer to Basrah than anywhere else, but it was here that most of the remaining battle support group could be found. All of the different units were spread out over the whole of the area. The guys who had been up there, mentioned that the place was one big, dry dustbowl, but that it had two things going for it ... there was a small Pizza Hut and Burger King trailer which was doing a roaring trade with the company of US Marines also based here as well as the Brits.

Well, as far as I was concerned, it was another place to go and check out (as well as a burger). We would be up there working for the next week, during which, a small team of 'Tigers' would head over to Basrah International Airport and 'recce' the situation there.

Within the next several months, Shaibah would become the main 'Log(Logistic)Base' for the Brit-force in Southern Iraq. For those troops to be deployed here later, on subsequent 'Telic's, this place would dramatically change as living conditions and the overall welfare package would improve things beyond all recognition. But, in its current state, it had to be experienced to be believed.

As a complete aside, if you drove further into central Iraq, you would come across the village of Medina, believed to be near the site of the Biblical Garden of Eden. But sadly, Eden was now an area littered with unexploded ordnance, which was causing no end of problems for the bomb disposal teams. This was because the local populace did not realise just how dangerous the unexploded ordnance was. Kids were actually playing footy with mines as villager's used plastic explosives for fuel as though it was firewood. Despite warnings to the locals, the Royal Engineers were working as fast as they could to clear what was believed to be around 100 plus ammo dumps full of explosives (courtesy of retreating Iraqi forces).

It looked like one or two of the guys were starting to suffer the first effects of the dreaded 'D and V' or 'Montezuma's Revenge' as the Americans referred to it. And, in this heat there was nothing worse. It did mean not having to stray too far from a porta-loo of course. There seemed to be a number of cases around and about. I just hoped that good hygiene practises were enough to keep me from catching the bug. Depending on how many team members we had in good health would dictate how we operated over the next few days. So far, nothing other than obviously getting a little too hot had affected me, and then that was mainly in the 'foot region'.

I just hoped that it would stay that way.

Next morning at 0800, our team minus one (incapacitated by 'D and V') drove out of the port and headed off for the dust-bowl that was Shaibah Airfield. Prior to exiting the check-point, we'd loaded full mag's onto our weapons (as per long-standing SOP's). It felt good to be back out driving again. Hooch and I followed the lead vehicle as we took the route that led in the general direction of Basrah.

This was all new territory to me, and it was quite a different prospect driving this side of the border. The one thing that I did notice, was that the landscape appeared a lot harsher than in Kuwait, although there was a little more desert scrub, there was no golden coloured desert here.

We passed an oil refining plant with its weird looking spherical-shaped tanks, like something out of a sci-fi film, but it did make for a handy reference point. We then started to come up on some small hamlets with just a few ramshackle houses. The kids from within ran towards the edge of the road, waving frantically with beaming smiles. It was as though the sight of a British vehicle had made their day, especially when we responded likewise.

To say that these kids lived in reasonably primitive conditions didn't detract from the fact that they all looked clean and appeared be quite happy.

They had very little, but could still manage to smile.

As we passed another group of 'munchkins' further on, some were waving again, whilst others made the drinking or hand to mouth, "give me water, give me food" gestures. At the very least, fresh water was obviously a priority for their daily survival.

The scenery changed little as we got to within a few miles of our turn-off, except for maybe one or two roadside fruit stalls, a little more traffic, and a few severely overloaded donkey carts. I really felt for one poor beast, as his tiny cart was loaded with half a metal factory on the back. There were goodness knows how many sheets of tin and other bits of metal fabrication, that it was doing its best to pull.

Animal Rights Campaigners would not have been happy at all.

We had to pull over to the left and cut across the carriage way to get on the route we needed for Shaibah. This was one time that I was so glad that I wasn't riding in the back, the road was a real 'bone shaker' in places.

A few K's out from Shaibah, I could see burnt out and battle-scarred Iraqi armour amongst an avenue of trees. Nothing had escaped the onslaught from coalition armour or aircraft.

As we neared Shaibah, we passed a bunch of kids who were not only holding up Iraqi money, but military medals too. We slowed to see what these 'mini hustlers' were asking for in return for the medals. A couple of dollars seemed to be the going rate.

Anyway, 10 minutes later, we slowed up to the checkpoint at Shaibah, flashed our ID's and pulled over whilst we unloaded our weapons and made them safe. The airfield was indeed a large area, spread out over a 3K grid square, with an artery of roads leading off in all directions, but the place was nothing like you could imagine in terms of a modern day airfield. And, what's more, the guys had been right in their previous assessment of the place – it was a dust bowl and no mistake.

Due to the fact that there were about ten of us out on the ground, it was decided that we would 'blitz' a given area of the airfield each day that we were here. That way, each unit that we visited could be systematically wiped off the slate, as it were.

As we divided up into two's to cover a given area of a unit, I came across the very RLC Support Unit that my buddy, Gordon (who I'd last seen at Camp Fox some several weeks previously – for all of 10 minutes) was serving with. When I enquired as to his whereabouts, it turned out that he'd been tasked up north to '16 Air-Assault' for a couple of weeks. So, I left a message with one of his guys to let him know I'd been around. I was sure we'd catch up at some point.

There was quite a bit of light armour that we needed data from – '432's and other tracked stuff. As the sun rose, so did the temperature of the armour plating as we clambered over the kit, raising more of a sweat in the process. This was were the issued sweat rags helped a little, and were particularly good as neckerchiefs (especially when dampened with cool … .well, tepid water). Another little snippet of information that I remember my dad telling me, how in the days of yore (World War Two), the desert troops used to cook eggs on their scorchingly hot armour .

I could begin to understand how that was possible now, and I found out rather quickly, that it bloody well hurt if you let any part of your anatomy touch the metal for longer than a millisecond.

There was also an area just outside the main entrance, where some of the battle-damaged Iraqi armour (mostly 'T-55's and a few light guns) had been assembled, so we had a look on our way out, being mindful that some of the armour might have been taken out with 'DU' rounds, and so were careful. (Depleted Uranium ammunition is the most effective material available, due to it being twice as dense as lead, and having the capability to punch through armoured vehicles).

Out on some of the tracks and routes that ran parallel to the desert up and around the Shaibah area, there were still many pieces of Iraqi hardware that lay scorched in their dug-in's, and others that were stopped dead, literally in their tracks. On a couple of the tanks it was possible to make out the neat hole of an armour piercing round that had punched its way through, where it had then wrought death and destruction on the inside. They sat there with their immobile gun-barrels pointing across the expanse of the desert.

One of the Engineer units had, I believe been given the challenge from their CO to get one of the lesser damaged 'T-55's up and running in a given amount of time as a side project – most probably as an actual working war souvenir to be returned to Blighty. We saw one tank being towed about on the airfield. Now, whether that was the 'project' tank, I'm not sure.

With our move further north, came a different BFPO address, but despite this the mail was managing to get through to us reasonably well. I'd received one really welcome package from my Sis back in Blighty, which happened to contain amongst other things, another much-needed bottle of 'foot soak'. One of my first priorities when we got back in each afternoon was to sit with my 'plates of meat' in a steel bowl (now courtesy of the QM's department). It was such a pleasure to immerse them into the tepid water. Add a brew to the equation and what more could you ask for. The combination of these two factors whilst listening to my cassette version of 'Black Adder Goes Forth' went a long way in the wind down for the day. If we weren't needed for anything specific, I'd lovingly tend my tootsies, powder them and leave them out of my boots for a while. They were the one thing that I'd really have to keep an eye on. Fortunately, I'd managed to get hold of a large pack of thin cotton socks from the American PX, and they were just the job for my desert boots. But, no amount of pampering would stop my feet from becoming 'redders'. I'd just have to do what I could to keep them in good nick.

In one of our post evening meal briefs, the Sgt Major reiterated the point about sticking to recognised and designated tracks and routes, as a Lance Corporal had been killed when his vehicle hit a mine, somewhere in the region. When we'd been out and about during the day, I'd heard the unmistakeable 'crump' of an explosion, but that had most probably just been a coincidence as the 'EOD' guys were in the area, destroying ordnance.

And, talking of 'EOD' bods, Gaz, one of the team members that we'd shared our tent with way back in 'Hammersmith', turned up around this time.

He and his small crew had moved in just across the aisle in 'Tent City'. We'd got to know him a quite a bit, and so he became a good buddy to Tiger. It was really great to be able to compare notes, with regard to where and what we'd been up to since we last met.

During the week's tasks, we were due to head up to BIA – Basrah International Airport, which from Shaibah is around a 40-minute drive. However, the route varied greatly from dirt track, salt flat desert plain to multi-lane highway. It was a strange experience to pull off a desert track on to a 6-lane highway with its large overhead signs that pointed in the direction of Basrah. These were signs that we'd seen in news bulletins as the forward battle-group was advancing on the city, where plumes of smoke could be seen beyond, and not all that long ago, either.

As we finally approached the long strait that ran towards the 'A Pod' (Airport), I could make out a long line of battle-damaged Iraqi armour that had all been dragged into one area, like some heavy duty parking lot. Once through the heavily armed check-points, we parked up outside the main terminal building, then headed into the departure lounge.

It was eerily quiet, and although it was a hub of activity elsewhere within the building, the layer of dust on the floor of this massive lounge with its beautiful brown marbled floor, gave it a look of sudden abandonment.

All I can say is that there was something very strange about it.

Anyway, we'd managed to book in for lunch, which was a welcome change from eating MRE's 'on the hoof'. They served their purpose, but just sometimes, a bit of fresh salad (when and where it was available) made into a sandwich, hit the spot just nicely at lunch break, followed by several thirst quenching cupfuls of juice.

After we'd completed our task at 'BIA', we headed back for Umm Qasr, with me launching a few bottles of saved up water towards the kids at the side of the road as we passed. Because the kids were always making the gesture for 'drink' I'd started to collect the partially filled bottles back at base – most of which would more than likely be tipped down the drain, especially when it became rather tepid, or otherwise used to top up the cooling systems of the vehicles. Anyway, I would top up the bottles to make full ones, that way – no waste and a good cause too. When I launched them out of the Rover, I was always very careful to allow enough distance for the bottles to come to rest, without knocking one of the kids over like a skittle. Plus, I made sure that the bottles skidded in off the road away from harm, as we had heard that an over-excited 'munchkin' had got a little too close to a vehicle and had been knocked down. I think I only ever had one bottle split on me, due to a bad landing.

Whilst passing the homesteads one morning on our way out towards Shaibah again, Hooch in the passenger seat, started to give the kids a double 'thumbs-up' sign whilst making an up and down motion, and in turn the kids did likewise. There was also one little boy who, for whatever reason was holding a dead lizard at the edge of the road, maybe he was showing us his latest trophy? The lizard was about three feet long and it looked like it took all of the boy's strength to lift the beast by its tail. I remarked to Hooch that had it not been dead it probably would have eaten him. Maybe he was hoping that by holding it up in the sun for long enough that it would bake in time for 'vittles'? The funny thing was that as we returned at mid-afternoon, he was still at the roadside showing off the lizard. Not only that but the same group of kids remembered our vehicles and gave us a dancing version of the 'two thumbs routine' without being prompted. We both burst out laughing and called the routine 'The Hoochie Dance'. It was basic level communication but it worked. We joked that the kids must work a rota system in the daily grind of waving and dancing to the Brit convoys that went past, with the kids that we regularly saw, doing the early morning and mid-afternoon shift!

Prior to one of the later trips past the homesteads, a few of us had decided that we would 'donate' the unwanted bits and pieces from the Brit 'rat pack's and US MREs. This was I suppose, our little bit of 'feel good factor'. We were never going to eat all of the stuff that was left over, so we thought, "Why not?" But as a cautionary tale, I did remember a situation one time when I was on holiday in Egypt, where somebody had a pile of sweets to give out to the local kids, probably with good intention. But, because of the number of children, it caused a sickening spectacle as they fought each other for the sweets. So we had to make sure that this didn't happen here, and the last thing we wanted was to make full-time beggars out of these people.

At the hamlets that we passed, there were only around half-a-dozen kids so it was reckoned that things could be done sensibly and without problem.

So, the next time we were out and about, we'd pre-arranged that the vehicle behind me would slow up whilst one of the guys distributed his 'ex-rations', with me easing off the gas a little too, so that he could kept well in sight.

Bearing in mind that we still had to ensure good convoy drills and be aware of any potential threats to our safety. Anyway, he managed to distribute them without problem, and drove the rest of the way back feeling rather satisfied with himself.

We realised of course that it wasn't possible to make much of a difference in the lives of these people, but it was just something that we wanted to do.

(Although, some time later, signs were posted back at base telling everyone not to feed locals.)

One of the afternoons we'd returned a little earlier, which allowed us a little down-time, so a few of us headed over to the edge of the quayside, to find a number of the locals swimming around the bottom of a slip-way. The best we could do, was to park the up vehicles, take our shirts off whilst remaining out of sight, and attempt to 'bronzie' anything above the waist-line for half an hour. We'd armed ourselves with soda's from the small 'EFI' shack – still 4 for a Dollar.. … .and they were superbly cold, straight from the cooler, what more could you ask? Well, it was a case of you had to take what you could get. As we watched the goings on around the quayside, we spotted one of the waterway patrol boats that happened to be moored alongside, and went to have a chat with the guys on board – it turned out that they were Aussies. It made for a welcome change, being able to converse with other coalition members who didn't hail from the US or Blighty. They'd even offered us a spin out on the waterway at some point when operational duties allowed. So, we said thanks and would gladly take them up on their offer if the chance arose. Needless to say, it didn't happen.

A little while later, we inherited a beat-up little fridge (courtesy of a new addition to 'T-Team' who'd brought it from her last location) that was still in working order – or just about.

The only area close to a 240v supply that was hooked up at this point was, in Gaz's 'EOD' tent across the way. He was more than happy to be 'fridge custodian', providing that his Senior Ammunition Technical Officer (SATO), who he'd introduced us to, was happy with the arrangement. We just had to ensure that we didn't disturb any of his team when we were in and out of the fridge.

We could now fill this little god-send with cans of pop. The only problem was that it was so full all of the time that it just about managed to keep its contents cool. But never the less, it was a real bonus. You just had to remember how many drinks you'd stashed away or you'd find a far from cool can where your lovingly cooled one had been, and there was nothing more disappointing when the 'old pipes' were expecting the gloriously cool feel of 'throat gargle' hitting them, when instead, all that you got was luke-warm fizzy liquid. The answer to this was for everyone to marker pen their initials on the side of each their tins.

We trusted each other implicitly and didn't really mind if someone else took a drink so long as they asked first and replenished it later – one for one, simply because it took so long for the contents to chill down.

BFBS – British Forces Broadcasting Services radio had been doing sterling service since day one, keeping everyone amused and entertained, mind you this was its glorious 60th Anniversary Year on the airwaves (1943 –2003). Apart from the touching recorded messages from loved ones to and from Theatre, the station was taking requests that seemed to reflect the feelings and overall situation of the troops. There were a common handful of songs that were replayed again and again, such as Thin Lizzy's *The Boys are Back in Town*, The Animals *We've Got to Get Out of This Place* and The Clash's *Rock The Casbah,* to name but a few. BFBS Middle East was getting upwards of 2000 requests a day, and this desert-friendly service certainly kept a lot of people's spirits up. Back in '43', it would have been a different brand of music that the boys out in the desert would have been listening to. But they would have still been given the same morale boost when listening to Glen Miller or Vera Lynn, whilst conjuring up wistful images of Home.

For our own amusement when not listening to my 'Black Adder' tapes, some of us also started to rack our brains for topical song titles that also reflected our current circumstances – some songs were authentic, and some were the creation of warped minds. A couple of tunes dedicated for instance, to the Iraqi Republican Guard; Iron Maiden's *Run For The Hills,* Gary Moore's *Run For Cover,* Del Shannon's *Runaway,* amongst many. We came up with some crazy song titles and added to originals such as; *Walking Back To Happiness ('cause we've blown the tracks off your tank!),* the alternative version of the

Bon Jovi tune *Living on a Prayer (Mat)* as sung by the Muja Hadeen All-Male-Voice-Choir, and *Saddle up and pack your (pony) camel.*

We thought up quite a few, and there were one or two really excellent ones that had us rolling about … .literally. Humour is such an amazing thing.

Not only that, but for weeks I'd been humming *Horse With No Name* to myself, whenever we ventured out into the open spaces of the desert, and it drove me nuts because for the life of me, I couldn't remember who'd originally recorded it. Then one day, Barney, one of the newer Tigers 'in-country' simply answered, "America" – that's who it was … .problem solved. Now perhaps I could try and get some sleep instead of rooting through the filing system in my head, looking for the name of the band that had recorded the damned song in the first place.

Maybe I was 'Sand Happy', as time spent in the desert combined with the heat will do that to a person. But then I got to thinking, well, if this was insanity, then it wasn't so bad.

During one of the nightly briefs, it had transpired that one of the Kuwaiti mini-teams required an additional bod to assist with things in the south, as whole units were now starting to head out of theatre, and we needed to 'tag' the kit that was going out. The lucky 'Joe' just happened to be me.

The Sgt Major knew that my being up here with my '1 Div' team buddies meant a great deal to me, but that I was to be "on loan" for no more than a couple of weeks. In the words of 'Arnie' … .. "I'll be back!" I sure hoped so. Three more Tigers were also needed at Ali Al Salem Airbase for a week or so.

Our briefing parade that evening was a little more formal than usual, due to the fact that the Colonel (of JFLogC) was to address those gathered.

We got to thinking that something really serious had happened, or was about to happen, or maybe that one of us, or maybe all of us were in for a high ranking 'kicking'. It couldn't have been further from the truth. As we stood at ease, he informed us that he'd been taking an interest as to our operational role out here, and was basically giving us a 'pat on the back' for our efforts thus far. But the other reason that he had assembled us, was to present both Geordie and Taf – our two 'VM's, with their Sergeant's stripes, as they had been due them from their respective units prior to mobilisation. This meant that they could both carry the rank as 'local', but that they would still only receive Corporal's pay until they were back on their unit's strength, once they were back in Blighty.

I've got to admit that it did make me think about my previous recommendation for immediate promotion following my UN tour.

What with this being a 'war tour', any promotion gained during such a time would mean a great deal more to anyone in such a position. Although, I will say that the OC was very pro-active in as much as he was all for contacting several individual's units on behalf of those he believed to be worthy of promotion to see if it was achievable out here, or at least to endeavour to set the 'promotional wheels' in motion. But alas, due to circumstances outside of his control, this would not be possible. (By the end of the tour, most of us would get another recommendation). It was a case of, 'nothing ventured, nothing gained'.

At this point, Saddam's minister of military industrialisation, Abdul Tawab Mullah Hwaish, who had been suspected of playing a central role in developing Iraq's weapons of mass destruction was now in the hands of the US, along with one Taha Mohieddin Ma'rouf – one of Saddam's vice-presidents. This now brought the total of the regime's "most wanted" to 17 having been arrested out of the original '55' being sought.

4th – 18th May

I'd been up around 0600 and had virtually all my 'parrots and monkey's ready to load on the vehicle that was to take me south. I managed to enjoy a relatively fat free breakfast, with an option of fried or poached eggs – "Wow, an actual choice"! The day could only get better from here on in. By 0800 hours, our two Rovers were through the 'DMZ', and back into Kuwait. I wondered how long I would actually be out of Iraq, or was that it for the rest of the tour? The 'bigger picture' also now allowed for a realistic time-frame in which we could reasonably expect to head out of theatre – it looked like being the end of July. At least now, we had a rough 'end ex' date to work to, which meant that I'd got around three months to do out here.

After 200 K's we reached 'Kohima' and I unloaded my gear (again). I was billeted in a tent with the boss and a few of the other seniors, but that didn't bother me one way or the other.

So long as I could have my few small comforts, nothing else particularly mattered. It had been planned that a bunch of the guys, including myself would head over to a Kuwait Naval base, some 20 minute's drive away. This was a chance for a bit of quality down-time … and a swim. The base had an indoor pool and a small outside diving pool. A few of the port-based Tigers had been there before, once or twice. It sounded too good to miss anyhow. And, as is typical with the Spam's, they had the usual 'Burger King' and other outlets set up there. I didn't need any further persuading.

My god, just being able to immerse my body in water was a real tonic and no mistake. Whilst there were a fair number of people around the diving pool outside, 90% of whom were US soldiers – understandably. Half a dozen of us wallowed inside and had a bit of a chuck-about with a water-polo ball.

After an hour or so we got dressed again and headed over for coffee and ice-cream in the air-conditioned atmosphere of 'Baskin Robbins'. This made a 'down-time' day even better. And so, after the compulsory visit to the small PX, we headed back for 'Kohima' and the cool of the mess tent.

I still had stuff to get squared away and some news to catch up on before 'gonk time', so I finished off the bits and pieces that I needed to do to make myself that little bit more comfortable, after which I headed across to the TV tent complete with 'bum-achingly' hard benches, which I'm sure were designed to ensure that you didn't stay over-long as you lost the power of your legs, or ended up with a numb posterior, or both. Not dissimilar to spending too long a time spent on a loo seat!

It appeared that one Huda Ammash otherwise known as "Mrs Anthrax" for her alleged role in furtive Iraqi biological weapons programmes, was now in US custody. And it was also claimed that one of Saddam's sons, Qusay Hussein had originally fled with $1bn (£620m) in cash just hours before the war had begun. So, had he really been seen just several days ago, or had that been one of his own doppelgangers, such as his father had used on many occasions. There were believed to have been that many "Saddam's" planted at various locations, that it was a case of, "I'm Spartacus!" … "No, I'm the real Spartacus!" …

After another night in another location, I was up washed and heading for breakfast not much after six a.m. Having said that, one of my Artillery compadrés, who was known to be an early riser, was already up and had been on the hunt for a washing machine over at 'Spam Central' not much after five a.m. This was probably due to him being conditioned by his civilian job's truck driving hours, where he was usually out on the road at 'sparrows fart', if not before.

With breakfast out of the way, we (four of us) headed down towards Shu'aiba Port, to see if there was a vessel docked, and ready to take 'assets' (kit) out of theatre. There was still a lot of activity going on around and about. And in particular, there was still US rolling stock being unloaded from a rather large cargo ship. "These guys certainly don't do things by half," I thought at the time.

Not only that, but there were 'Kiowa' helicopters, Humvee's and other stuff dotted around the place, but more impressively to me, there were a handful of 'Blackhawk' heli's winding up their rotors on the quayside. We weren't sure at first whether they were just running them up to speed and going through their operational checks on the ground. But as the pitch of each motor picked up, they lifted off, one by one, banked round in formation, and were gone in several seconds. It was quite a sight to see and no mistake.

Once we'd scouted around and assessed our tasks for the day, we managed to grab some lunch where the 'port guys' were located. Even down here at the port where you'd think a breeze might do some good, it was stiflingly hot.

I got to wondering what the '1 Div Tigers' were up to up across the border in Iraq.

Later, as we went over to have a word or three with the '17 Port and Maritime' guys, based down here, I caught sight of one guy who was fishing off the edge of the quayside. There was obviously a lull in-between all the usual port activity that went on. Anyway, he pointed towards his keep net, where a Catfish was deciding whether or not it liked being contained in its watery prison. The fish was around two feet long, which to me looked absolutely huge. It was a good job that the fish had no idea of its intended fate … it was to end up on a BBQ that the guy's were gearing up for.

Finally, back at base, I proceeded to wash my only set of desert kit (I didn't really want to have to resort to putting on the 'greens'), hoping that the Boss's earlier comment about trying to acquire some further desert gear from the RAF up at 'Ali' had paid off.

After evening meal whilst chilling out (wrong term with regard to the current temperatures), and attempting to relax on a small makeshift bench that had materialised outside our tent, I watched the sun making its rapid decent towards the horizon whilst enjoying a damned fine brew – Asda's tea bags from home … just the job. Up strolled the boss with his arms full of desert kit, he'd obviously been busy. This looked like being Christmas all over again. Anyway, as it turned out, I got two further sets of gear out of it plus a 'boonie' hat into the bargain too. There was no doubt about it now, the 'green' kit would be going home. Cotton sleeping bag liners had also materialised, which were to be put to good use, and they were ideal in the extreme temperatures. They were just enough to cover you and add a little protection from anything 'bitey' as well. Because of the early starts at the sea port, it was decided that we would temporarily bed down for a few nights at 'Spearhead Camp' – another enclave of Spam's here in the South. The '17 Port and Maritime' guys 'n' gals, plus a small RAF contingent were also based here, but there weren't that many Brits in total. I couldn't believe it, I would be back amongst our Colonial Cousins once more … .outnumbered and out-talked again!

During the initial stages of the war, I knew that we were outnumbered by around six to one. But judging by the influx of US kit and hardware coming in at the 'A Pod' and 'S Pod', I reckoned that the ratio had had increased quite considerably.

The only saving grace of being located here, was that the port was only a ten minute drive away. We'd shifted some of our gear into another large tent, which actually had 'air-con' units set up, which was a real bonus. The only major down-side to being in this particular location was that across the main route some few hundred yards away, there was a cement processing plant with formed heaps of its product outside. This was okay until the wind picked up the cement dust from the surface of the heaps and blew it all about the place. Sand was one thing, but cement dust was another.

One particular evening, when the wind decided to pay 'Spearhead' a visit, I stepped outside to find a strange mix of fine sand and, what was no doubt, cement dust swirling round, which made for a very strange kind of blizzard. Fortunately, the storm subsided in a reasonably short time, and nothing like as bad as some of those experienced out in the northern desert. But anyhow, paradise this definitely wasn't!

On an adjoining piece of ground was the US vehicle parking area.

In the convoys that we'd seen earlier during the build up to conflict as we headed North on the highways of Kuwait, it looked like a good half of the entire US of A's armour was parked up here. There was desert painted rolling stock everywhere. Looking around as we passed in and out of the camp, I was convinced that if I just simply drove one of the many Humvee's into a spare ISO container at the port, and addressed it to myself, they were that numerous that nobody would miss one, surely? Now, I don't hold with theft itself, but a re-location of assets … .well, that's different!

A few yards to the front of our tent, the Spam's had a volley-ball court set up, which was all well and good until they started getting a little excited and the noise levels went up (especially when it got to around 2230 hours and they were still able to play by spotlight). "Oh no!" it was 'Hanger 10' all over again. In the end I think it was one of their own who recommended that the volume on the whole proceedings be turned down a little.

Out beyond the rear of our own tent, (but fortunately not close enough to become an annoyance), they even had an outdoor screen set up, where you could pick your spot, hunker down and watch whatever was being shown. Mind you, due to the location and relative lack of welfare amenities down here (compared to other US camps), any additional activity where you could 'lose yourself' for a couple of hours, was no doubt welcomed by most.

For the few Brit's based here, there was very little – not even a phone.

The best we could do was to go and ask the small RAF 'det' if we could borrow their 'sat' phone as and when. And, I've got to say that they were extremely obliging in that respect, but it wasn't the easiest piece of kit to try and get connected at first try. All in all, this was not a particularly brilliant situation really, but as I was fond of saying, "home was where you parked your camp-cot".

It transpired that 'Kohima' would be closing in a week's time, which meant that the remainder of 'Tiger' could either move up to Ali Al Salem Airbase or remain here. There was no way that I wanted to stay down here, if I was indeed given the choice. Even though it meant a good hour and twenty minutes drive each way to and from the port and back to 'Ali'.

As it was, you needed to don a 'rezzie' when the cement laden wind picked up. Thanks, but no thanks. Having said that, over the next few days, the decision would be taken out of my hands anyway. Our tent had started to swell with numbers, which meant a slight re-shuffling of bed and gear. The space was diminishing bit by bit. What's more, we'd learned that there was another port team coming into Kuwait within the next week or so, to replace the '17 Port and Maritime' guys, 20 of which were to bed down in here with us. Next, it would be standing room only!

A 'BBQ' had been arranged on board one of the ships in dock for any of the Brit's who worked with '17 Port'. To be honest, I was too knackered to attend (despite the excellent sounding sea-food on offer … ..no catfish though), and two of us still had to bring across all of our remaining kit from 'Kohima' – that in itself was a ninety minute round trip. All I was fit for was a brew, then bed. However, two of the other 'Spearhead Tiger's certainly made up for our absence, that much was for sure. Apparently, we missed a very good night, but there you go. Sometimes you have to make these little sacrifices I suppose.

America and Britain laid out the blueprint for post-war Iraq in a draft resolution to the United Nations Security Council, naming themselves as "occupying powers" and also giving them control of the country's oil revenues. But, Iraqi agriculture was also on the brink of collapse, bringing the fear that many of the population (some 24 million people) would be going hungry when the summer came.

Our small team of four had completed what we needed to do for the day, as we were reliant on other factors to do our job, which meant that we had some clear time to ourselves. So, it was suggested that a swim at the naval base would be a good idea. I wasn't going to complain. When we arrived, I just fancied a coffee and a sit in the shade as the Americans showed off in the diving pool, doing the usual stuff like jumping mob handed off the high-dive platform, whilst displacing half the water in the pool. I was glad that I was far enough away from being swamped. Still, it was so nice to be somewhere else for a spell and out of uniform.

We made it back in time for evening meal – US style. The grub wasn't too bad, but it wasn't a patch on anything that was served up over at Arafjan. Meat-loaf and mash was the order of the day.

That night, after sorting out my kit for next day, I turned on my mobile phone. I wasn't bothered too much about the use of my mobile out here except for the very occasional text home. But something this evening told me to switch it on. Once the phone had finally locked onto a network, it highlighted a text message that had come through. It was Linda with a text that read, "Txt me asap". As soon as I read it, I knew immediately what it referred to. I had that leaden feeling in the pit of my stomach and in my heart of heart's I knew it was about mum … .. .and that she'd gone.

Giving myself a moment, I sent a text home to have Linda reply, almost instantly confirming what I already knew. It was getting late but, I needed to go and see if I could get the use of the RAF's sat phone, and make the two calls – one to Linda and one to my Sis. Finally, I found one of the guy's with the phone and fortunately managed to get through in my first attempt. Linda then proceeded to tell me that my Sis had phoned her in work that afternoon. Apparently, mum had slipped away peacefully at around 3 p.m. with my Sis and Brother-in law at her bedside. I was saddened and relieved, both at the same time, but I knew that mum's suffering hadn't been prolonged. And I felt some comfort that the two of them had been there with her at the end.

Frustratingly, I couldn't get hold of my Sis. I got the ring-tone, but no answer. At 2330, there shouldn't have been any reason for her not being around. But as I later found out, there had been a fault with the phone at her end.

It was almost midnight, and it also happened to be my birthday. A handful of the family's cards had been sent out to me, so I sat there with my thoughts of mum and opened my cards. It didn't really matter whether I opened them now or in the morning. The strange thing was, that my Sis had got mum to scrawl on a card that she had already bought some weeks before (whilst mum was still capable of holding a pen – just about). Anyway, the sad thing about this was that the card, despite being sent off in good time, never arrived in theatre. And for whatever reason, it ended up being re-directed back to Blighty after doing a world tour. This made for quite a sad moment when I eventually returned home some three months later and opened the card to see mum's frail bit of writing. Sitting on the edge of my camp-cot in the dark, except that is, for the blue beam of light from my micro-torch which illuminated my cards, my watch bleeped midnight as I thought, "What a birthday".

And, this would be one birthday that I would spend most of travelling home.

We were out and down at the port for 7a.m. A couple of hours later during a lull in activity, the Boss and the 'Staffy' drove up. He came right over to me and said he'd like a quiet word. I just said, "It's ok Boss, I know already". The OC had come to get me out of there just as soon as was possible. As it turned out, the Compassionate Cell had wasted no time after having received the official phone call from my Sis, the previous night. With a quick 'au-revoir' to my buddies, we shot back to 'Spearhead' were I'd grabbed an already packed travel bag, and we were at the 'A pod' in less than an hour. I'd been booked onto a 'Jumbo 747'. With grateful goodbyes said, I was in the air approximately two hours after the Boss had come to give me the sad news. This was to be no repeat of the previous 'hurry up and wait' scenario a month earlier. And, this time, I had no hop over to Cyprus either, just a direct flight back to Blighty, were a car was waiting for me. Once again, all the flight staff were marvellous. I was home within three hours of touching down at Brize, which was pretty good going by anyone's standard.

My Sis had wasted no time in getting the arrangements sorted. In fact things were arranged so quickly that I didn't really have time to think about it, which was probably just as well. It was now Tuesday and the funeral was on the Friday. So in reality, I wasn't really required to do anything as everything had been taken care of. Apart from the sad reason for my return, it was great to be home just to touch base again. My compassionate leave would give me just less than a week, for which, I was extremely grateful. It was also a chance to recharge the batteries. I also understood that unless individuals were in similar compassionate circumstances, no-one would be getting leave on this tour. Only when things were stabilized would the successive 'Telic' tour personnel get proper operational leave.

On the Friday morning prior to the funeral, I'd confirmed my return details with the 'head-shed's at HQ Land – Wilton, because what with it being the start of the weekend and all, I wouldn't have been able to contact anyone.

I was actually on my way to the funeral, when the Sgt Major phoned my mobile phone from Iraq to confirm my return travel details (which I'd learned only an hour previously). Still, despite the inauspicious timing it was good to know that the lines of military communication worked and that doubling up on same information did no harm, and at the very least, it was good of him to do so.

When this day was out of the way, I could start to make plans for my return to theatre, now that I knew that I was scheduled to fly back early on the Monday morning, which would mean catching the train down to Oxfordshire and RAF Brize, late on the Sunday afternoon.

21st – 28th May

The Monday flew around, and with the sad but inevitable day behind me, I, and about 30 'new' Kuwait bound bods took off for the Middle-East (new looking desert kit and British sun-tan's were a dead give-away). I was thinking to myself, "So, you lot are after decent sun-tans are you? Well, just slap on your 'Factor 55' and prepare to be Bar-B-Q'd!"

Being back in the departure lounge at Brize was certainly a case of 'Déjà vu'. The Sgt Major had also previously informed me that as soon as I touched down, then I would be heading back the 200 K's further North ... back to Umm Qasr with the rest of the Iraqi Tigers. Now, despite the fact that I'd just lost my Mother, I couldn't wait to get back and get stuck in as it were.

It was quite a cathartic experience, I suppose, which is the only way that I could sum everything up.

We would be heading over to Ali Al Salem AB just for a night, then carry on Northwards the next day. It was just over a fortnight that I'd originally left Iraq to head South. It felt so much longer what with all that had happened. But a 'hop, skip and a drive' would rectify that. It was good to spend a little time at 'Ali' and re-charge my batteries after the journey. The Boss had basically given me some time to square away a bit of admin, due to the fact that I was to be here for a day. The other Tigers that operated at Shuaikh port had enough bods to crack on with the work, which left me with some chill time to myself, for which I was grateful.

With the spare time that I did have, I wrote the boss a note of thanks for his consideration and assistance with the whole bereavement situation. It meant a great deal.

I had a wash bag full of stuff that I'd previously left at 'Spearhead' prior to my rapid departure out of theatre, that required 'dobying', so I set to and got the lot hand-washed and dried in less than an hour, thanks to the the 'Kuwaiti tumble dryer' – the desert wind.

Whilst I'd been flying home the previous week, a mass grave had been found near Baghdad – with the number of bodies found estimated to be around 15,000. These were people believed to have been missing since 1991 following a Shi'ite uprising. A British-trained microbiologist Dr Rhihab Taha, also known as "Dr Germ" had surrendered to the coalition forces. She was another individual believed to have played an important role in the development of Iraq's biological weapons programme. It was around the same time, the British foreign secretary Jack Straw conceded that hard evidence of weapons of mass destruction might never be found in Iraq.

He basically said that it was "not crucially important" to find them because the evidence of wrongdoing was overwhelming. "Well, Whoopdy-doo!," Tell us something that we didn't already know.

My 'Spearhead' buddies had shifted all of my kit up to 'Ali' for me, so that I only needed to throw it all on the vehicle which would take me across the border. It might have sounded strange, but one of the most sought after things round here were … .clothes peg's, and most definitely scarce up north. There never seemed to enough of them. A quick trip to the 'EFI' shack' saw to that. Plus, it meant I'd have spares to share out with my Iraq based 'Tiger's. I thought, "What an exciting life I lead, and no mistake!" You can never have too many pegs. I'd also heard that the terrorist threat had gone up a notch in Southern Iraq, as there had been sporadic sniping in and around Basrah. Still, it didn't put me off.

I still had one or two pieces of essential kit down at the camp near Shuaibah – body armour, battle-bowl (helmet) and 'rezzie'. The 'staffy' would take me down to collect them after breakfast the next morning, prior to heading north.

After a really good night's sleep in an air-conditioned environment (being cool enough to require me to actually sleep inside my 'scratcher'), followed by a top notch RAF breakfast, we were on the road. It wasn't quite 0900, and already it was blisteringly hot. There'd been a slight change of plan, as once I'd retrieved my kit we were then to double back to 'Ali' to collect the OC, who had to attend a station brief. There was a traffic accident on the highway, which had us baking in a traffic jam for 20 minutes or so, but the delay wouldn't really affect our trip north. I'd get there soon enough, but now we wouldn't be moving out until after lunch. So, I could enjoy what would be my last bit of RAF hospitality for a while.

And so, we set out for Umm Qasr, a fair number of K's up the road. The journey was so uneventful, being a repeat of my trip three or four weeks previously. So much so, that I can't now recall anything about it. A bit like being on 'auto-pilot', I suppose.

Once I was installed in 'Tent Tiger', the guys filled me in on the latest happenings. They'd now been up and around the city of Basrah itself, and were due up that way again, so I hadn't lost out on an opportunity to see inside the grounds of one of Saddam's palaces, which was currently occupied by 'The Black Watch' amongst other units.

One or two of the team mentioned that they had been appalled at some of the sights and smells regarding the poverty to be found in the poorer sectors of the city. However, after having seen such conditions in other countries I'd visited in times past, I couldn't comment as to whether it was any worse than anywhere else until I'd seen it for myself. We'd be back up that way during the next few days.

The night temperatures were 'humongously' hot now that we were a month further along on the calendar, so trying to sleep was even worse. I wondered how long it would be before we could get out of these damned tents and into the air-conditioned environment of the 'TDA', across the port.

Next day, a mini-team – myself and two other 'Tigers', had the task of heading up to the 'Al Zubayr' naval base, around twenty minutes drive up the road. Due to the fact that we cleared the task for the day before it got too hot meant that we could have a steady day without killing ourselves. We had plenty of cool juice-stops courtesy of the well set-up cook-house in one of the port hangers, which helped considerably as the day wore on.

One of the key points in our briefing that night indicated that we would hopefully be moving over to the 'TDA' on or around the 1st June.

I wasn't so sure about the "on or around" bit. As somebody commented later, was that June the 1st of this year or next?

It was around this time that the OC had agreed to take part in a charity walk with some of the Ali Al Salem Base Fire Team. It was to start at 'daft oclock' – 5am, with the Fire bods and the boss donning full kit for the few K's they were to walk. I would take my 'boonie' hat off to the OC for his efforts.

The update on the current situation was that the UN Security Council had voted fourteen to nil to lift sanctions on Iraq and hand temporary control to the US and Britain. Syria had boycotted the vote. The former US ambassador and head of America's counter-terrorism office, Paul Bremer had now been Iraq's (temporary) civil administrator for a fortnight, as the hunt for the remaining of the 'Fifty Five Most Wanted', with Saddam, Uday and Qusay Hussein right at the top of the pack. However, there was still no sign of either of the three despot's.

We were tasked to head west of Basrah to visit '2 Royal Tank Regiment's location. The only problem was that I was to travel in the rear of the rover, and due to the fact that we had one or two team members who were off doing other things, it meant doubling up in a couple of vehicles. Painful memories sprung to mind as we set off. On the approach to '2 RTR's location, we had to negotiate the junctions and cross-roads on the outskirts of the city. I realised that there were no "normal" driving conditions in this country and that every junction was akin to a game of 'Russian Roulette'. In some ways, it was an even more scary prospect trying to get through the traffic unscathed than the thought of some unseen Saddam hard-liner taking a pot-shot at us.

It reminded me of the local drivers in Nicosia – Cyprus, who all thought that they were taking part in an episode of 'Wacky Races'. Vehicles around and about, were barely roadworthy, with the great majority having no lights or indicators (none that worked anyhow). You always had to be prepared for sudden manoeuvres. Most Iraqi drivers would most probably not be too upset to hear that they were pretty low on the list of contenders for the 'Advanced Driver Award'. I'm sure that every Iraqi behind the wheel of a vehicle held to his belief of 'Inshallah' – 'If God wills it' when approaching any and every road junction. To my way of thinking, that could be the only answer as to the way that they drove, believing that they had devine intervention on their side. But it wasn't just us westerners that had to contend with the insane Iraqi drivers, as the local donkeys had to compete with these maniacs as well. They were quite resilient beasts I suppose, and they always managed to carry on unhindered and unharmed, apart that is, from the tickle of the lash from their driver.

When we finally arrived (safely) at '2 RTR's location, I breathed a sigh of relief at being able to get out and try and piece my spine back together, and I did start to wonder as to whether there might have been a reduction in my height due to several compressed vertebrae – I started the tour at 5ft 11 and would go home 4ft 6 at this rate!

Anyway, today we were in the company of the 'big stuff' – 'Challenger 2' tanks. So we set to and proceeded along the line of this formidable tracked armour that had proved itself in battle once again. This was after all, the most advanced main battle tank in the world.

I always found it a humbling experience when standing next to something like this. Whilst clambering up and onto the turret to get the data I required, it made me think back to the recent events when the fiercest of sand storms had hit the region, and drove a disorienting blanket of sand across the desert. During the maelstrom, the crew of one of our own 'Chally 2's had mistakenly fired upon another, believing it to be enemy armour. And, as a result of a direct hit with a 120mm armour-piercing fin-stabilised, discarding sabot rounds, the turret had been literally blown off, killing two of its occupants and seriously injuring the other two. The turret on this particular beast weighs several tons itself, and what with the tank's up-rated second-generation 'Chobham' armour, the overall weight comes in at around 70 tonnes. This was certainly no light-weight piece of military hardware.

Eventually, we'd completed all that we needed to do in reasonable time and headed slightly south, to another location, where the Royal

Regiment of Fusiliers were to be found. The sun was really starting to beat down as we pulled out to head back to on our (my) spine-numbing journey, and dicing with death at the road junctions as we went.

For the first time in a while, we actually made it back for lunch, where there was fresh salad available … .. flies not so fresh. Well, they were an integral part of every meal. It reminded me of an old joke, where a man, sitting in a restaurant is being annoyed by flies buzzing round his table, and say's to the waiter, "Waiter! I don't like all of these flies in here!" To which the waiters reply is; "Well Sir, point out the ones that you don't like and I'll do my best to get rid of them for you!"

The rest of the day was now ours, so long as we were around for the evening brief. Outstanding! A spot of hand 'dobying' was first on my 'to do' list, followed by a foot inspection and soak of the feet next.

Having given my 'plates' the once-over, my stainless steel bowl was at the ready – water temperature just right, and invigorating foot bath added, all that I needed to do now was to submerge them in the rather soothing foot-wash.

As my feet felt the blissful sensation of the medicated liquid swirling around them, I noticed a slight movement out of the corner of my eye.

It was a little mouse, come to have a nose about. I was hoping that it was a Jerboa, the emblem of 'The Desert Rats, but no, it was just a little brown mouse. I sat still as stone as the rodent scurried closer. Standing on its hind legs it appeared to be sniffing the air. Maybe it liked the vapour coming from my foot-bowl, as the combined ingredients of mint, witch hazel and calendula, did a cracking job of soothing the sinuses as well as the feet.

The mouse continued to stop, sniff and rummage, and seemed to be in no particular hurry to move on. I could have maybe clobbered it with my boot, but seeing as there wasn't anything for it to nibble on that would keep it returning, I decided to give it a reprieve. Had we been out in the 'boonies', I may well have seen it off simply because mice make great hors d'oeuvres for other beasties higher up the food chain … .snakes. But for now, the little fellow was pardoned. And anyway, I didn't want to be known as 'The Mouse Butcher of Umm Qasr', there were enough tyrants in this country already.

That evening, our brief made only scant reference to military affairs.

No attacks, no shootings, no explosions, no-nothing, which made a refreshing change. The key subject matter was all about who was to attend the first night of the CSE Show (Combined Services Entertainment) the following week. Over the two nights that the show was to run, it was to feature the Abba tribute band, 'Bjorn Again', another tribute band, 'Bee Gee's Magic' and some comedic juggler who's name I'd since forgotten.

I was to be in the first 5 from 'Tiger' who would be travelling up to Shaibah with a bus-load of others from 'JFLogC'.

We'd also heard that Jim Davidson was due in to at some point during the next week too, as well as the new 'forces sweetheart', Nell McAndrew. I definitely wanted to see Jim if I could. He'd been entertaining the troops for around twenty-odd years – ever since the Falklands Campaign, and he always made time for them, despite the "colourful" reputation that he had. So, I thought that it would be a damn shame to miss out on the chance of seeing him perform live out here in the desert. It was also rumoured that he would also be performing at 'Ali', back over the border. That was, of course, if it didn't interfere with the night duty stags that we now had to do on a rota basis.

In the meantime, a team BBQ had been planned, with the 'Southern Tigers' having been invited to attend. I thought that it was a good idea in principle, as the whole team hadn't been together for a while, but that it was a fair old drive for the southern guys.

To make things a little more enticing, a few slabs of beer had magically materialised, and of course the fizzy stuff was plentiful.

As it would turn out, a few of the guys couldn't make it, but we had pretty much a full team in attendance.

Anyway, we'd borrowed some tubs to put ice in (we'd actually frozen several bottles of water in the kitchen's ISO freezer), set up trestle tables out in the open, and got the cut-in-half oil drum BBQ lit in good time. Permission higher up the chain of command had previously been granted, but it was decided that the whole shebang should be kept low key and out of sight, so as not to attract too much attention. Discretion being the better part of valour.

Trying to break up the frozen bottles with a pick axe was a real pain (that was all we had), so we just left the big chunks to help cool the water – it would still do the trick, once the tinny's were submerged. Nick, our other 'long range sniper' was Chef for the evening, and so with a bit of salad and pre-requisitioned meat-stuff from the kitchen, we were set to go. I'd cut down a plastic bottle to turn it into a reasonable sized drinking utensil, what with not liking to drink straight out of tins (not because I was a snob, but for reasons of a related health hazard horror story I'd always remembered). With Sprite and a beer, I could make a refreshing Shandy, and with not having had an alcoholic drink in a while, the couple that we were allowed would be enough, and I'd probably just end up bloated anyhow.

A good example of intolerance to alcohol after a period of abstinence can be born out by an incident that had occurred whilst I had was at home on compassionate leave. Being rather an aficionado of red wine, I had the chance to enjoy a few glasses of the said liquid. Without realising it, in no time at all, the few ordinarily harmless glasses had gone to my head.

And, due to the wine being an extremely rich one, I ended up being as sick as a dog, which surprised even myself. It wasn't as if I'd made a pig of myself with the vino, it was just that after having spent an amount of time away in 'dry mode' (you couldn't really call it anything else, out in the desert – no pun intended here either) my system just simply couldn't handle it.

Here endeth the temperance lesson.

Anyway, by the end of the evening, we'd all had a laugh, having taken part in the pre-arranged quiz, swapped a few tales, compared notes, and it had also given me a chance to get to know one or two of the other guys who's company I'd not been in very much – due to our geographically challenged team. All in all, it had been a pretty good night, with the added bonus that our 'Chef' had managed not to give anyone food poisoning – well, nobody was suffering the next day, put it that way.

Next day, some of the team disappeared down to the Kuwaiti Naval base, but a couple of us needed to get an oil service done on our vehicles as best we could, and decided to stick around to get on with the task – service components permitting of course. Getting new oil into the old engines was our main priority, so Barney and myself ended up assisting the REME guy. Or should I say, he was there just to supervise, as it was the two of us who'd end up on our backs underneath the vehicles. I'd done many an oil change in my time, but certainly not in these conditions or indeed, this kind of heat. First time for everything I suppose.

We had the barest of things to work with, and as we were checking the various oil levels, things got a little messy during the removal of the oil filters and oil sump plugs. Despite being as careful as possible,

I still ended up with oil patches on my recently acquired desert trousers, which I was not at all happy about. That was the final insult!

When it came to refilling the engines, we barely had enough oil to top them up. There wasn't a single drop to be found anywhere to hand, so had we required a little more, even as little as half a litre, then we'd have been out of luck. The REME guy didn't even have a clue as to the whereabouts of any more right at this very moment in time. For whatever reasons, supplies were short. I wouldn't mind, but we were more or less standing above some of the largest oil reserves in the bloody Middle-East! Figure that out?!

Anyway, we finally completed our servicing task as best we could under the circumstances, and at least we'd give the engines a bit more longevity by easing the wear and tear a little. What with the state that some of the vehicles were in that we were driving, the thought of an engine packing up in the kind of the places we'd visited (and were likely to visit) did not bear thinking about. So, with task done, it was lunch-time and then … ..nothing! nada! zip!, for the afternoon as the rest of the team would not be back over the border from Kuwait until late afternoon. So I would at least make an attempt to try and remove the oil stains from my long sought after deserts. There was no 'Vanish' stain remover out here, just a bit of old soap powder and a nail brush, and even then I had to be careful not to rub the thin fabric through with the brush. Although they faded a little, I didn't manage to get the stains out. Well, they would have to do until I could get my hands on another pair.

The boss had intimated that there was a chance that a small team would quite possibly be flown up to Baghdad to visit '16 Air Assault' as the 6 to 7 hour drive was a little too much, despite also still being a rather risky proposition into the bargain. So, if it was to happen, then a 'Herc C130' would be tasked to fly those that were chosen to go along with two rovers, which would then be used to run from the airstrip to '16's location. One could only hope, but we'd have to wait and see. Myself and one or two others were certainly up for it. I wanted to look (given the opportunity) down the mile long Triumphal Route, where the two giant arms (allegedly modelled on Saddam's own) held scimitars that crossed over the roadway. This was where Saddam had, on so many occasions watched his troops parade past. But, that was something now that he would never do again. Not unless it was with the divine assistance of Allah, which could put him firmly back in power. Put simply, there was more chance of Lord Lucan winning the Grand National riding Shergar!

(For those that remember the mysterious disappearance of both man and horse).

In the meantime, we had the remit of starting slightly earlier with the prospect of being finished on or around mid-day, work-wise (due to the temperatures).

Another of my serving TA buddies from my old 'King's unit back home had written to me, telling me that he had received his mobilisation papers to deploy on what was to be 'Op Telic 2', within the next month.

He'd been expecting it since I'd volunteered, but now he was 'good to go'.

I wrote back to him just as soon as I was able, with the main thrust of the letter explaining about the heat and to prepare himself for a shock once he stepped off the plane. I mentioned that even if it was 80°C back home, he could expect another 20°C on top of that. At least we'd had the cooler months to gradually acclimatise and get used to things out here, but to come straight out mid-June was something else.

I was also hoping that by the time that Derek got established out here, with me still having around two months to serve, I would hopefully cross paths with him. On the same subject, I was still determined to track down my 'RLC' buddy, Gordon, whom I'd narrowly missed up at Shaibah.

That was a separate mission. Well, I reckoned that there was still time.

After spending another roasting day up at Shaibah, we were to return that evening for the 'CSE' Show. I armed myself with a hand-full of pre-cooled tins of fizzy stuff that I'd been saving for this very night (I really knew how to live). As those of us mounted the buses around six p.m. you could still feel the hot air as the sun made its decent towards the horizon. And, as if to add insult to injury, we just happened to be on the very bus on which the 'air-con' wasn't working … ..marvellous.

After passing through the familiar check-point, an hour and a bit later, the buses pulled up in an open area away from where we usually operated.

It was a bit like attending a 'gig' as all the other buses started to come in. There was still an hour or so to dusk, so we could find ourselves a suitable vantage point to see the show. There was quite a large stage set-up, with decent light rigs and sound system. The stage itself was offset with two 'AS90' Guns at either corner, and what with it being set against the back-drop of the desert, it made for a most impressive sight.

The six of us moved to the rear of the space in front of the stage and climbed onto the flatbed trucks where we could sit, raised above the heads of those in front, but still directly opposite the stage which gave us a great vantage point. As hundreds of bodies wearing desert kit filed into the area, the patch of desert in front of us started to fill up as dusk descended rapidly. It was estimated that there were around two thousand people in attendance, and although things were running a little behind schedule, we didn't mind.

It made the build up to the show all the more special. This was going to be a good night, and no mistake – you could just feel it.

Finally, the compare-cum-host came on and gave us a run-down of the evening's events, in between his line of jokes which started to warm everyone up nicely. Most of 'The Black Watch' squaddies had taken up their position near the front of the stage, no doubt to ogle the 'CSE' dancers when they came on to strut their stuff in the slots between 'Bjorn Again' and 'Bee-Gees Magic'. There was a very pleasant breeze blowing which kept things just right. As the juggler-comedian came on, one of the show 'helpers' came round handing out different colour 'Lumi-Sticks' to everyone. "Wow, treats"! It was time to be a big kid again. Soon there were little strips of luminous colour everywhere. As the juggler did his best to try and keep the momentum of his act going, he was taking a fair bit of flack from The Black Watch guys at the front. Every time he came out with something funny whilst attempting some rather difficult juggling or balancing manoeuvre, he was met with mocking remarks. It looked like the poor guy was dying on stage until he appealed into the microphone, "Come on guy's, give me a break, I'm only trying to entertain you!" With that, he totally turned the audience around, not least, the hard bastards in the front. Finally, he exited the stage to whoops and cheers, so in the end, he went off triumphant.

Well, at least I think he did.

After the dancers, came 'Bee-Gee's Magic' who weren't half bad at all. Then more dancing, a few jokes from the compere, then it was 'Bjorn Again's turn. They played faithful renditions of 'Abba's finest, which had us all singing along and waving our Lumi-Stick's in unison.

At some point, the Lumi's started getting launched across the audience area, which made for a colourful spectacle as they were thrown back and forth. It was a bit like a safety firework display but without the sparks. Everyone was in really good spirits, and that was without the aid of a few beers, just Fanta and Cola mostly.

As the proceedings came to a close, we all agreed that we'd all had a great time, and one to remember, not least because of the location and the atmosphere. The other team members would have the chance to attend the next night's show, which meant that no-one would miss out. It turned out that anyone who had seen the first night's show could attend the second night if they didn't have any kind of duties and of course there was room on the transport. A couple of my compadrés enjoyed themselves that much that they did actually attend the next night's show.

I had now been told that Jim Davidson was to be doing a show at our old stomping ground at 'Hammersmith' at the end of the week, but it happened to be the one night that I'd drawn the short straw for a 24hour duty … "Bugger!"

So this turned out to be a right old week for famous visitors. Nell McAndrew was due in at Umm Qasr, as was the 'PM', Tony Blair (though not both at the same time). The 'PM' was to address the troops based here as well as those at other locations in Iraq. Despite us actually living here, we thought it most unlikely that we'd see him, as we were due to be up at Shaibah when he would most probably be visiting.

I certainly wanted to hear what the guy had to say, but the 'audience' had already been selected, after which, nobody else would be able to get near.

We'd heard in our brief that evening, that 2 US soldiers had been killed and 9 injured in an attack on an army checkpoint in the town of Falluja, about 30 miles north-west of Baghdad. And, there was still no mention as yet, about any of us flying up to the Iraqi capital, but then again, the idea hadn't been vetoed either. Nell McAndrew was due in sometime the very next day, but again, we were out and about. We'd just have to wait and see how the day panned out.

Well, what do you know? We headed back into the port that very afternoon to find one Miss McAndrew still about and talking to all and sundry. To be honest, she was just about finishing up when we parked up. However, she was very obliging and before she left, a few of us managed to get one or two photos with her before she departed.

Well, she certainly brightened up the place anyhow. A lot of garbage was later printed about her in the press, over this and that, but that didn't matter to those of us out here – she'd taken the time and trouble to come a-visiting, so "Yah-Boo-Sucks!" to her detractors, was all we had to say.

Later on, following a melt-into-your-food evening meal, I went across to the secure ISO container where Gaz, our 'EOD' buddy was logging the day's weapon's find. "Have a look at this," said he with a knowing look on his face. With that, he placed a towel on a box and unfolded it with due ceremony. An intricately etched Browning 9mm pistol met my gaze. But more than that, it was gold plated. It was a bit like the power of the ruling ring in 'The Lord Of The Rings', in as much as it made you want to reach out and pick it up. But, Gaz just handed it to me anyway so that I could have a closer look. If a weapon could be beautiful, then this thing certainly was. Give or take a few quid, he said he'd been informed that it was estimated to be worth around $13,000 – not a bad bit of loose change by anyone's standards. This was where a discreet photo was called for, as we didn't want this 'baby' getting too much attention. There was all manner of other captured weaponry; 'Dragunov' 7.62mm sniper rifles, any amount of 'AK47's, 'RPG's and something that resembled an ancient 'Blunderbuss'.

Then again, most of this stuff seemed to be quite old, but it still had the means with which to bring about maximum damage – not least the 'Dragunovs'.

A couple of days later, he showed me a stainless steel 'AK47', but no gold plated ones, such as those that had been found a few weeks earlier at one of Saddam's palaces.

Our old friend, the 'Camel Spider' had made an appearance, not physically. Well, not to me, but in conversation, as someone else had encountered one of these frightening beasties. The aforementioned rumours surrounding it and what it was capable of (some way back in this tome) had been exaggerated beyond belief. But, the funniest and most outrageous story that somebody made up was, that during the night a victim had been attacked whilst he was asleep, and all that was left next morning, was an eyebrow on the victim's pillow. It was crazy stuff like that, which kept you going, or scared you stupid if you were an arachnophobic.

29th May – 6th June

Following another stint up at Shaibah, we unloaded weapons on the way back into base, sorted vehicles and then hit the showers. We'd had a sweltering few hours up at the old airfield, so it was even worth the risk of going "OOH! AAH!" under the shower head as the supposedly cold water would still be rather hot, due to the sun boiling the tank. And although, you would be sweating the minute you stepped out of the shower, at least it was clean sweat. As our small convoy of vehicles swung round to cross what was usually a spacious area of the port, it now looked like a car park.

What's more, our hope of getting back to "Hot Home Sweet Home" for that longed-for shower and throw on clean desert kit was suddenly dashed by an RMP thrusting his hand out to halt us in our tracks. "Sorry, you can't go any further for the next hour or so, the 'PM's over there, giving his speech, so you'll just have to park up and wait it out". Not two hundred yards away was a gathering of the "chosen," surrounding Tony Blair whilst listening to what he had come to say. Well, that just about put the top-hat on it.

We couldn't move on past the assembled throng to get to our hanger, and we also couldn't get any closer to hear anything the 'PM' was talking about.

It was a bit of a chess stalemate – we couldn't move one way or the other. So, with nothing more to do for a while, a few of us simply stripped off our shirts and lay on the top of our vehicles to get a few more UV's. It was better than sitting, baking in a vehicle.

'BFBS' would be covering the 'PM's visit on the box that evening. It was definitely a case of, "So near, yet so far". The 'PM's visit was indeed covered on the news that evening, and the following is the speech which we unfortunately missed hearing, verbatim:

"It is really good of you to have me here today. I would just like to express the sense of pride that everybody has in Britain over the magnificent job you have done. I know there were a lot of disagreements in the country about the wisdom of my decision to order the action, but I can assure you of one thing, there is absolutely no dispute in Britain at all about your professionalism, and your courage and your dedication, and not just the way you won the war, which was extraordinary, but the way you are conducting the peace, which is remarkable. The taking of the Al-Faw Peninsular and then the taking of Basra in the way it was done, with the minimum loss of civilian life, is famous right round the world now, and you should know that you have brought tremendous honour on our country, and respect and admiration everywhere for the way that you did that. And I know too this was real war, this wasn't the pretend stuff that happens in films, it was real war, it was real bloodshed and real casualties. And there will be people you will have known that aren't going back home, and we grieve for them and we pay respect to them for everything they did and the sacrifice that they made.

And I just wanted to tell you very quickly the two things that I think have come out of this that are going to be important not just for this country but for the whole of the world. The first is in Iraq itself. You will know, having talked to local people and having been on the streets in Basra, you will know the sheer misery of the tyranny they lived under. And there are people here who in years to come will look back and will remember what you did, and recognise that as the start of their future and a life of hope and the possibility of prosperity. You probably know this country – Iraq – is one of the wealthiest countries potentially in the world, and yet its people live in appalling poverty. Now in the years to come, as a result of what we have done, they can rebuild their country, and we have got to help them do that, and the liberation from Saddam is one huge thing, a momentous and a mighty act for the people of Iraq, which you did, and of which you can be proud.

But something else is happening right throughout the whole of this region. You know I think that this area of the world has been the source of probably more instability, more terrorism, more difficulty in managing world affairs than any other region in the world. And it is interesting to me to talk for example to the leaders of the Gulf countries, most recently last night in Kuwait, and see the changes that they can see happening in their countries as a result of the removal of Saddam's dictatorship from Iraq. You can see in relation to countries like Syria and Iran, where we have still got big issues we need to discuss with them and we need to resolve with them, and yet we can do that now in a completely different atmosphere than was possible a few months ago. And you can see it too in the Middle East peace process in what is happening in Israel and Palestine, where for the first chance now in several years there is just the beginnings of the hope of a different way forward for the future. And all of that has arisen out of this action and what you did. And I would like to think that maybe in a year or two years time it is going to be possible for some of you to come back here and see the changes in this country that have arisen from what you have done today. Because in a way what you did I think serves as a model of how Armed Forces anywhere in the world should conduct them-selves. You fought the battle and you won the battle and you fought it with great courage and valour. But it didn't stop there. You then went on to try and make something of the country that you had liberated, and I think that is a lesson for Armed Forces everywhere the world over. And the other thing I think will be very clear is that when people look back on this time and look back on this conflict, I honestly believe they will see this as one of the defining moments of our century. And you did it. It was your courage and your professionalism that did it.

And I just wanted to say to you, because I know people back home, you know you will read lots in the media and the newspapers, I just want to say this to you. People back home are incredibly proud of what you have done. You have made this whole country, our country, hold its head up high, and I think that is a wonderful, wonderful achievement. It is your achievement and thank you".

Over an hour later, the gathering dissipated and the black unmarked vehicles carrying the 'PM' and his entourage, sped off to whatever location he was due at next. That night, just around the time I was about to head off to bed, a tired looking Jim Davidson also appeared. He was only stopping off to get his head down for the night before moving on to Basrah.

I later found out that he was filming in and around the area for a documentary called 'Basrah Bound', which was to be screened sometime in July. The last thing he wanted, was a crowd of squaddies badgering him when all he wanted to do was get some shut-eye (if indeed he could in this heat).

My 24hour duty rolled around, which was 9.a.m one day through to 9a.m. of the next. The checkpoint and main entrance, where everything and everybody had to pass through was manned '24/7'. In a building, 20 or so yards away, was where the duty guard and QRF (Quick Reaction Force) were to be found. In the event of an incident, the QRF could be called out at a minute's notice.

The two positions that we were required to cover, were the checkpoint barrier and the watch-tower that gave a view all the way down the several-hundred metre approach that led to the archway from which all pedestrians and vehicles had to pass under to approach the check-point. Nothing could pass through this point without the correct ID. As with any protected area, its security rested on the diligence of the personnel at its point of entry, and for the next 24hours, we were 'it'. The daytime duty 'stag' operated on a rota of one hour on, two hour's off, because of the heat. And that was split down too – half an hour on the barrier and half an hour up in the tower. Although, the tower had a roof, giving just a little shade, the hot breeze that enveloped me still produced a lather of sweat under my body armour.

At night during silent hours, the 'stag's changed to 2 hours on, 4 hours off. With PRR's (Personal Role Radio), we could speak to the comm's desk and to each other. This way we could alert whomever we needed with a minimum of fuss (albeit you needed one hand to depress the pressel switch in order to give a voice response), but again, the heat and the sweat made the earpiece feel like it was sticking to your ear, and it was a relief to take it off once the duty was over.

When having our rest periods, our 'Des Res' was just a bare room with a desk and a bit of a brew area, plus a line of camp cots for whoever was on duty, along with the 'QRF'. I'd already picked a camp cot near the wall and threw my overnight kit next to it. Still, it was a case of, roll on 9.a.m, and hope that the duty passed without incident.

In between the night stags, I'd found it extremely hard to get much shut-eye, mainly due to the heat that emanated from the walls after a day spent absorbing the sun. They just seemed to pulse with it. The saving grace was having access to a brew. 'Norgies' (insulated containers) filled with coffee were available, but late night, look-warm refreshments didn't appeal.

It wasn't that I was fussy (well, I suppose I was if I'm being honest). Besides which, I made sure I had my mini-jug to hand. So, if sleep wasn't forthcoming, it was a good excuse to get a brew going.

Now that the locals were being allowed back into the port to work, the morning 'rush-hour' coming in could be bedlam. Most seemed to arrive on bicycles and would have to queue up at the barrier until checked through.

It got to be a little crazy sometimes, where it was necessary to tell the throng in broken Arabic (and with the help of one of the newly established local port security guards) to line up and wait their turn whilst each and every ID was checked. If something was going to happen, then this would have been the ideal time what with so many people milling around.

Whoever was in the tower, had to keep a keen eye on things down below.

Eventually, one of my 'Tiger' buddy replacements got dropped off by some of our team, who were heading out – 9 a.m. had at last arrived.

It had been a long and fortunately uneventful duty apart from having to stop one local who's bicycle was barely rideable, due to the fact that it was weighed down with bags full of what was believed to have been contraband – tins and tins of corned beef. It turned out that he had been given the almost 'out-of-date' tinned stuff by the US contingent based here, but that they hadn't bothered to give this particular guy the paperwork to say that it was legally his. Judging by the look on the poor blokes face, he must have thought that he was going to have the lot confiscated. Finally, with everything cleared up and him much relieved, he pushed his cycle away up the road, with tyres nearly flat with the weight. It wouldn't have surprised me if he'd not been 'mugged' for his hoard of 'bully-beef' on his way home.

With my duty over, I headed back across the port to our 'hot-house' hanger where, following an "almost" cool shower, I would do my best to try and get a few hours kip. The rest of the team would be out until early afternoon, so I knew that I could get a little peace and quiet without being disturbed too much. However, after having lain on my bed for about an hour, I realised that there was no way that I was going to be able to settle with the building heat, it was simply too much. So, in the end I got up and decided to have an early lunch. I bumped into the Sgt Major who informed me that Jim Davidson was to perform at 'Ali' that very evening. And, knowing that I'd requested to go and watch JD previously, I'd been given the green light to use the 'Pajero 4x4' that we had at our disposal to head over the border to 'Ali', providing of course that I could find another bod to ride 'shotgun' in my vehicle, and find 2 more willing bod's with a second vehicle (because at that time there was a minimum 2-vehicle move anywhere in theatre for obvious safety reasons, whether it be a break-down or contact situation).

I was now on a mission.

I knew that I could count on at least one other … .my buddy, Gaz. He'd already said that he wouldn't mind seeing 'JD', and what's more, Gaz also had a similar vehicle at his disposal, and another of his team was more than willing to accompany him in his vehicle. So, I was 75% sorted.

After doing the usual bit of 'doby' during the afternoon, I'd asked around for interested parties and found a Signals guy, who was more than happy to come along.

The trip over the border would require us to detour to 'Camp Coyote' in the 'Hammersmith' area, because Gaz needed to sort out some 'EOD' business with some of his people there. Then we would need to shoot across to '61 Ammo Squadron' at 'Fox' where he then needed to pass on some urgently needed paperwork. So by the look of things, it was going to be tight schedule, but we figured that the hour gained as we crossed the border, would give us just enough time. Although we had no time for any further delays once we set out.

We had evening meal as soon as it was served, fuelled the vehicles to the max, and headed off for the border, 'DMZ' and off into Kuwait like two proverbial bats out of hell. (Of course, we were mindful of our speed). Apart from a few US convoys, we didn't encounter anything at all – the highway was ours. It was the complete opposite of the 'M6' near Birmingham on a Friday afternoon. We had no problem eating the kilometres up.

We flashed our ID's to the US sentry's at 'Coyote', and as soon as Gaz disappeared to complete his task, I grabbed a brew.

We were off again in around 20 minutes, but realised that by the time we arrived at 'Fox' it would be a little 'close to the wire' in order to arrive at 'Ali' with any time to spare. Finally, we hit the sand track that ran the 20 or so K's out to '61 Ammo'. With Gaz in front, we kicked up a streak of dust behind us. It helped that we'd both been up and down this route before – prior knowledge of terrain is invaluable, as we drove reasonably fast but still within safe margins … there was no room on this trip for "Driving Miss Daisy". With the important paper-work handed over, we made our way over to 'Ali Al Salem AB' and finally pulled up at the guard post at the entrance to airbase just as dusk was falling. However, we still had to adhere to the frustratingly slower speed limits on the approach road through to the next check-point, then once through, head for the base gymnasium.

With handbrake on, we'd made it! As we entered the gym, 'JD' had already been on stage some ten minutes. But, overall, we'd done extremely well to get here within the time constraints.

There were 'desert' covered bum's filling all of the benches, so Gaz and I simply stood to one side against a wall. Jim was in fine fettle, as he took the 'Michael' out of the officers and 'fly-boy's, who made up most of the audience. There were a few army bods here. (I also caught sight of a few of my 'Tiger' compadrés sitting in the audience, but 'Tommies' were pretty much in the minority). There were one or two funny's I'd heard before, but like one of my other favourite comedian's, Billy Connolly, Jim's humour came from general, every day observations. He joked about the never-to-forget experiences of 'Thunderboxes' (portaloos), something that was not lost on us either. After a rather warm hour later, a sweat-soaked Jim closed his show with a rather heart-warming message to all those in attendance.

He was most sincere in telling us that he had been proud and honoured to entertain 'the troops' in the various theatres in which they (we) had served over the years, and that despite the fact that Iraq was not front page news any more, our folks at home were justly proud of us, and that the UK hadn't forgotten we were still out here. It was a really touching gesture and one which meant every bit as much as what the 'PM' had come out here to say.

So with that, the guy had gone up a couple of notches in my estimation.

Giving Jim a few minutes to chill outside (if that was possible), Gaz and myself requested a photo with him before we had to take off for the border. He kindly obliged, and so after shaking hands whilst thanking him for his heart-felt words, we were gone.

The disposable camera I'd used that night later developed a problem, and I sadly lost a whole film full of photo's, including the image taken of Jim and I. However, I did end up with a souvenir every bit as good when watching 'JD's documentary, 'Basrah Bound', once I eventually got back home … . Gaz and I had been caught on TV camera during Jim's show at 'Ali'.

We were minor celeb's without even knowing it (at the time)!

We made good time again, heading north due to the deserted highways, and despite having to take a minor detour and brief stop-off at 'Coyote' again on the way back, we finally rolled into base at half past midnight. By the end of the evening we'd covered a few hundred K's, but getting to see the show was worth every kilometre. Because of the nicely chilled temperature in the air conditioned vehicle, I didn't break into a sweat, and so did away with the late night shower option – that could wait till morning. I crept back into 'Tent Tiger' and clambered under my 'mozzie' net, whilst my team-mates grunted and snored around me. I drifted off to sleep thinking about the good old ribbing that Jim had given the RAF top-brass, which made me laugh quietly to myself. It had been a rather eventful night.

The one thing that I'd noticed with Iraq, was that you didn't have to look too far across the landscape in any direction to see the burn-off towers of the oil processing plants. At night, just as in Kuwaiti desert you could clearly see the glow and flicker of the flames from the towers all the way across the horizon. The desert terrain here in southern Iraq had a harsher look to it, if that's a suitable way to describe it. The landscape surface was covered with shale and desert scrub, giving it an unwelcoming look to it. But, there was still something about the vastness of it all that I liked.

It just felt that I somehow belonged in this unforgiving environment.

Back over the border in Kuwait, I'd made a point of learning a little about the 'Bedou' or Bedouin Tribes. These nomads were known to be one of the most welcoming people on earth, and apart from those who'd made the transition from Camel to motor vehicle, they existed pretty much as their 'Amorite' ancestors had some 4000 years previously. Bedouin customs are universal all over the middle-east and North Africa, and one of the most sacred of those is hospitality. Their code holds that anyone is welcome in a Bedouin home for three days, and in that time, the host is duty-bound to give their guest the best of what he has to eat and drink, and also to protect him from harm, even against his own family. The sacred code holds that that even if the guest is an enemy with whom the family has a blood feud, and when the guest has left, the host and his family cannot pursue him until the bread and salt he has eaten in the Bedou's home is reckoned to have passed out of the system.

One of the worst insults that can be lodged against a Bedouin, is that he "did not know a guest". They live by the cult of reputation rather than possessions. Families and individuals would actually compete with one another to gain renown for open-handedness. To pass a Bedouin's tent without stopping, for example, is considered an insult. They are immensely curious about anything that goes on around them, and are so avid for news, that they will travel many miles to get it. The Bedouin 'grapevine', coupled with powers of observation honed sharp by years of experience in a landscape where nothing is hidden, is extra ordinarily efficient. Deep down, I felt a strange curiosity about these most hospitable of people.

I was thinking that maybe I should learn a little more Arabic and head off into 'the wild blue yonder', when this was all over … at least for a spell.

On this particular day, we were Basrah bound ourselves. This would give me a chance to see what the inner city was like, to experience some of the sights, sounds (and smells). As we weaved in and out of the chaotic traffic, with me stuck in the rear of the Rover again, I could take a look at typical Iraqi city life. There were road-side stalls selling all kinds of weird and wonderful stuff – anything from fruit to vehicle bits. One particular stall-holder was doing a nice line in engine bits, except that some of the larger looking components could not have come from any standard road vehicle (even theirs). I reckoned that some of the bits and bobs that I could see came from pieces of knocked out or abandoned armour.

These people were quite adept at stripping any kind of vehicle down to nothing in no time at all. I'd seen it myself, when passing some stranded vehicle along desert routes, whether car or tank. Anything was game. Obviously, copper wiring figured highly on the 'strippers' must have list – especially where tanks were concerned. But until all of the knocked out armour had been removed from where it lay, the 'strippers' faced a silent and deadly enemy – 'DU'. Leaflets had been distributed which warned the local populace about the risks that they and their children faced if they messed about with the de-mobilised hulks, and in particular, the 'scrap-heap challenge' entrepreneurs.

The thought of carrion stripping a dead carcass came to mind, or a pretty similar example of what Piranhas could do in minutes. Anything, whether it be a wheel or other such component, it would somehow find a use – and most definitely, anything shiny.

The image of seeing a young boy furiously pedalling what would ordinarily have been a light-weight cart, springs to mind. We had to overtake him to get past, mindful of all the other 'Wacky Racers' around and about.

He was having to put some considerable effort into pedalling, in order to maintain the momentum of the car wheels that he had stuck on either side of his cart. They looked like they weighed more than the cart itself. So, I'm sure that if he was to keep it up, he would no doubt grow up to have the calf and leg muscles of an Olympic athlete.

The kids themselves could be quite funny in that everyone called everyone else an 'Ali Baba', or thief. They'd point at another individual and say, "See him? Him, Ali Baba!" The only thing was that they all were, if indeed they could get away with it. But that was the legacy of Saddam.

Finally, out of the chaotic traffic, we rolled into the grounds of the Shatt Al Arab Hotel, which was currently occupied by the Fusiliers battle-group.

This hotel had a commanding view across the adjacent Shatt Al Arab Waterway (not least from its control tower, as it was once 'RAF Basrah' until the British withdrew from here in 1955). Looking out from the very edge of the hotel grounds, the waterway with its palm lined banks opposite, gave me the impression of a scene out of a Vietnam War film. I half expected to see black-garbed figures with broad conical hats standing atop rice paddies beyond the palms. However, it did make for quite a pleasant sight.

After a recce of the location (this would be another of our locations to visit), we were off. Next on the list was the Ba'ath Party HQ which was at the moment, home to the Black Watch until they handed-over to the next lot. Weaving in and out of the traffic again, we eventually came upon the partially destroyed building that had previously been the Ba'ath Party's central hub of activity. This place had taken a right hammering during the bombardment. And, I could recall the reports that were coming in as each of the key buildings were being targeted, during the fight for Basrah. We dismounted at the rear of the HQ whilst the Team Sgt went to pay his respects to the Black Watch 'head-sheds' and have a word regarding our task. Whilst having a few minutes to have a careful look around, I could see where one of the bombs had literally scythed through several floors of the main building leaving a reasonably neat hole in its wake. It may well have been one of the very bombs that I'd 'eye-balled' over at 'Ali Al Salem', which seemed an age ago, now. Outside, was a crater, were some heavy duty ordnance had also impacted, the ground scooped out as though by a giant spoon. The scene instantly reminded me of an old sepia-coloured photograph that I had of my father, going about his War-time trade (Bomb Disposal back then – now 'EOD'), rubble and debris strewn all around, whilst he and his buddies carefully searched for mines and booby traps – the scene was very similar, except that the photo was taken near Florence and that it was some sixty years apart.

A little later, we retraced our route back through the hub-bub of every day Basrah life and back onto the main highway. As we jostled for position at the road junctions, the image of a couple of cool 'Fanta's straight from our wonderful little (though nearly clapped-out) fridge, entered my mind.

Well, I had to concentrate on something to make me forget the bumps and hollows which threatened to knacker my spine. Due to the visual land marks which had now become all too familiar, I could estimate the travelling time back to base with reasonable accuracy. Eventually, I caught sight of the blue cargo cranes at the port, which were a much welcomed sight.

Thank goodness … .we were back.

It was around this time that I wrote a short poem which reflected the situation of lives disrupted, whether Reservist, Territorial or Regular Soldier, and the war and its consequences. My Uncle who'd inspired me to write this, had also written a moving piece in honour of his Brother-in law, David (a Driver with the King's Regiment), who'd been killed in France a few weeks after D-Day in 1944. My Uncle had been stationed in Arras at that time, with the Royal Army Service Corps, and had found out through 'the grapevine' that his Brother-in law was holed up in what I believe was an 'R&R' position somewhere near Caen, and had managed to get a 24hour pass to get across to see him. In the meantime, there had been some kind of explosion, whether mine, shell, I do not know, but David had been mortally wounded.

As my Uncle arrived at his Brother-in-law's location he learned of the tragedy and that David had already died of his wounds, which must have been a terrible shock, especially after having expected to find him hail and hearty. After reading the poem that my Uncle had penned all those years ago, I found it not a little sad, and very touching.

Like my Uncle John before me, I'd also read the First World War Poems of Sassoon and Owen and their hellish existence in the trenches that they communicated through verse. So, it was the example set by these three men that led me also to write a short piece when serving on the UNFICYP mission, that I simply titled 'Peacekeepers', and which I recall the Padre requesting to use at one of his services .

However, the following is the piece that I wrote for 'Telic':

A Call To arms
When called away by Royal decree,
We travelled far, to foreign shore,
To rid the world of heinous foe,
No knowing what our fate would be.

Some went gladly, bold and true,
With sense of purpose, full of pride,
Some left their lives in disarray,
With heavy hearts, the lives they knew.
None wavered when the storm did break,
They held their courage banner high,
Some paid the highest price of all,
Their sacrifice for peace's sake.

With duty done, they fight no more,
In honour now, their home-land rest.
With grateful thanks, our safe return,
A call to arms they'll hear no more.

Back 'at the Ranch', and under canvas once again, the sweat rolled off. Somebody mentioned that just outside the rear of the hanger, it just happened to be a bit of wind tunnel (well, breeze tunnel – when in fact there was any breeze). This corridor of space that ran the length of the building was shielded on the far side by ISO containers. It was out here that all manner of Iraqi field guns and one 'T-55' tank were kept. I called it 'Souvenir Alley'. Each piece of hardware had been claimed by the various Regiments looking to have them shipped back to Blighty as war trophies. Apart from this area also being a bit of a sun trap at a certain time of the day, a few individuals had already started sleeping out here during the night, plus it was a little more protected, although if any of the local hounds came sniffing round, there wasn't much you could really do except to try and shoo them away with perhaps a bit of harsh language. Although it sounds cruel, shooting them wasn't an option as we were no longer in what could be a declared a war zone at that point in time, and all rounds had to be accounted for again. (Plus, we couldn't exactly go round loosing rounds off – as much as we'd have liked to).

During the last few days', a make-shift bar had been erected a few hundred yards away across the port. Basically, it was a hollow square of ISO container's, with a few trestle table and benches in the centre, covered over with some cam netting. But, all in all it made for a great little social place – somewhere else to sit, chat and have a laugh with the two beers that you were limited to (despite the 'two–can rule' it was infinitely better than no can's at all, and an improvement on fizzy 'Fanta'). It was sometimes pot-luck as to what was available to sup, but that didn't really matter. It felt like you were going out for the evening. Well, ok, maybe an hour or so. I mean how long can you make two tins of beer last?

But to be honest, after having been "dry" for so long, having just the two beers (or cider when it was available) didn't particularly bother me in the slightest. Whatever, it made for a rather pleasant distraction and it was a lot more comfortable than sitting on plastic chairs under the canvas of the mess tent, which meant that we didn't have two ceilings above us to contain the heat, just a bit of cam netting, then nothing but lovely night sky.

A regular duty had started up apart from the 24hour guards that most of us were already doing. The threat state regarding suicide bombers had elevated again and additional bods were needed to cover the 'JFLogC' checkpoint. However, we couldn't complain because we had sufficient numbers to be able to rotate the duty fairly evenly, giving each of us a once-a-week duty, and then that was only for a few hours of an evening. And during the daylight hours, we were mostly out and about anyway, so it didn't really impact on us too much.

On one of our trips up to Basrah, the traffic was just as heavy as ever it was, hampering our progress somewhat. As we approached one of the main bridges, there was a great deal of commotion going on over to our left. As I looked, I could see looters running in and out of a breach in the wall of what appeared to be some kind of building or steel supplies yard. People were coming out with lengths of steel rods, and anything else that they could carry. British 'Warrior' APC's were on the scene in rapid fashion, deploying troops to try and quell any further looting. That was the way things were in these here parts. Anything that could be utilised, bartered for, or sold, was fair game – everything had some kind of value. As my father would often say, "They'd steal the eyes out of your head and come back for the sockets."

6th – 13th June

Fifty-nine years ago on this very day – 'D-Day, June 6th 1944', the greatest military operation in the history of the world succeeded in landing 155,000 men of allied armies – US, British and Canadian, on the shores of northern France. The great majority were facing battle for the first time: many were just ordinary men sent far from their home. But before the battle for Normandy was won in late August, these troops had endured some of the most savage and costly fighting of World War Two.

With the 60th anniversary year (2004) approaching, this would quite possibly be the last time that this event would be commemorated on such a large scale, as could be seen with every successive year, veterans were dwindling, most of whom were already in their eighties.

But, so long as people didn't forget …

At the evening brief we had been informed that there would be a handful of 'new' Tigers coming in at the end of June, with another dozen or so coming in during the middle of July. So that we could ensure a smooth hand-over, we needed to get them out on the ground and start to prepare them for when we eventually 'bugged out'. Realistically, this meant that I and the rest of the team still had just over two months to go, now that the Sgt Major had given us a flexible end of tour finish date – on or around the 20th of August (but obviously subject to change). However, he did mention that when the new bod's did arrive, there were liable to be too many Tiger personnel about, and so, half a dozen of us would perhaps get the chance to head for Blighty a week or so earlier than the 20th, and although it was just supposition at this stage, he wanted to find out who wanted to go, given the opportunity. There were however, one or two of us who had every intention of staying until the finish date, and made our intentions known – the point was noted for future reference.

In the last week, the news reports from home were showing that Tony Blair was facing mounting pressure from the House of Commons to hold an independent judicial inquiry into the case for the Iraq war after Claire Short levelled the allegation at the Prime Minister that he had lied to the cabinet. However, the PM rejected the idea of an inquiry. Hans Blix, the Chief Weapons Inspector hit out at the quality of intelligence given to him by the US and Britain on Iraq's alleged chemical and biological weapons programmes, stating, "Only in three of those cases did we find anything at all, and in none of these cases was there any weapons of mass destruction, and that shook me a bit, I must say". This led to the most senior minister to admit publicly that Downing Street was wrong to publish a "dodgy dossier" on the military threat posed by Saddam.

Well, even though that appeared to be the case, there were still a fair number of us who would be out here for a good spell longer, and there would be those that would say that we had gone to war based on a lie. But, when all was said and done, everyone out here still had a job to do.

We were operating in and around the nearby port of Al Zubayr and could manage with two-man teams for a few days, so that in itself made for a change. A 10K marathon that was to be run around Umm Qasr had been organised for the weekend, with the proceeds going to the local community. A few of our guys 'n' gals had agreed to take part. The only downside was that it would be run at 6am (or earlier) because of the heat. I had drawn the short straw for the next 24hour duty over the Friday-Saturday, which ruled me out anyhow. But, if I was being honest, I didn't have the inclination (or the feet) at this point in time, to run the 10K's at 'daft oclock' in the morning. But, I did have to take my 'boonie' hat off to those that were going to crack on with it, and in the process, I made sure that I handed over a couple of bucks for the cause. Those that were not running would act as markers along the route, whilst encouraging the participants to the finish line.

And so, with an unmemorable 24hour duty over, that was me done for a while. We'd been informed at our usual evening brief that there was a job to do "up north," although not as far as Baghdad (everything had gone quiet on that particular subject – in terms of 'TT' heading up that way, that is) but somewhere short of half way – a good 250 K's anyhow. Al Amarah was the place, where elements of '16 Air Assault Brigade' were to be found.

This place, or certainly one of its nearby south-westerly towns would later become extremely news-worthy, but for the wrong, tragic reasons. Originally, the plan had been to send two 'Tiger's to complete the task they were given up there, but that was the scenario if a 'bird' could be organised to fly them with a vehicle in to the location. It would mean that whoever got to go, would spend maybe up to a week up there. But at this point in time, the flight arrangements looked a little tentative to say the least. Failing that, plan 'B' would be put into operation, which was to send four of us with two vehicles for the obvious reasons of vehicle break-down and contact situation. It would be a reasonable drive, but no one would be sight seeing. It would be a case of, eyes peeled for trouble and 'pedal to the metal'. Geordie and Billy were the original two 'Tigers' nominated for the trip, with Hooch and myself as additional back-up.

There were only a couple of days to go until the day of the pre-arranged flight, but as time rolled on it looked like being a non-starter. The boss reckoned that plan 'B' was now definitely the more likely of the two options.

So, it looked like Hooch and I were on the trip. And even though it meant a drive through unfamiliar and less than benign territory, at the moment, anything was better than staying put here. Some may think that there's a certain amount of comfort to be had in reasonably safe, familiar surroundings, but that was the way of things. What's more, our move over to the new air conditioned 'des res' had been put back again … maybe to the 16th. We all agreed in unison that the move would most likely take place the very week that we were due to leave theatre, and heading for home … just a little too late.

That night, not content with broiling inside our tent, several of us simply lifted up our camp cots and carried them outside, positioning them along the wall of the hanger. So, with just a pair of shorts and a cotton sleeping bag liner covering me, it did indeed make for a more comfortable night's sleep. It was a big improvement on the airless confines of 'Pigeon Central'. And until our situation improved, this would be the nightly practise – sleeping under the stars … ."Ahh, nothing quite like it!"

Next day was a vehicle and admin day, but during a respite in the afternoon, the Sgt Major tasked me to go and round up the other half dozen 'Tigers', four of whom were knocking about the port area – he wanted to brief everyone on the latest developments. As it happened, I'd just had a wash-down prior to throwing on clean kit, so I clambered into my sun-baked Rover, ready to go on the 'tiger hunt' and instantly went, "Yeeeoww!" as my behind made contact with the roasting hot vinyl of the seat. Even the steering wheel was 'redders'. I'd only just started the engine and I was already sweating buckets. "Well, so much for putting on clean duds," I thought. Eventually, I found the others. Making good use of a couple of hours down-time, they'd gone over to where there was a small US contingent who had a 'plunge pool', where you could go and immerse your body in an attempt to cool down for a little while.

When I say 'plunge pool', I mean a round soft sided storage reservoir that looked like a high sided cauldron, which was about five feet tall and could accommodate about six people standing. This thing was ideally situated near the edge of the dock with a view across the waterway. As I approached, it looked rather comical to see several heads sticking out of the top of this strange looking container, four of which were ours. It was a shame to have to break up the party, but with a, "Sorry guys, the Sgt Major wants us all for a brief," they clambered out of their watery haven one by one and hurriedly dried themselves off. I must admit that I was sorry that I hadn't taken up the offer of joining them in a dip. Whilst we remained at Umm Qasr, I never did get the chance again, either.

As we sat around one of the cook-house tables, trying not to become liquid on the plastic chairs, the Sgt Major gave us a 'heads-up' on the latest happenings. The news was that the port was to be handed back to the locals in the near future and that Umm Qasr's own port security would eventually have full autonomy in controlling things, once it was safe for the Brit force to back off and leave them to it. Next, on the agenda … .our trip up north.

It appeared that air transportation was a 'no-go', but that we did have the clearance (as it was deemed safe enough at that time) for our four-man team to free-wheel it to Al Amarah. And as such, we were to set out the very next morning.

Al Amarah is the capital city of Maysan province which straddles the river Tigris and was once a military outpost in the days of the Ottoman empire. Interestingly enough, it was only around 50K's from there to the Iranian border too.

Anyway, once the maps had been pored over, with the best and safest route discussed along with all the pre-task details, it was decided that we would take all of our kit, as it looked like we might, just might be moving straight across to our new accommodation the moment we returned. What with us being 'up-country' for maybe up to a week, which depended largely on the scope of the task, taking all the gear seemed the best option. Well, that was the plan anyhow. So, it was "pack up your troubles in your old kit bag," again. I'd lost count a long time ago regarding how many times we'd 'upped sticks'.

That night was our 'Party in the Port' where we had the brass section of the 'AGC' band to entertain us at our watering hole. Admission fee was two bucks with the proceeds also going to the local community as per the 10K run. It was a cracking music night, with a selection of blues, soul, jazz and whatever else was thrown into the mix.

A really good time was had by all, with some of the braver (mostly female) members of the audience getting up to dance. It was, 'score cards at the ready' – "Come in number six, your time is up!" It was 'end ex' at 2300 hours, and we did have a long day ahead of us.

It was also around this time that a small group from our Kuwait based team were to head up and across the border to Tallil, just a few kilometres from Nasyriah, which was north-west of our current position. This mini-team comprised of my other long time buddy Tony, Taff, one 'Staffy', the 'OC' and the 'CO' of 'JFLogC'. They, complete with a couple of rovers were to be flown by Herc, to spend a few hours 'tagging' some of the rolling stock belonging to the unit based at the airfield.

Tallil itself is very close to one of the Old Testament's holy spots; the city of Ur (as I mentioned earlier, Iraq is home to some of the most ancient civilisations and most significant religious sites). This place was said to have been where Abraham was born, and also where he began his journey which would eventually take him and his family to Israel.

Further north, between Najaf and Baghdad, was the settlement of Kufah, where Noah is believed to have built his ark. And, the Euphrates river which bisected the country from north to south is one of the most biblical of rivers. So, if you cared to look just below the surface, this was a fascinating country, steeped in history. And, that was one of the interesting things about being a part of an autonomous team such as 'Tiger'. It gave us the opportunity to move around and take in so much.

6. "How are things in Al-Amarah?"

I awoke around 5a.m. with quite a thirst on. Reaching for my strategically placed bottle of water, it meant that in half-sleep mode I could just reach out and grab it without having to scrabble around for it. Anyway I took a swig – "Yeeeuck!" You could tell how hot it had been during the night as the water was more than tepid. I'd decided that for the last night before our 'expedition' up north, I'd sleep back under canvas … most definitely a bad move. Anyway, that was it, I was awake, so I thought I'd better make good use of the time as we had a few hours before leaving. After my morning ablutions ritual, I dismantled my camp cot as quietly as I could, pulled down my mozzie net and loaded the remainder of my belongings onto the Rover as some of my comrades-in-arms started to stir. Because we needed reliable, speedy vehicles that could get us out of potential trouble fast, we'd temporarily swapped our usual rides for the best two vehicles that we had amongst the whole of the team, and at least they were 'Wolf's.

So now, with me having sorted myself out, it allowed me time to have a reasonably leisurely breakfast and that all important second brew. I managed to grab a bit of CNN news on the box. It appeared that Hans Blix, the UN chief weapons inspector was not a happy chap at all, calling those that had tried to undermine him during the three years that he had held the post, "bastards".

Finally, the remaining three Tigers had risen and had started to make ready for heading out. With final vehicle checks complete, weapons planted in the weapons rack between driver and commander, and fully 'bombed up' mags ready to load up on the way out, we set off for the north. As per our earlier brief, we needed to be fully alert for the slightest signs of trouble.

Before long, we had crossed the Basrah bridges, negotiated the road junctions and started into non-familiar territory. Just under 2 hours into the journey, we started to leave the Basrah region behind. The road began to open out in front of us and there was much less traffic about, which aided our progress. Still, eyes were peeled as our mini convoy headed north with all good speed.

As the clutter of Iraq's second city receded, we came upon little hamlets, pretty much the same as we'd seen on our previous journeys up to Shaibah. The local kid's up here also came running out, laughing and waving and giving us the 'thumbs up' or the "give me water" drinking gesture. I had also remembered to stow a few additional bottles of water for such occasions, and as accurately and carefully as possible, I threw them out with no damage (to either child or bottle).

It appeared that we'd left the desert behind a little, as greenery had taken over, and palms overhung some of the stretches of road near some of the homesteads that we passed, reminding me a little of the small villages that I had once passed along the roadsides in Kenya.

As we continued to eat the kilometres away, we headed in a slightly more westerly direction. We caught sight of the signs for Al Amarah and Baghdad, only that Baghdad was a damn sight further on from were we were headed – maybe a good three to four hours drive on top of that. We were headed for the British base – 'Camp Abu Naji', just off 'Route 6', the main Basrah to Baghdad highway. 'Abu Naji' wasn't strictly in the town of Al Amarah itself, but 5 K's south. As the coalition had advanced on the surrounding area, around 50,000 tons of shells, rockets and explosives had been discovered near the town, and what with there being such a great number of UXB's spread across a wide area, it really gave the RAF EOD teams something to think about.

As we got nearer our intended location, the landscape changed again. The outlying areas of Al Amarah were certainly not what could be described as being picturesque. Dotted about the skyline, I could make out old brick-built chimney stacks from which black sooty smoke issued. The nearer ones looked like brick kilns or some such, but whatever, they marred the surrounding landscape, giving it the look of an ancient, drab industrial area. The place probably hadn't altered in hundreds of years.

Finally, we turned off the junction that took us to '16's location. Once through the archway that led into the base proper, and ID'd ourselves with the Sentry, we booked in, then went in search of '1 Para's RQMS who been told to expect us. After an introduction, the 'RQ' obligingly squared us away with a small 'cell-like' room in his stores complex, which would give us enough space in which to stow our gear and put up four camp cots. "Home from home again," I thought. Once we'd got ourselves sorted, we went off to do a 'recce', to familiarise ourselves with the layout of the place and break down the areas where the different units were to be found, so that working in pairs, we could systematically clear the whole location's vehicles in maybe 3 or 4 days.

There were several Regiments up here, all operating under the banner of '16 Air Assault', or certainly those elements of '16 AA' that were here. When 1 Royal Irish had been here several weeks before, they'd called this place 'Killaloe', which just also happened to be the title of a jaunty military march that the Queen Mother had loved.

So it looked like we had a fair bit of work to accomplish. But if necessary, we had the week anyway, in which to complete our task, which was to include a run out to a disused sports stadium on the edge of the Hayy al Muallmin district where one of the other 'Para' company's was located.

With our gear dumped, we found the cook-house, which heat-wise was something else (and we had thought 'Tent City' back at Umm Qasr it was hot). Mind you, it did have its own "ventilation" in the form of a missing section of roof that looked like it had been blown in by an air-strike, with the area directly below it having been taped off. As with any situation, adaptation is the key thing, in order to be able to cope with your surroundings, which is something that the chefs were having to do in this all-but-condemned building. But all things considered, the grub here was really good. So, it was a bit like the 'Ritz' with the roof stoved in, except there was no dance floor, chandeliers, decoration or … well, just about anything else for that matter!

As the sun shifted across the sky, it came round to beat down upon our little 'cell', warming it up for when we finished at the end of the day. So, in terms of heat (not trouble), it was definitely a case of "out of the frying pan, and into the fire". Daytime temperatures were up to maybe around 50°C, so our water intake increased in relative quantities too.

That night, the walls of our abode just seemed to radiate and pulse with the heat – it was something akin to sizzlingly hot armour to some extent, and I reckon that if I'd managed to get a raw egg to stick to the wall somehow, it may well have cooked. Mind you, if I had managed to make an egg stick to the wall, I would be calling myself 'Paul Daniels'.

The four of us cracked on with our data capturing task, moving from one unit to the next, whilst paying our respects to the 'Head Sheds' of each – to let them know who it was that would be clambering all over their rolling stock. We were doing well, despite the heat – the sun was taking no prisoners.

The armour plating on the tracked vehicles of the 'Household Cavalry' was exactly as I'd just mentioned, ferociously hot (and definitely egg-frying temperatures!), as were my feet, which were not doing as well as the rest of me. No matter what I did, they constantly felt like they were simmering in my boots and becoming increasingly more uncomfortable by the day.

I'd just jumped down from an APC when a guy working on a nearby vehicle said the usual "Hello" and enquired as to what I was doing. When he realised what we were about, he smiled and said that he too had done a stint with 'Tiger' a couple of years previously, and that he had thoroughly enjoyed the experience. We crouched in the shade of his APC to swig some water whilst he mentioned some of the previous team members, including 'some real characters' – none of whom I knew or had heard of. "The job can't be that bad then," I thought as I moved onto my next bit of armour.

Up near the Chinook HLS just outside of the camp (it had to be there because of the man-made sand storms that the rotor wash created), choppers were flying in and out, and we had been informed that some 'big cheese' was due to fly in at some point, and for us to keep our eyes open out for the high profile visitor, just in case we accidentally stumbled across him and his entourage, whilst going about our business.

A little later, we'd adjourned to the cook-house in an attempt to spend a few minutes out of the sun and get some cold juice down our necks. As I turned around I did a double-take, for who should just be walking into the place, but my long sought after buddy, Gordon. He hadn't quite noticed me, so I hollered, "Hoy Gordy, Ya wee bastard!" With that, he looked at me, and a broad grin formed across his face, as we instantly shook hands in the process. "So, I finally found you at last!" I said, followed by, "In all of the cook-houses, in of all the camps in Iraq, you just happen to walk into mine!" adapting that famous line from 'Casablanca'. And with that, we spent a few minute's catching up, agreeing to meet up after evening meal and have that brew that we were originally going to have, in the dim and distant past at 'Fox'.

Well, that certainly cheered my day up, no end.

When we did catch up, it appeared that Gordon had been here, there and everywhere by all accounts, and that he was due to return south to our neck of the woods in a couple of days – to Al Zubayr, to be exact.

Although there were reasonably decent washing facilities somewhere around the area, the closest was a man-made, wooden enclosure with a solar shower bag hanging from a hook on a piece of wood. The whole contraption looked like something out of a western, except with the water bladder doubling for an old wooden bucket. "Ain't no never mind, anyhow," I thought to myself. It was still water from above, and gravity would do the rest, and that was all that mattered. It still got the job done and it made me appreciate it all the more. After all, three months previously, I'd been happy to stand in a bowl with three inches of water at my disposal, which was a lot more than a lot of soldiers had. Ahh! … the appliance of science! But it was so luxurious standing under a shower again, although I needed to top the bladder with a bottle of slightly cooler water in order to bring the temperature down a little … well it had been basking in ridiculous temperatures most of the day.

I noticed that some of the Paras had taken to sunbathing on the flat roofs of the buildings when they were stood down from immediate duties, and although it was discouraged (as far as I know), some of them also slept up there at night, as did Gordon too, on occasion. In that respect, I couldn't blame them.

Once evening meal was over, entertainment options were limited. It was either, stay in the cookhouse and watch TV and broil, or spend the remainder of the evening in our 'cell' where I'd also broil. But whatever, you risked heat over-load either way. With the decision made, I grabbed a brew and decided on the latter, where I sat with my headphones on listening to some sounds, whilst attempting to scribble notes in my pad, and in the process, trying to stop the paper becoming a sodden mess as perspiration rolled off me. My three compadrés just chatted amongst themselves.

I'd decided to try the welfare phones in order to speak to my nearest and dearest, but alas, they were off-line. So, I'd have to wait and see if the Paradigm Engineers managed to get them up and running during the few days that we were to spend up here. However, I did cross paths with one particular engineer who 'Tiger' kept bumping into at several locations around and about. Wherever we turned up, he (Godfrey) seemed to be at that particular location. So, we said hello etc, followed with a, "Fancy meeting you here!" I did jokingly ask him if he had a twin, due to the fact that he seemed to be everywhere. (I will say that the civilian comms engineers moved around as much if not more than some of the units in theatre, and despite their pre-requisite for armed escorts (in most cases), travel between locations wasn't without some risk).

The next night however, I was in luck, even if it did mean waiting in a long queue. I'd almost forgotten what it was like to stand amongst a long line of people – it was shades of the American PX back at Arafjan.

It was around 3 a.m. as I woke in a lather of sweat with my throat parched. So, rather than drink the tepid H^2O at the side of my cot, I remembered the stacks of bottled water kept just outside the rear of the building. I was determined to find something a few degrees cooler to drink. Stepping outside, there was no other form of illumination except for that of the moon. As I gazed heavenwards, rubbing the sleep from my eyes, the view that greeted them was amazing. Because of the near total darkness, I'd never seen so many stars, and the deeper I looked, the more I could see. Rummaging through the boxes of bottled water, I found a few slightly less than tepid. So, I spent a few minutes quenching my thirst whilst availing myself of God's majesty. It was a sight never to be forgotten, and unless I was ever to find myself in a place of all encompassing darkness again, it was a sight most probably never to be repeated. It was worth the disturbed sleep for the spectacle.

Back in doors again, I spent the next three hours drifting in and out of sleep. Even the merest hint of a breeze would have been most welcome, but there hadn't been a breath of air. I wished that I'd been able to follow the example of the local Paras who'd set up their camp cots and 'mozzie' nets on the flat roofs of the buildings. It must have been wonderful to have been able to drift of to sleep with the whole of the starlit heavens as your canopy.

But in the end, having had enough, I got up and headed for the shower, before my fellow 'Tiger's started to stir.

I breakfasted as I caught some news in the half bombed out cook-house. Once I'd finished what must have been my third cuppa, I went and found the guys and got ready to move at 8a.m. We were headed the 12 or so K's over to the sports stadium where '1 Para (A Coy)' were to be found. Not far away from the stadium, on the southern bank of the river lay 'Chemical Ali's old house, and although it was now hard to believe, Al Amarah once basked in the shade of thousands of ancient date palm trees and was no doubt something of sight to behold in long ago days.

Initially, we'd been told that there had been a "little trouble" in and around that particular area, and to be on our guard. However, we didn't meet up with, or find anything untoward happening as we approached, thank goodness. Once we'd identified ourselves on the way in and were parked up, Geordie went to introduce himself to the Para 'head-sheds' and inform them of what we were here to do. Because there was only one company based here, there weren't a great many vehicles, which meant that we would more than likely complete our task in just over an hour. A little later as the heat started to build, a couple of the Paras invited us in for a brew before we headed back to our 'home from home'. Well, it was rude not to accept, and certainly not with the 'Para's.

Their makeshift TV room was also the brew-room – something there was never any shortage of. Just like every other location we'd ever visited, they'd tried to make themselves as comfortable as possible. The stadiums viewing boxes and other rooms that overlooked the running track and sports field were being used as billets by the soldiers based here. The track itself was abandoned and quiet – its inner sports field still quite green. So whilst I had a minute or two to myself, I walked out to the edge of this now hushed arena, trying to imagine a time when it was filled with 25,000 people cheering their local 'homeboy' to the finish line. In a way, it was quite sad really – this desolate arena, once a place where individuals gave the best of themselves, and now it just echoed with ghosts. On the other hand, this may well have been a place where Saddam publicly 'dealt with' anti-Hussein, anti-regime Iraqi's, but I preferred my thoughts on the former notion. In better times it must have been some place.

We paid our respects to the Paras, mounted the vehicles, then headed back for 'Abu Naji' – it was still only mid morning. Our task up here was all but complete, so we could grab a spot of lunch before the trip south. But at least I'd managed to catch Gordon again briefly, as he and his team started to load up their kit and equipment for a move out later in the day. So in the end, I'd managed to find him, albeit by accident. After lunch, we loaded the rovers, paid our respects to the 'RQ' and gunned the vehicles in a southerly direction. All that we needed to do now was get back without incident.

A hundred or so K's into our trip, I could feel myself starting to tire – mainly with the heat. So, I mentioned to Hooch that I wished to swap over with him, and that he could drive the last half of the route. After flashing our compadrés in front, to make sure that they slowed down in tandem with us, I checked out a suitable piece of roadside in which to pull over. With nothing or nobody else about, I quickly ran up to their Rover to inform them that we were swapping positions. And, with that we sped off on the last leg of the journey. We still had the 'fun' of Basrah to negotiate. If having to concentrate with your eyeballs glued to the windscreen for any 'crazies' didn't keep you awake, then nothing would.

250 K's later, we rolled into home territory, thinking that we could be moving directly over to our new air conditioned accommodation that very afternoon – no chance! That was still not likely to happen for around another five days, as things would turn out. So, we just simply unloaded all of our kit back into 'Pigeon Central' again. You win some, you lose some! But it wasn't all gloomy news, as we were informed that very evening during our brief that despite there being no actual leave on this tour, soldiers were starting to get three-day 'OSD's (or Operational Stand-down) packages across the border in Kuwait, at Ali Al Salem Air Base to be exact.

The Sgt Major hinted that the team was due for theirs anytime soon, and we were to keep everything crossed in the hope that it would come off. To add to this, our little Al Amarah team got a pack on the back for a job well (and speedily) done. Well, that certainly brightened a few faces up anyhow.

The news from around and about indicated that sporadic incidents were still happening, and for us not to let our guard down. It was at times like this, when things appeared to be reasonably quiet that it was possible to be lulled into a false sense of security where something would invariably catch the unwary out. There were also other incidents that had taken place that the news teams would not get to hear about, but "that," as they say "is another story," but not one that will be related here. As the US had moved in on Iraq's resistance, some 400 suspects were being questioned after the biggest military operation since the regime had collapsed two months previously.

After our brief, there was a chance to avail ourselves of one or two 'cool one's in our make-shift bar, as a small stock of beer had been replenished … .something that was more than welcome, especially after our return from the north.

Next day, we were to be up at Basrah Palace visiting the '7th Armoured Div', which would give me a chance to see one of Saddam's strongholds for myself. That was of course, once we'd played 'dodgems' with everything that moved on the roads on the approach to Iraq's second capital city.

14th – 21st June

We had three rovers on the move towards Basrah, and boy the traffic was just as mad as ever it was. As we made for the older and just as congested parts of the city, I scanned around, taking stock of our surroundings as we passed. I was 'riding shotgun' again in the rear, but it gave all my senses the chance to take everything in. A number of the local inhabitants smiled and gave us the 'thumbs-up' – to which I responded with a smile and a wave. Some of the younger elements of the population occasionally shouted bursts of Arabic (which, accompanied with a grin, I assumed was friendly).

On the opposite side of the coin though, we knew that lurking here and there, where those who also wanted to be rid of the 'infidels' who roamed freely around their home-land. All that we could do, really, was take as soft an approach as safety and security allowed, particularly at this point in time. We were not an occupying force as such, and although we formed part of the coalition, Americans, we weren't either.

As we checked in through the archway of the Palace, the sounds of the city began to recede as we took the avenue that led into the grounds proper. This place was somewhat different to what I'd imagined. It was more a complex of buildings surrounded by man-made lakes and pools linked by a series of ornate arced bridges, although, there was one main building in the heart of the grounds. However, here at the centre of one of Saddam's (many) provinces, it was as far removed as you could imagine from the sights, sounds and smells that lay beyond the palatial archways where the city dwellers lived. The main building was also the central feeding place for all the Regiments and units based here. When we did eventually break off for lunch, we dined in one of the larger air-conditioned rooms designated for 'Other Ranks'. The grub was very good, or maybe the surroundings had something to do with it? No, I think that the food stood on its own merit. Mind you, that's not to say that the elaborate ceilings and facades weren't impressive, as I remembered thinking that I mustn't shovel a fork-full of food in my ear whilst looking around at the Palatial décor. I bet Saddam never envisaged "the friends and helpers of Satan" sitting down and having lunch in one of his beloved palaces (and this was only one of around 80 such palaces that Saddam had dotted around Iraq – talk about excess!)

But sitting here in this rather grand room was definitely one weird experience though. It was grand in terms of Arab taste and style … ..although it was a whole world away from what a western eye would consider grand in a traditional sense.

Before finishing for the day, and mounting the vehicles for home, we had a few minutes to take in a little of the exterior surroundings. Nearby one of the ornamental bridges, there was a lovely view between two stone lions across the Shatt Al Arab Waterway – very picturesque indeed. And as if in contrast to this, looking beyond the bridge down the road that led towards the gates and arches, a long line of sand painted APC's of the battle-group, lay neatly parked up against the kerb. I'd certainly be taking some striking memories back home with me, that much was for sure. Apart from the reasons that we were all out here in the first place, the chance to see and do so much was in some ways, a privilege. That's not to say that it was all 'sunshine and roses' … ..well maybe the sunshine, but still, sometimes you do have to seize the moment, or 'Carpe Diem' – seize the day.

We still had one or two days up here, so it would hopefully give us the chance to see anything that may be of interest. However, we still had to get back to in one piece, and as it turned out, we did have a close call at a road junction with one of our own coalition 'Warrior AFV's, due to the bad road manners (or plain crazy road sense more like) of an Iraqi driver. So much so, that several tons of tracked armour travelling at somewhere near full belt, narrowly missed re-arranging our Rover into something that would have resembled a giant dustbin lid. That was definitely enough for one day.

Our three-day 'OSD' was confirmed. We would be heading for 'Ali' the next Monday and returning on the Wednesday. With travelling time, it would realistically give us two days really, but a break is a break, and we were ready for it. We were told that we'd have the chance to use the facilities at 'The Marble Palace' as it was called – a complex located at a power station, that had a swimming pool and other activities laid on, cheap food, and that it was mostly full of our 'Colonial Cousins', seeing as 'Camp Doha', the giant American base, was only a couple of miles away.

But another good reason for paying this place a visit (well, for me anyhow) … .it had a 'Starbucks' coffee shack. It may be considered a long way to go for a coffee, but I'd have travelled to the moon for a decent cappuccino or latte. However, that's not to say that the subject of brews of any sort pre-occupy a major part of my waking life … .but then again who am I kidding! Although I will say that my original alternative title for this book may well have been, "Stop the War, And Get a Brew On!"

Now that we knew what was available to us, I just hoped that nobody 'pulled the plug' at the last minute. But then again, anything was possible.

There were still an unknown number of extremists and insurgents out there who thought that the coalition was fair game, and it was generally agreed amongst us, that "things weren't over until they were over". Time, effort and a large amount of trust were required. As I understood things, and as far as the Iraqi people were concerned, Saddam was overthrown, but he was still at large and still posed some kind of invisible threat which created an air of unease amongst those who wanted rid of him and his regime. Despite his absence, his spectre still cast a shadow upon the people of Iraq.

I made what was, to be my final trip up to Basrah Palace, and my last chance to look around. This time we made the journey without incident. And this time we didn't nearly get written off by the crazy local drivers. We were required to detour to Shaibah Airfield once we were finished up at the palace. As we checked through the sentry post, we did the usual weapons unload and headed for the parking area across from the 'EFI' shop which had undergone a slight transformation. It now had more variation on the kind of thing that it had sold previously. But it also had the addition of half a dozen patio sets plonked outside, complete with umbrellas. At least it gave people a little shade whilst devouring a couple of tins of cool stuff, or when munching on a burger from the adjacent 'Burger King' trailer. When we'd completed what we'd come to do, we had a short respite before heading back to Umm Qasr. Despite the warmth, it was enough to be able to get out of the glare of the early p.m. sun. As I went back into the shop to buy a couple of extra tins for our fridge back at base, who should come in, but my buddy Gordon, again. "We're gonna have to stop meeting like this," I said. And, with that he started to tell me of his next location move. He was finished up north, and was now waiting for details on his return back to Blighty, somewhere within the next couple of weeks. He had even managed to get back over the border to 'Ali Al Salem Air Base' where he'd bumped into Tony, our southern Tiger Team buddy. Of the 'Four Musketeer's out here in the Middle-East, Derek was the one that none of us would see again for almost another six months. As Gordon and I went our separate ways again, we reckoned that the next time that we would see each other, would more than likely be when we were both back home, and meeting up for a beer in one of the local haunts in which we RV'd every few months. That would indeed turn out to be the very case.

But little did I know that I and one or two others would also be re-locating within a week or two, and as far as the Basrah region was concerned, I was all but finished here as well.

The remainder of the journey back to the port was damnably hot under the canvas of the Rover, but we finally rolled in through the check-points and parked up outside our luxurious 'des-res', the 'hot-house' hanger. Apart from the possibility of being summoned for some kind of additional task, we were more or less done for the day.

After grabbing a light lunch, the news reports coming in declared that almost 100 Iraqi's had been killed in two of the bloodiest attacks since the fall of Baghdad, whilst an independent research group stated that as many as 100,000 civilians may have died in the war. Well, whether the alleged numbers totals were correct or not, war, sadly is a grievous business.

So, the afternoon consisted of vehicle prep, weapon strip, 'doby-ing' some kit and soothing the feet, in that order. Although it was necessary for us to remain in uniform, the washing tables in our open-plan 'laundrette' made for a pretty good place to stretch out in the shade whilst waiting for the sun to do its job on the wet washing. And, if you were discreet, you could take your shirt off to let some fresh, if hot air, get to your body.

There were however, those individuals who would openly sun-bathe in whatever down-time was to be had, but with the 'HQ' so close, it wasn't wise for 'Tiger' to attract any unwanted attention, as some additional duty could always be found for anyone that looked none too busy.

A little while later, with no further team tasks on the menu, a few of us grabbed our fold-up chairs and headed for the rear of the hanger, amongst all the captured weaponry. It was a bit like 'Steptoe's back yard out here, and I bet that there were more than a few bob's worth of scrap around and about. "Hmmmm," I wondered, "Now what would an old disabled Iraqi field gun fetch in scrap weight?!"

There was a young local lad who helped out around the cook-house, (as some of the locals did), and on a couple of occasions, would come out to our 'sitting area' to chat, and seeing that he spoke pretty good English, we would attempt to converse, mainly trying to learn a few bits of Arabic that weren't on our Arabic Aide Memoir cards. We were always wary about what we said, but he seemed content just to talk about the differences in our two cultures, and found our slang for things rather amusing. It appeared that his older brother had fought in the '91' Gulf War against the coalition.

"My, how things change," I thought. In the general swapping of phrases, we picked up one or two useful bits and pieces. One such phrase, which my compadré Hooch really liked was, "Hadini Bicycle!" or, "Give me your bicycle!" – not a million miles apart I suppose, what with 'bicycle' being one of the only two words present. Hooch proceeded to use this on his next duty stag at the check point where he apparently got some bemused looks from the locals riding in and out of the port, who were probably thinking; "Wow! These Brit's are strict. Now they want to confiscate my bike!"

It was all just a bit of banter between two very different cultures. And anyway, the local Arabs could have been calling us 'fit to burn' amongst other things, whilst still managing to smile, and we'd never have known. Not unless we started to become a bit more fluent. However, half a dozen key phrases seemed to be our limit, really.

My previous vehicle commander, Nick, and I had been tasked to drop the CO down to 'Ali' airbase in the south. At least we had the Pajero at our disposal for the day, which meant that we'd travel the well worn route in relative comfort, and at least remain somewhat cooler with 'air-con' on board. Once we'd dropped the CO off at 'Ali', we had to shoot across to Shuaybah port – and 'Spearhead Camp' to be exact (my former address for a short spell). This time I was glad to be making a brief visit, knowing that when our simple task of delivering and collecting some information was complete, we were out of there. We couldn't hang about anyhow, because we knew that we still needed to do a quick call to 'Camp (America) Doha'. So, when we'd spoken to the few 'Tigers' based down here, we grabbed a coffee and a doughnut in the newly opened coffee shop, and then zoomed off in the direction of 'Doha'. By the time we'd left the US base, the sun was way across the sky and beginning its descent. As it headed for the horizon, the desert took on an altogether different appearance. Not the bleached inhospitable look, but a softer more 'lunar' looking environment. This was the time of day that I liked, as the sun made longer shadows upon the terrain, completely altering its appearance as you drove past.

As we parked up, it had just turned dusk, and it appeared that we were just in time for our evening brief. The 'Tigers' were already assembled near to where we pulled in, so as we stepped out of the vehicle, we could get the latest news from the Sgt Major without someone later having to repeat what had been said. All in all, it was pretty good timing.

Next day was to be the start of our three-day 'OSD', and coincidentally, at the very location where we had dropped the CO off, earlier this very day. We could probably retrace the route blindfold, not to mention the fact that our tyre imprint on the road surface would still be fresh, but you can't have everything, and there were three days off into the bargain. It was well worth the mind-numbing route again.

So, the very next day, we did the same trip again and made it in good time to 'Ali'. One of the buildings had been set aside for 'OSD' visitors, which had a number of rooms squared away with bunk beds, proper quilts and pillows for those that would be taking advantage of their three-day break. When we arrived, we signed out our bedding, threw in what little kit we had with us and decided to head over to 'Doha', where we could pick up the transport laid on by the Americans that would take us to the 'Marble Palace' for a day of sunning ourselves (without wondering whether someone would take umbrage at us being out of desert kit). There was an outdoor pool, which was absolutely mobbed, almost standing room only.

So, it was a case of, try and find a sun-lounger, slap on the factor 'minus twenty' and soak up some rays. One of the guys had actually concocted a mixture of stuff with which he was quite happy to coat himself, but I declined his offer of what I considered was more than likely a 'skin stripper' rather than protector. In all honesty, good old chip fat would most probably have been kinder on his skin. His "tanning oil" was something akin to brake fluid, baby oil and power steering fluid (to give it that nice deep colour), or something very close. But as I jokingly pointed out to him, he might well be walking along one day as several layers of skin decide to detach themselves from his body. Similar to the way in which a snake sheds its skin, virtually in one piece. Anyway, after a while, I'd had enough of the din from the pool, so I thought I'd explore a little. Plus, the call of 'the cappuccino' was overpowering me too, so I parted with my dollars at the 'Starbucks' shack for a 'super-duper all-in-special', complete with chocolate, coconut, the works. If a tad pricey at what was about four quid, it was still worth its six bucks anyhow, as it turned out to be absolutely delicious. Then after queuing for ages at the snack-bar I finally managed to grab some typical US style food …

.. a burger, fries and a Coke. I'd had enough of the heat for one day, and decided to stay a little cooler and remain in the air-conditioned 'atmos' of the reception area. There were a few distractions, such as a video games area, ping-pong table and a music room complete with instruments, which you could simply sign out and have a play (I use the word "play," loosely). People were generally enjoying themselves, but every time the music room door opened, there were a cacophony of noises coming out. Some good, some excruciating.

To put it bluntly, the lesser players sounded like they were torturing the instruments, not to mention ears. For those that were attempting to 'chill' in the reception's seating area, it sometimes proved to be a little too much, especially when you were nodding off, and all of a sudden the door opened with the noise of what sounded like somebody doing a "Keith Moon" and kicking over or falling into the drum kit, rather than playing it. "These little things are sent to try us" I thought, as I gritted my teeth and attempted to get back to my 'zen-like' state of being one with the rather comfortable settee, situated under an Arabian styled canopy.

A little while later, the rest of the guys 'n' gals appeared at our mutually agreed meeting time, so that we could jump on the transport for 'Doha', where we'd left our vehicle.

Later, back at 'Ali', after having been fed with some rather good RAF nosh, a few of us decided to spend a little viewing time in the superbly chilled welfare portakabin, complete with large rear-projection screen TV and comfy seats. There was the additional bonus of a fridge and kettle at the other end, which meant that we could 'view and brew'. There were only a handful of us, and it was like having our own personal film theatre, except no popcorn, thank goodness – the noise of which would have proved too much of a distraction!

So, after catching a little of the news from around the world, we settled in to watch a couple of episodes of 'Band of Brothers' – one of the guys just happened to have the DVD boxed set out here. Around the time that it was first being aired on TV, I was deploying for Cyprus and had missed half of the episodes, so it made for a great viewing experience in our wonderful surroundings.

On the whole, it had been a really good day, apart that is, from some of the cat-a-wailing non-musicians. But I suppose even they had the right to enjoy themselves, even though it was at expense of other peoples suffering.

Prior to getting our heads down for the night, several of us had agreed that we would take advantage of the available transport and take the 50-minute drive into Kuwait City the very next morning.

As we headed towards the capital, some of city's unique looking towers hove into view. The one in Kuwait central looked like a strange hypodermic needle, whereas the others that we could see on the coast resembled pickled onions on fat cocktail sticks, but upon closer observation they were quite a feat of engineering and design. We found a multi storey car park, locked up and went exploring. We were heading down a street where the 'Marriot' hotel was located and continued on through the main reception doors. At first I thought we'd gone a little astray, and I was thinking that I was a bit under-dressed walking into a swanky looking hotel. However, to the side of the reception, there was another doorway which led into a really sumptuous shopping mall with beautiful marbled floors and retail outlets where window goods didn't display any prices. No doubt 'megabucks' were required here. Further along I caught sight of a familiar sign and alerted those that were interested. A 'real' Starbucks! So, whilst a few of the gang wandered around, a couple of us decided to spend a little time sampling the delights of this famous coffee emporium and wait until the others had returned. Anything could have happened at this point, but we didn't care as we were in 'caffeine heaven'. Whilst we were sitting there enjoying a deliciously chilled chocolate-cream 'Frappucino', it was fascinating to discreetly people watch, as the local Kuwaiti's sauntered by. Most of the males were wearing the whiter-than-white customary *'dishdash'* (robe) and *k'fir* (headdress), whilst a great number of the women wore black, full head-to-toe ensembles with only a slit for the eyes. There were however, a few women who dressed in a more westernised fashion, wearing jeans and such.

It certainly made for quite a different experience from sitting in the same coffee outlet in my own city, and it seemed such a long, long way from bombs and bullets. But having said that, in the whole scheme of things, it hadn't been that long ago when Saddam's missiles had reached the city – killing and injuring a number of people.

We continued our stroll on towards 'Liberation Tower', with its hypodermic pointed communications mast, (not dissimilar to Toronto's CNN Tower, which I'd visited some two years previously) and ventured into the reception area to ask as to whether visitors were allowed to ride the elevator to the viewing platform, but we were politely turned away. Well, it was worth a try.

We headed back through some of the more market-like areas and souqs, which couldn't have been more different from the marble encrusted mall that we had left earlier. A slight error of judgement with regard to where we'd originally parked the vehicle gave us a moment or two of panic, thinking that the Pajero had been stolen … .wrong level. Phew!

As we took the scenic route out of the city, we passed the interestingly shaped Kuwait Towers, with their bauble-like structures skewered through the centre. After duelling with the city traffic, we were once again out onto the freeway and back at Ali in pretty good time.

The following day was spent in situ, just having a spot of relaxation. Unfortunately for us, the small but ideal plunge pool with its raised sun-deck and sun loungers wasn't yet open to us which was a real pity.

It had been planned that we would head for the border after evening meal, giving us just enough time to get back to before the sun set.

Once we were back in 'UQ' again, we'd learned that 'Sultan Lines' was ready for us to move into at long last. So we proceeded to move everything from our tents and into the vehicles, then transfer it all the few hundred yards across the port to our new address. It took a couple of hours to sort ourselves out, as unloading the gear in the dark was no easy task, what with the numerous things to bump into and trip over. Eventually, we had our stuff stowed into our allotted air-conditioned accommodation, and by then, it was getting close to midnight when we'd finally finished. The funny thing was that, Herbie and I would only get the chance to spend the one night here, as we'd been informed by the Sgt Major earlier on, that the two of us were required back down at 'Ali' again to work with the port team for a week or so. What's more, we were due to leave again the very next morning at 0600 hours! So, it was a wonderful shower in the adjoining ablutions and then slide into the 'old scratcher', which made for a very pleasant experience at actually having to sleep in a sleeping bag again, instead of on top of it. But, that's air conditioning for you. Next morning, before we headed south, the two of us went off to find the new cookhouse, which was to be located a couple of twists and turns away. It was a bit like 'follow the yellow brick road', in that you simply stayed on the plastic walkways and followed the signs to whichever part of 'Sultan' that you needed to get to. It was quite a neat set-up. One of the 'tented' units even had some basic gym equipment in there, which was part of the welfare package set-up, as was the case with most of the other locations which were also being kitted out in similar fashion.

At the rear of all the accommodation units, low-noise generators and air-conditioning hummed whilst trying to keep internal air temperatures constant. With the building summer temperatures, this new equipment would be tested to the limit.

After 'brekkers', we were south-bound again and heading for the very place that we'd only just left around twelve or so hours previously. However, there were much far worse places to be based than 'Ali'. On the plus side, the two small plunge pools had been built just across from the welfare and TV room known as the 'Oasis Club' were now open. This was to be another one of the real bonuses of being based down at the airbase. And, given that the pools were now in use, 'Ali' based personnel could avail themselves of this added luxury (work and duties permitting of course!). Those RAF bods certainly didn't mess about when it came to creature comforts. The 'Tigers' down here, were pretty much sorted too. Once the southern team had got established they'd moved out of tents and into air conditioned portakabins, which were kitted out with decent beds and furniture. The guy's had even bought their own fridge, and had quite rightly got themselves as comfortable as they could be. When the two of us showed up and were given our allotted beds, with me in one portakabin and Herb in the other, it quickly became apparent that we would be somewhat more comfortable here than up north as it was easier to maintain cooler indoor temperatures than a tent-like structure, where the 'air-con' is constantly trying to do battle with the heat coming through the fabric, no matter how heat reflective or resistant it was.

Over the last couple of days, hundreds of US troops had swept through Fallujah in an attempt to extinguish the last vestiges of guerrilla resistance, but this was something that was easier said than done. Whilst in Baghdad, new searches were being conducted after a US soldier had been shot dead on patrol by a sniper. It was also now believed that the trail leading to Saddam was getting warmer, and that he was still in Iraq, despite the very different notions that had been expressed some several weeks previously. Not only that, but one Abid Hamid Mahmud Al-Tikrit – the 'Ace of Diamonds' in the pack of '55 Most Wanted', had been captured. He was the most senior member of Saddam's closest aides. Thus far, 32 of the pack, along with another 50 of the Special Republican Guard and security forces had also been nabbed. It looked as though the US were not going to give an inch, and their aggressive stance may, or may not have had some effect on the slowly escalating fatalities on both sides. My own humble opinion was that the Iraqi people in general were certainly a little more tolerant of the Brit's than our American counterparts, although it must be said that they (the US) were operating in the more northerly and overtly hostile areas of the country, whilst we kept the south-eastern sector under control.

But sadly, as the months ticked away, the whole situation would deteriorate rapidly. Again, in Baghdad, it was believed that a gunman nicknamed 'The Hunter', had allegedly sniped at least 6 US soldiers, which brought the total of US 'KIA's since May, to 41. The latest killings took place in a northern suburb of Baghdad, during the city-wide 11p.m. – 4a.m. curfew.

US night patrols had been plagued by ambushers in several parts of the city. It was also believed that the sniper was an ex sharp-shooter from Saddam's Republican Guard Special Forces, and had been hand picked by his son, Qusay, for his deadly skills.

The previous Sunday had marked the ending of a two-week gun amnesty, whilst 'Operation Desert Scorpion' was launched to hunt down guerrillas blamed for the deadly attacks on checkpoints and convoys.

In the northern cities of Tikrit and Kirkuk, almost 400 people (mostly Ba'ath Party loyalists) were arrested during night-time raids. The US were stating that 'Op Desert Scorpion' was an attempt at achieving two goals – trying to win the 'hearts and minds' of the Iraqi populace as well as hunting down loyalists. The Iraqi's were claiming that the raids were conducted in a far too heavily handed manner, with houses having been ransacked and civilians assaulted. This in itself would further incense those who already hated the coalition with a passion, and would only increase their desire to be rid of the 'infidels' whom they saw as an occupying force in their country'.

Only time would tell, but the long-term prospects didn't look good from where I was standing, especially for the Americans. In fact, it could be said that the whole situation looked extremely dire.

21st – 28th June

The boss came in to task Herb and I with heading up to the 'Hammersmith' area where '2 Battalion REME' were ensconced at the old Kuwaiti base. This was where '10 Transport Regiment RLC' had their rolling stock, and so we needed to get the kit tagged as soon as was possible, as they, like many other units, were to head for the shipping ports and out of Theatre, bound for the UK in the very near future. So once we were up, about and breakfasted, we didn't waste any time in gunning the Rover northward. Fortunately, there weren't a great number of vehicles around and about, for varying reasons, which meant that we could accomplish what we came to do in about half a day. Subtle changes in the weather told us that a storm was brewing, and we weren't wrong. As it reached mid-day, the wind started to build rapidly, but thankfully, we had all but finished. We decided to forgo lunch and high-tail it out of there, and see if we could make it back to 'Ali' in time. Or, failing that … .'MRE surprise'. The wind was by now, frenziedly whipping the sand across the open areas of the desert as we got to the main highway and took our route south. Every time we were buffeted and blasted by the hot air, fine sand was doing its best to get in through every aperture on the vehicle. But, we managed to get back to base without mishap, and just in time for grub, which was later followed by the removal of the Kuwaiti desert from the vehicle and the engine's air filter element for good measure too.

Because we'd completed our task in good time, the boss stood us down for the afternoon, which meant that we could do whatever we wished. My first thought was to get the old swimming shorts on and take a dip in the pool. We'd been here a couple of days and this was the first time that we had the chance to take advantage of the 'Hotel-Del-Ali's plunge pool. It was only around 25 feet by 20 feet and about 4 foot deep, but it was more than adequate. Our northern 'Tiger' comrades, Billy and Hooch, had been allowed a 'chill' day, and permission granted to come down here, so long as they were back safely across the border by a given time that very evening. So, they too could enjoy the sensation of total body immersion (and short swim). Once out of desert kit, I threw on my shorts, grabbed my towel, sun-oil, and went off to find the others. It was "reet grand" (to coin Hooch's phrase), just being able to immerse oneself again. Even the sun loungers on the sun-deck were proper solid wooden jobs. So after a bit of a float around, the four of us sat there, all 'slicked up', and chatted about recent events.

It was good to catch up, as it was so easy to miss out on information that couldn't be relayed on the old 'jungle drums'. Billy did tell us of an alleged incident of 'over-reaction' by other coalition forces, where a child had been shot and killed, but that is about all that I will say concerning the matter. However, this then started a whole other conversation on the current situation regarding our guys up in the Basrah region. By the time we'd finished chewing the fat, the sun had travelled a good way across the sky when we decided to call it a day. Once our compadrés had showered and had grabbed an early evening meal, we said our goodbyes as they took their leave. It had turned into a pretty good day and no mistake.

Now that I was a temporarily 'adopted' southern team member, I thought that I may as well show a little solidarity by 'mucking in', and buy a slab of pop from the American PX. Whilst having a mooch around in the store, I grabbed a pack of 'Mountain Dew' which was rather pleasant when chilled. Because the guys had the fridge, anyone could take a can of whatever was in there, so long as each individual helped to replenish the current stock from time to time. It seemed liked the civilised thing to do, and for the sake of 6 or 7 dollars, that wasn't bad at all. It was so good being able to open a real thirst quenching 'cool one' when you felt like it (although back in Umm Qasr, the little fridge did its best, but was so stacked full most of the time, that it struggled to do its job). Some of the newer 'Tigers' were based down here, which gave me a chance to get to know them a little better too.

The current situation over at the two sea ports – Shuwaikh and Shu'aibah, meant that we could operate in three small teams of three, thus allowing us to work in rotation, in shifts basically. And the way it worked out, it meant that everyone would get a little more down time each day.

Over in the 'land of the free', George Bush was having to address the ever increasing disquiet over the number of US troops killed in Iraq. More than a quarter of the casualties had occurred since the President had declared an end to all major military combat operations on May 1st.

It transpired that there was need to send a four-man team to Oman, to tag the RAF's kit at their base near Muscat. Two of the guys that were originally lined up to go, weren't overly bothered about the trip, one way or the other, which left the door open for other interested parties. The OC would be going, accompanied by three others. Herbie and myself were more than interested, so much so, that he ran the idea by the boss, who said he'd consider what, and who was to go. For the trip to come off, the logistics of the flights had to be sorted, along with a request to the RAF detachment at Seeb (in Oman) for the 'fly boys' down there to be able to accommodate us without too much hassle.

For me, the possibility of a being able to travel and experience an altogether different part of the Middle-East was an additional bonus.

So, we'd see what was decided.

On one particular day, the mini-team of which I was a member, had an afternoon stint, which allowed us the chance to sign out one of the base mini-buses and head off into Kuwait city. One of the guys was on the hunt for some sports gear, and once we were safely parked up, we then proceeded to scan for suitable shops. It appeared that we were heading back towards the 'Marriot' again, and the only thing that I had on my mind, was an ice-cool, refreshing and ultimately delicious 'Frappucino'. Once we entered the mall, I made a bee-line for the 'Starbucks like an Exocet missile locked on to its target. Whilst the others wandered around the mall, I was quite content to sit and chill for a short while until they returned. We were only out for a couple of hours, and I got to thinking that if the coffee was the only thing that I'd got out of my second visit to Kuwait City, then that was no bad thing. But I was in for another treat. "Surely the day couldn't get any better than this?" I thought (sometimes, it's the simple luxuries that count). Upon leaving the city, we took the route out along the gulf coast road aptly titled, 'Arabian Gulf Street' towards the intriguing looking Kuwait Towers and pulled into the parking area below them. This was Kuwait's most famous landmark and it turned out that we had just enough time to go and have a closer look at these amazing 'Arabesque' features, unlike the previous day when we only had time to do a drive-by. We'd timed it just right, as the viewing tower was open, and so we handed over our Kuwaiti Dinar notes at the turnstile – 500 'fils' to be exact (equivalent to a pound), and proceeded to the elevator. Once out and onto the revolving observa-tion deck, there was a commanding view out over the city, where a heat haze shimmered, courtesy of the afternoon sun, with the 'Liberation Tower' (at 372 metres, the fifth-tallest communications tower in the world) rising above everything else. Rotating 180degrees, the waters of the Arabian Gulf looked rather inviting too, as did the 'Aqua Park' directly below. From up in this lofty perch, you could see all the water slides and complete layout of the water park. Now that really looked like the kind of place to have a bit of fun, should 'down-time' permit. A few of the guys had already talked about the possibility of spending a little time in there, if given the opportunity.

As I peered through the glass at the sphere of the slightly lower tower, its exterior tiling gave the impression as though it was decorated with giant blue sequins, if not as sparkly, like some kind of Arabian bauble, which was possibly the effect that the designers intended. (The towers were actually designed by a Swedish architectural firm, and were opened in 1979, and the tallest of the three rises to a height of 187 metres).

As I descended from the viewing platform into the café area, I caught sight of black and white images on the walls – photographs of the destruction and mayhem that the Iraqi's had caused following their invasion of Kuwait some twelve years earlier. They'd certainly made a right mess of the interior of the towers, doing their best to inflict as much damage in their rout. They'd also given the city itself 'a right kicking' too. Physical signs of the Iraqi invasion are hard to find in today's Kuwait. With its gleaming shopping malls and new hotels, it is becoming something of a shopper's paradise (some would argue that it's beginning to rival Dubai for prices and the variety of goods on offer). However, despite Kuwait's efforts to put the destruction behind them, the emotional scars still run deep, especially concerning the whereabouts of around 600 Kuwaiti nationals.

Anyway, with a little sightseeing over and done, we pointed the bus back in the direction of the airbase, and back in time for our change-over with the morning team.

That evening, the boss called myself, Herbie and Ibby, (our recently joined Signal's Sgt) to his quarters next to ours. In the background, whilst we went about our everyday tasks, he had managed to set up the trip to Oman, and we three, were 'the chosen'. There was no time to be wasted though, as he informed us that we were on a 'C-130 Hercy-Bird' the very next morning at eight o'clock sharp. "Not bad at all," I thought. We assumed wrongly, that we would be flown from the airstrip just a couple of hundred metres away, more or less on our very own door step. But instead, our flight was leaving from Basrah International, which meant that we had to be up around 2a.m., and high-tailing it for the border in rapid fashion. Well, you can't have everything I supposed. We were also required to pack all of our worldy goods again, as we would be repatriating with the team straight from the airport on the return journey. As we packed our gear for our five day sojourn, along with the rest of our personal belongings to leave in the vehicles, we thought that it was goodbye to 'Ali' for good, but no, we'd be back. It was becoming a little like Arafjan in the early days out here, the place kept pulling us back. But as I remarked earlier, Ali Al Salem was no bad place to be.

With gear stowed, I got my head down around ten p.m., so that I could attempt to get about four hours kip. The next thing I knew, my watch bleeped 2a.m., and it seemed as though I'd only been asleep for a very short time. By torch-light, I grabbed my stuff and headed off for the ablutions and decided to throw on my clean kit over there, so as not to wake the rest of my slumbering companions. The 'OC', Ibby and Herbie were also up and about, so once we had ourselves sorted, it was just a case of jump in the Rovers and go – Basrah bound, with the Boss mentioning that we would more than likely be able to grab some breakfast when we arrived at BIA. We were bang on our pre-arranged leaving time of 3a.m. as we headed onto the absolutely empty freeways that would take us north. Empty except for the twisted car wrecks that lay off to the side, and there were a few. (Kuwait has one of the highest road accident rates in the world, with a third of all deaths being driver related). With an empty road ahead of us, there was no hanging about, as we sped through the night, with the boss and Ibby in the lead vehicle. I nattered on in an attempt to engage Herbie in conversation, to make sure that he didn't flag. But, all things considered, he was pretty alert, despite the ungodly hour. It had been a while since I had been in the passenger seat of a Rover, due to the fact that I'd either previously driven, or had the misfortune to end up in the back, (the painful memories lingering). As the sun started to creep over the horizon, we were up and across the border, past and back on the well worn route that we had taken several times now. The main source of traffic out on the roads appeared to be mostly donkey carts, but there were very few vehicles to be seen as the population started to stir, which was probably just as well for us, as in a couple of hours it would be like an episode of 'Wacky Races' again, where defensive driving was the only way to survive (just like in Kuwait).

But, by that time we would more than likely be airborne.

As we reached Basrah International, the sun was already starting to warm the air rapidly. Once we were finally parked up, we unloaded, wrapped and labelled our weapons as per SOP's for military flight, then checked them, ourselves and our luggage in at the RAF flight desk. The boss's previous hopes concerning breakfast had been dashed, which was a real bugger. He wasn't best pleased, stating that the whole situation was a "cake and arse party". That was definitely a bit of new vernacular on me. However, we still had over an hour before we could board for take off, so rather than sit there listening to our stomachs, we decided to sprawl out in the seating area and snooze the hour away.

Eventually, we were given the word to pick up our belongings and head out across the tarmac to our waiting 'bird'. As we strapped ourselves into the 'onion bag' seats on the Herc, I noticed that there were only another half-dozen bods on the flight with us. With ear plugs wedged, the four props wound up to maximum revs as we took off and climbed rapidly in what I can only assume was a 'combat' take-off due to the steep angle and height gained ASAP (no doubt the pilot's were taking no chances of someone using us for aerial target practise, as there were still those amongst the population on 'Terra Firma' below, that would have loved to have bagged themselves a coalition plane). "So, I guess there's no steward service or in-flight movie?" I thought, as the plane thrummed, throbbed and vibrated as we climbed for cruising altitude. It was strange to see rods and cables above our heads move, as slight flight adjustments were made. Anyone the least bit squeamish would have wondered what the hell was going on. I remembered the first time that I had ever flown on one of these 'crates', to RAF Guttersloh in Germany, some fourteen years previously – and bone-shaking memories at that. I can also remember the look on the face of one of the young lads in our party as we were buffeted about by turbulence, and what a white knuckle ride it had been for him. Plus the fact that he'd never flown before. I would imagine that any first time flyer who can get through a 'Herc' flight with nerves intact, can thereafter, fly in anything. But, having said that, these stalwart aircraft had been doing sterling service for around fifty years and there was plenty of life still left in this most flexible of air transport. And, apart from a few modifications over the decades, it was still basically the same aircraft that evolved from the drawing board. As the trip progressed, one of the air-crew handed out scoff boxes, and whilst the contents certainly wouldn't challenge the taste-buds, at least it would fill the void where breakfast should have been. After about 90 minutes we started to descend into Saudi Arabian airspace, where we were to get off and stretch out legs for an hour whilst the plane was re-fuelled. On our second leg, we flew the remainder of the 900 mile journey, heading for Muscat in the Gulf of

Oman. In the space of several hours, we'd 'bunny-hopped' four countries, Kuwait-Iraq-Saudi Arabia-Oman, which wasn't bad by anybody's standards. But, despite the air miles travelled, nobody was getting any points. You win some you lose some.

As we disembarked, we had someone from the RAF 'det' meet us in a vehicle. The first thing we all noticed as we stepped down from the Herc, was the humidity. Basrah could reach hellish high temperatures no problem, and although it wasn't as hot here, the moment you stepped outside, you were soaked in perspiration, instantly. This 'sticky heat' was even more uncomfortable than what we were accustomed to way up north.

I also noticed the two 'Nimrod' jets through the shimmering heat haze across the air strip. That's what this was … . an RAF 'Nimrod' detachment. We very quickly and discreetly got our weapons out of the way, as we were reliably informed by our 'chauffeur' that weapons were not allowed to be brought into the state of Oman, period. Despite us being British Soldiers and the fact that the weapons were bundled and wrapped for air travel. We'd previously not been told any different, and it was a must that we had weapons about us prior to and after our trip. We needed to be able to defend ourselves if necessary (when on Iraqi soil) but, the last thing we wanted was to cause a diplomatic incident. So without any further ado, we were whisked across the runway, all of about seven hundred yards to the base.

Right next door was a USAF camp that Brit's had access to. But, within about three or four days, it would be closed with virtually everything being moved out. I was somewhere near needing a 'hack and whizz', and was also informed that the Spam's had a barber shop and a PX. So, given the chance, I would visit both before they disappeared.

We were shown to our accommodation, which was a small portak-abin-style unit, two bunks in each and superb air-conditioning which could make it feel almost sub-zero if you so wished. But the 'piece de resistance' was, … ..a small fridge. Outstanding! We even had to go and sign out lightweight quilts and bedding. "No need for a maggot here," I thought. That could just stay in its compression sack until we got back to Iraq. Well, this was the RAF. So far, so good. We got rid of the weapons into the 'det' armoury, which meant that we didn't have to see them again until we were leaving. Even the cook-house was available at most times to make a brew or grab a light-bite, it was never off limits.

Later, we met with the detachment head honcho, introduced as 'Sheds', who came across as a really decent chap, and seemed to be genuinely pleased at having four army bods on his turf. It made for something different in having us here. We passed the outdoor 'det' bar on the way to the cook-house, which was not dissimilar to the set-up that we had up north, except for the fact that you were liable to end up even more of a 'sticky' mess, what with the humidity. And, it didn't let up in the evenings either. After a superb night's sleep, on a rather comfy mattress, I was still feeling a little jaded from the rigours of the previous day, but we breakfasted and carried on with the day. After speaking to the flight-line guy's about what we needed to do, we were granted permission to roam out onto the runway to 'tag' some of the specialised kit. Out across from us sat a couple of US planes, the equivalent of our 'C130'. And, in close proximity, sat a 'Nimrod' jet. We got talking to a couple of the crew who just happened to be around, and who also offered to take the four of us up on a 'sneaky-beaky' mission, tasks permitting. That was of course if we were willing to sit in on the 0430 hour brief, prior to the mission with them. They just had to clear things with their direct boss, which they believed to be a mere formality, and they would let us know which morning they could take us up. I'm sure that there aren't that many people who get the opportunity to fly a surveillance mission in one of these jets.

I would come to chalk this up as yet another unique experience.

As it happened, we cracked on with the work we had to do and were virtually finished in about half a day. We still had a couple of things to do before we were to leave on the (alleged) Sunday flight, as apparently, there were no guarantees on it being the Sunday, but task-wise there was nothing that would take any particular time. Once it had been decided by the OC that we'd done all that we could for the day, it was a relief to get into the cool of the accommodation. This heat was sapping in a different kind of way, so it paid to get out of it when it was around early p.m., and a fair few of the detachment personnel disappeared after lunch. Now whether they were upholding the traditions of the 'Siesta', I wouldn't know, but it was damn uncomfortable out there. So, it wasn't necessarily a case of, "Mad dogs and Englishmen" because these particular Englishmen seemed to have adopted the right idea. Anyway, after a refreshing, almost cool shower, there didn't seem much point in drying myself off, thanks to the humidity. All that I could do was hurriedly get back over to our cool little haven that was not too many degrees above chilled. I can only liken the experience to being something that had been taken from the fridge, then wafted over a steaming pan of water and returned to the fridge again. At least that's what it felt like, when going from accommodation to shower and back again.

Evening meal, later on, was a slightly different affair to what we were used to. There were more, spicy, curry orientated selections on offer (mainly due to Asian chefs that prepared these culinary delights). But, the other thing that I noticed was that the chefs and kitchen staff were extremely polite when serving you whatever you requested. Was it because RAF personnel operated on a different level to what we were accustomed to, or was it that politeness was a way of life for these people and the fact that these were civilians and not serving personnel. As we were the 'new kids in town', it made it all the more refreshing and it was something that was certainly not lost on me. Especially when after trying one dish I was told to have a little more of something else that took my fancy, which appeared to make the head chef's day. We had the detachment 'head honcho' come over and join us whilst we finished our meal. Apparently, because there were only the four of us army 'bods' who'd come-a–visiting from the Basrah region, we had a little celebrity status. What with us being 'those chaps on the ground', so to speak. He also mentioned that we were welcome to use their 'watering hole', and that any and all of the 'det' facilities were at our disposal, even suggesting that time allowing, we might like to head out from the airbase to the smart shopping mall across the highway from the main entrance.

My ears picked up when he mentioned that it even had a small 'Starbucks' outlet … now there's a thing! We were even asked if we would like to attend their own 'CSE' show on the Sunday night, (that was of course if were still here by then). Anyway, the boss thanked him for his generous hospitality and that the offer was much appreciated.

As I caught up on recent events that were happening in Iraq, I was saddened to discover that six British RMP's from '156 Provost Company' had been attacked and killed in a Police Station that they had been visiting up near Al Amarah, in the town of Al Majar al-Kabir. We, ourselves, had only been up at Al Amarah a couple of weeks earlier, although not in the aforementioned town. The latest report read that their task had been that of an advisory role, patrolling the local Police Stations, assisting with the progress of the slowly re-forming local law enforcement. Due to other contributory factors beyond their control, the RMP's had been hemmed in by an angry mob, and were literally backed into a corner. Later on, it would come to light that they had bravely fought to the last man and virtually the very last round.

Whilst the tragedy of the RMP's was unfolding, the Paras, who were but a stones-throw away, were also taking casualties and having to fight their way out of the place as a hatred-fuelled mob were intent on killing every last 'infidel'.

The number of British military personnel killed in action during the war and up to this present time, were only into double figures, certainly not the kind of numbers that were to escalate later on. But, in spite of these relatively low figures, every additional death, seemed more keenly felt, which is not meant to demean or lessen any subsequent 'KIA's. However, this particular incident would have far reaching consequences much later on, once the truth leading up to the whole tragic event had been established (although, no one would ever know the full and exact details). All that I can say is that to those Brit's serving in the southern region, this was a really black day.

Our own 'Tiger Team' RMP, Alex, had personally known one of the '156' lads, and took the news rather hard. Had the roles been reversed, I would no doubt have felt exactly the same. Being a member of my parent Regiment's Pipes and Drums (103 RA), the incident prompted me to think about dedicating a simple piece of music to commemorate the six fallen.

After the first Gulf war, a stirring piece of music had been written for a Queens Own Highlander who'd been killed in action, and that piece was aptly called, 'The Sands Of Kuwait' – written predominantly for bagpipes, it was a really moving piece that never failed to raise the hairs on the back of my neck (whenever we played it in conjunction with our military band). We'd actually played it at Inverness Tattoo a couple of years previously, with the very guy that had written it, present in the audience – talk about pressure! I just hope that we did his piece of music justice.

Anyway, that was my inspiration I suppose. I'd had the idea for this slow melody floating around in my head for some time that kept nagging away at me, and it was driving me nuts. I wasn't hearing things … .at least I don't think so? So I felt compelled that this was what I should do with it.

The title I had in mind for it was simply, 'Majar al-Kabir'.

After, a none-too hectic day, the four of us had decided to try out the 'det' bar that evening. The OC had decided on a complete 'chill-out' day the next day, and we were not going to argue. So, after evening meal had settled and I'd been to check out the latest 'Op Telic' reports on the internet, we RV'd at the bar, finding an unoccupied table under the very "decorative" cam netting (these guy's even had a rope light around the bar for effect – I said that the RAF really knew how to live!).

The night air was extremely humid and close, but the 'tinnys' were superbly cold. I even managed to get my hands on a couple of tins of Blackthorne Cider, which Herbie and I were most pleased about (and what with him being a West Country lad and all). This was starting to feel like a very pleasant unwind, with a good selection of music playing, nice friendly atmosphere, especially now that some of the pilots and ground crew were becoming familiar faces, and some good banter going on between those around us. However, this air of relaxation suddenly vanished when someone spotted a couple of 'beasties' crawling amongst the table and chairs.

But what with the subdued lighting from the bar, I'm not sure what species of spider I was looking at that. I've never seen a group of people move so quick. Half of those that were seated only two seconds previously, were up on top of their seats in a flash, and that included a fair number of the fellahs too. I was more curious than scared to be honest, and reasoned that as long as my feet didn't pose any threat, I reckoned I would not warrant any further scrutiny as these two arachnids muscled their way across the floor area.

But, nevertheless, I cautiously watched the direction in which they were heading, which was fortunately not in mine. There were one or two guys'n'gals who were content to carry on drinking, but I think that had the spiders decided to stay put in the middle of the bar all night, there would have been some individuals also stuck on chairs for the duration too. Finally they moved off, with a number of people breathing a communal sigh of relief.

I could imagine one spider saying to the other as they moved off, "Well, 'arry, I guess we got em' that time, didn't we! Right, who're we off to spook next?"

Being out here taught you one thing. And that was to pay a little more attention with regard to what was happening at ground level, now and again.

Anyway, what with the effects of the heat combined with the couple of beers, I could feel myself starting to wilt. So, before I started to yawn myself silly, I paid my respects and said 'Adios' to my comrades. That was enough wildlife for one night. Anyway, it was indeed official … … we had a lie in next morning, and even I was prepared to miss breakfast and avail myself of brunch a little later in the a.m.

I woke around seven, but decided to take advantage of the luxury afforded us. My 'roomy' barely moved, and I think his plan was to remain as cool and motionless as possible for as long as possible. Mind you, he had mentioned that had he had to spend the duration of the tour in this kind of humidity, it would more than likely have finished him off, to which I also had to agree.

Eventually, I decided to brave it out, get up, and face the world. There was only so much that I could re-charge my batteries, and I could only be a 'pit-monster' if I was really tired and needed the sleep.

So, after a quiet brunch and a couple of brews, I went for a short stroll around to the USAF camp to try and get a 'hack and whizz' from the Barber employed by the Americans.

As I flashed my ID to the sentry at the barrier whilst replying to his "G'mornin," I could see that as the camp opened out in front of me, these guys also had quite a neat set-up here too. The basket-ball pitch was right in front of me, next to which was, an open air bar with seating area, a couple of 'Bling' shacks, PX, Pizza Hut and Barbers shack. I'd only walked the few minutes it took from our accommodation to the Barber shop and my T-shirt was already sodden. That was the reason that we'd all started to 'dobi' our few bits and pieces in the ablutions block, so that we'd have slightly fresher kit, which we could change a little more often.

The barber was just finishing off the occupant in the chair (not literally, like Sweeney Todd) and then I was next. I thought I'd have what our US counterparts around here usually had … a 'high and tight', but not quite as severe as some of the US Marines had had their heads shorn. Anyway, the barber set to work and was so meticulous in his approach, stepping back to admire his handy work, like an artist looking at the canvas to see where he needed to apply the next brush-stroke, or in his case, scissor snip, whilst ensuring that the beads of sweat were wiped from my face (as it was even hotter under the canvas roof). I have to say that apart from the heat in there, I've never enjoyed a hair cut as much, partly because he finished off with a short neck and head massage, final inspection, and eyebrow trim. Absolute quality! Even with a tip, it only cost me five bucks. What I'd just had would have cost me an arm and a leg back in the UK. Feeling slightly more refreshed and sporting a more streamlined bonce than when I first walked in, I perused the PX, bought a few tins of pop for our fridge then headed back 'home'.

In the meantime, we had to convert some of our cash to Omani Rials – the local currency. So now I was armed with Dollars, Kuwaiti Dinars, Iraqi Dinars, Omani Rials – a right load of coin.

That night, the bar was closed due to a lack of supplies, which was probably just as well for us, as the following morning was our pre-arranged 'Nimrod' flight and we had to be up before 'sparrows fart' to sit in on the pre-fight brief.

We knew that we could catch up on some sleep in the p.m. once we'd got back after the flight. However, that evening, a brief was to be given in the canteen by the det commander, and he'd requested that we be on hand to attend, along with most of the detachment who weren't tasked on other duties. Apparently, we four were to be used as 'live subjects' to add a little weight to his brief.

Basically, due to the fact that RAF Seeb was around 900 miles from where we operated, (and although the detachment itself operated in support of Operation Telic) the commander wanted to give the people here, some idea of what it was like up north, mainly to hit home that they led a reasonably charmed life down here in the Sultanate of Oman – and bearing in mind that RAF personnel do 4-monthly operational stints at a time, unlike the army who on average serve 6 months

Complete with a map of the Middle-East set up on an easle, he went on to explain a number of points regarding the whole scheme of things up to this moment in time, with the occasional reference made to ourselves.

It was a little embarrassing, standing to the side of the map, on show, whilst the commander crossed a few I's and dotted a few T's. It reminded me a little of the briefings that you would see in old black and white war films, except nowhere near as stiff or as formal … . "now we're going to knock out the bridges, here and here, cutting Gerry orf completely … " That was obviously way over the top, but it was something that popped into my mind at the time (and, there wasn't even a Brylcreemed moustache in sight, nor 'stiff-upper lipped' accent for that matter).

We had previously mentioned that although we had been here, there, and everywhere, we had not fired our weapons in anger (or up to this point, to protect ourselves) and we were certainly not trying to make ourselves sound any more combat hardened than those around us sitting in on the brief.

That didn't matter, as his intention was to try to give those present, an appreciation of what conditions were like generally.

He finished up with, "If you'd like to ask our guests anything about their experiences, or have any questions for them, then feel free".

Thank goodness nobody did. However, the sentiment was much appreciated.

Finally, we were off the hook and could get on with the evening.

Next morning at 'daft o'clock', the four of us made our way over to the briefing room, trying to shake the sleepiness away whilst listening in on the 'modus operandi' for the upcoming flight. Once the brief was completed and we'd been given our own safety brief, we headed out for the 'Nimrod' in the pre-dawn light. Once we were seated and buckled-up, the 13-man crew readied their various stations as we taxied out onto the airstrip for take off.

A little while later when we were at cruising altitude, we could move about and talk to the crew, so long as it didn't interfere with the mission. And, this, in simple terms is how a Nimrod crew's roles and tasks can broken down; two pilots and two flight engineers operate the flight deck, there are two navigators (who swap between routine and tactical responsibilities every other mission), an Air Electronics Officer (AEO) who co-ordinates sensor and communications. The sensor team includes three Air Electronic Operators (known as 'wet men'), who are responsible for monitoring both active (searching), and passive (listening) sonobuoys. The remaining four Air Electronic Operators (known as 'dry men') manage a wide range of avionics and weapons systems, essential in delivering the Nimrod's overall capability.

The object of this particular day's sortie, was to fly up and around the Straits of Hormuz and carry out surveillance on vessels within a given area, checking for ships that may be suspected gun-runners, or other unknown entities which may or may not prove to be (coalition) friendly.

This was one of the three main roles that this aircraft was capable of undertaking; 1: (ASUW) Anti-Surface-Unit-Warfare, which involved surveillance and reconnaissance, 2: (ASW) Anti-Submarine Warfare and, 3: (S&R) Search and Rescue. This was the only jet powered long range maritime patrol aircraft which was also capable of conducting a full 10-hour flying mission before requiring to re-fuel (and it was also fast, with a maximum speed of around 575mph).

We assumed that today's flight would be a few hours out and back to base. Were we ever wrong!

This was to be an 8-hour mission (you could have flown half way around the world in that time, or near enough). A fair amount of the trip was spent looking at the surface of the sea, until a vessel was spotted, then the plane would descend to around 200 feet in order for the ship to be identified, and if required, it would be photographed by our 'camera-man'. Information regarding the vessel would be transmitted to the necessary parties and appropriate action would be taken. Sometimes the Nimrod would fly over the 'target' and swing around in a tight arc. We were informed that when the plane banked round, we would feel the effects of a couple of 'G's.

Feel the effect of a couple of 'G's? I felt as if some great lead weight was compressing me into my seat, whilst at the same time trying not to laugh at the look on Herbie's face. But, not that I could have laughed anyway, as my body was in, how can I describe it? ... 'flattened mode' – a most strange sensation.

Donning head-sets, we could listen to the chatter that went back and forward, including the funny banter and a few jokes. I suppose a good sense of humour was needed on long missions such as this. As well as 'checking out' vessels, on this particular trip, the Nimrod would also act as protective early warning for one of the US Navy's 'Nimitz Class' Air Craft Carriers that was operating in nearby waters (there are currently several of this class in service). When I said, nearby waters, I meant around several miles. We had to remain at distance so as not to interfere with the carrier's own airspace, especially as she was deploying aircraft and conducting live firing exercises. At around 332 metres or 1,092 feet, and with a compliment of approximately 6,000 personnel, this particular class of vessel was the largest in the world – a veritable floating city. (As I write this, the tenth and last of its class, *The USS George Bush* is still under construction, with a completion date to enter service sometime in 2009).

However, from our lofty perch and despite being several miles away, I could still make her out. There was no doubting that what I could see through the viewing port was a very large vessel indeed.

As our flight progressed, we passed over dhows, cargo ships, and tankers, making a low pass over the vessel as and where required. I imagined the panicked look of a dhow skipper as we swung round to home in on his little craft – this large jet coming out of nowhere and heading straight for him (albeit at around two hundred feet), which would more than likely be the most powerful laxative that the guy was ever likely to have in his life.

In between all of this, one of the crew was up and down to the small, but well stocked galley. And, I thought that the guys on the ground ate well.

The stuff that was being served throughout the flight was amazing – trays of varied hot nibbles, samosas, onion bahjis, filot prawns, you name it, it was all here. The four of us looked at each other in wonderment. Everything was rounded off with a cheese-board, complete with about half-a-dozen types of cheese. Mind you, if you were flying for this many hours for one mission, you would welcome some tasty treats. It certainly beat a half-frozen, cardboard sandwich.

Anyway, by the time we landed again, we were well stuffed, which also brought back recent memories of the hospitality I'd received on my earlier trip home aboard the re-fuelling tanker, when I'd flown home for Mum's funeral.

As rubber made contact with terra firma again, we thanked the crew for their invitation to spend 'A Day in the Life Of' … , but they had been more than happy to have us aboard, as we were a welcome distraction (although not to the mission) and I think that they were genuinely pleased that we "army types" should be interested enough to want to experience a slice of their daily operational duties. No doubt we'd meet up in the det bar – time, tiredness and glugging supplies permitting.

So, with yet another unique experience committed to memory, we were back in the cool confines of our accommodation and feeling rather jaded, since we'd now been on the go for around eleven hours, given that it was still only 2p.m. I thought that I'd have no problem in getting a few hours 'gonk', but, no chance, as sleep just wouldn't come. So I decided to have a slightly later evening meal and try to get some shut-eye around normal sack-time.

By 10 p.m. I was beginning to flag and decided to call it a day and turn in.

29th June – 5th July

We'd been informed that the 'Herc' that was originally pre-planned to take us back to Iraq, simply wasn't going to arrive, but might possibly turn up on the Monday, but still no guarantees – "Maleeesh! Well, them's the breaks" and "what rotten luck!" I thought. What else could we do? We were at the mercy of flight schedules. It looked like we would just have to accept the det's offer of attending their CSE show that very evening.

A singing trio called 'T★40' were on the bill, plus the usual dancers and a well known Irish comedian (whose name escapes me). We had limited clothing with us, just enough for a few days – certainly nothing particularly smart. So, we managed to get some half decent track-suit bottoms from the local Carrefour shopping mall across the way. But, even so, I felt improperly dressed. And to think I was nearly going to bring my reasonably tidy light-weight jeans with me, as most of those present were only wearing jeans or Chinos and a shirt anyhow. So we boarded the coach that had come to collect all who were to attend the show at the 'Intercontinental Hotel' – some forty minute's drive away. Originally, when we'd arrived at Seeb, we saw the posters advertising the show, and I imagined some kind of outdoor stage set-up along the lines of Shaibah, up in Iraq. Except this one couldn't have been more different. Because there were only around a hundred and fifty personnel on the base, the numbers were just right for a function suite in the hotel. It was nearing dusk as we made our approach to the venue, but it gave me enough time to take in a little of the immaculate surroundings as we headed for Muscat.

The greenery was well tended and buildings were in keeping with the tradition of having domed or Arabesque windows. This was an attractive, clean and uniformed city. Even the roundabouts were adorned with things like giant colourful urns, coffee pots and miniature forts. It was a bit surreal really. I thought at one point, when passing a very ornate giant cup and saucer, that I'd shrunk like 'Alice in Wonderland'.

However, these sculptures made for something different to look at. Muscat proper is a small area wedged between the mountains and the sea, surrounded by a jagged spine of hills, which make a rather dramatic back-drop. Whereas Greater Muscat to the West, is home to the Head of State, Sultan Qaboos who, with the arrival of the millennium marked his 30 years of his reign. It is the Sultan's determined accessibility and his reputation for delivering promises that have made him such an effective leader. Whilst building a modern state, the Sultan has also shown himself to be a distinguished peace-maker – in 1998 he was awarded the International Peace Award from the National Council On US-Arab Relations in recognition of his insightful government, and his role in maintaining stability in the region.

Anyway, as our journey progressed, we passed a clock tower and interesting looking mural which marked the Rusayl (Risail) roundabout that appeared to be an important transport hub, and within a few minutes, we finally arrived at our destination and dismounted the coach. When the immaculately garbed door staff ushered into 'our' banqueting suite for the evening, the four of us couldn't believe the sight that met our gaze.

All the way around the room, circular tables were laid out in very 'posh' style – finest cutlery and everything, complete with two complimentary bottles of wine per table. Everything seemed to gleam and sparkle (I thought I'd need my shades), and to add to the spectacle, a hot and cold buffet table ran virtually the length of one side of the room. This kind of thing back in the UK wouldn't normally have registered anything more than a 'very nice', but what you have to remember is that we'd not really seen anything so grandiose in quite a while. So, to have all this laid out before us was a little overwhelming to say the least. What did I say earlier about the RAF doing it in style? Whilst we waited for the buffet and the show to start, some of the 'det' chaps that we'd got to know a little came and made up the numbers on our table. Apparently there was a Navy party due in at any time too. "This should be rather interesting," I thought. Well, at least all three services would be represented, even though we four represented good old 'Tommy Atkins' and the British army.

So we all tucked into the vino, making sure that we drank plenty of water, as we didn't want the alcohol going straight to our heads, and I remembered my last dalliance with wine only too well. Whilst queuing for the buffet, I was nearly salivating myself stupid as the covers were lifted from the many dishes that were on offer. I even asked Herbie to pinch me at one point in order to make sure that I wasn't dreaming. Mind you, he was just as 'gob-smacked' as I was. The Navy lads had arrived, and were of course in good spirits. The buffet was delicious, the wine pleasant and the comedian very funny. In between the various spots, the dancers came on, with most of the guys ogling – naturally, and the singing trio kept things ticking along with their brand of music and some reasonable cover-tunes. Towards the end of the evening as things were just about concluded, the Navy boys produced false 'World War II Wing Commander' style moustaches, stuck them on and with arms outstretched in aeroplane mode, started to chant the 'Dambusters' theme, "Naaaah-Naah-Naah-Nah-Nah-Nah-Nah-Nah-Naahh.." which segued into their own naval anthem, 'Hearts of Oak'. It was an absolutely hilarious moment, and one which was taken in very good humour by all the RAF bods in the room. We filed out of the suite, thanking the hotel staff for a most excellent night, (in surroundings that were a million miles from what we had come to know). However, on the return journey, there was a slight fracas on the coach, which very surprisingly was not between two opposing arms of any of the three services, either. Needless to say, those involved were later reprimanded and the det bar was to remain closed as a punishment the following evening, but enough said. However, the fact that the bar was to be closed wouldn't make much difference to us as we would be Basrah bound the very next day, or would we?

By mid-morning, we were up, packed and ready to take our gear over to the flight-line for our 'rumoured' flight. There was nothing definite, we were told. So, all that we could do, was sit in the 'departure's area' (which happened to be half-a-dozen seats under a tree) where it was now getting decidedly warm, and wait and see what happened (or didn't). 12.30p.m. came and went – this was the appointed time that the 'Herc' was supposed to be landing. It didn't happen. After a while, the Boss made a call to the relevant people regarding our ride back up north. For whatever reason, our transport was not going to arrive until Wednesday p.m. So, it appeared that we'd be here another two nights. If we couldn't fly, then we couldn't fly and that was it – period. Nine hundred or so miles was a little too far to hitch-hike across the UAE and Saudi anyhow.

Due to the fact that we'd vacated our accommodation, someone else had taken over the OC's room which meant that he had to bunk in with Herb and myself, but no real drama, and Ibby was sorted. But it was good to get back into the cooler confines of our room again after waiting around in the humidity after mid-day, for a plane that wasn't going to materialise. It so turned out that Ibby had not been slow in finding out about the use of a base vehicle. We could apparently sign one out. This meant that seeing as our task in Oman was now completed, the use of a vehicle was an added bonus, thus allowing us the opportunity to have a look around the Muscat and Mutrah areas, which included a brief exterior 'shufty' at the Sultan's Palace.

As we headed on the main route that would take us towards the harbour at Muscat, we spotted an Iranian restaurant. So it being Ibby's Birthday and all, it was decided that we'd double back and have lunch – it would cost us the princely sum of £16 all-in for the four of us.

We had soup, followed by a mixed platter of meat and fish which was mouth-wateringly tasty, but the mint yoghurt drink that accompanied it was however, fine for the first mouthful or two, but it was a bit of an acquired taste. In the end, the boss, who appeared to favour it, had half the pitcher to himself. "You're more than welcome to finish it!" the three of us agreed in unison. Lunch was followed by a quick wander around the Souq – although it was closing up for the afternoon by the time we got there. We finished up in a little corner coffee shop, with barely just enough space for a table and a few chairs, where four extremely strong (albeit tasty) coffees were brought over to us by the smiling Omani proprietor. As we were leaving, the tip we that we left our host, was actually greater than the cost of the coffees – they were that cheap.

In one of the gift shops on the harbour front, we followed the boss in as he had taken a liking to some of the silver bits and pieces on show in the window. Before we'd left the shop, he'd got himself a couple of silver trinkets and a very nice had-made rug for his own pad back home, so he was more than happy. The rug, and where it had originated from would no doubt end up becoming a talking point when he had people over to dinner.

With enough humidity for one day, we re-traced our route up and away from the corniche, and followed the jagged, teeth-like line of hills as we headed for Seeb on the main highway, passing once again, all of the ornately sculptured 'Alice in Wonderland' roundabouts.

These extra couple of days had been a most unexpected, if welcome turn of events, which made the trip all the more exceptional, and not least because of the RAF's hospitality. That night we had a final couple of beers, which just happened to be, 'Tiger Beer' – to celebrate Ibby's birthday. This would be some Birthday to look back on, certainly in terms of where in the world it had been spent, along with the experiences that had preceded it.

Next day we had said our goodbyes to the people of 201 Squadron, who would also be heading back home to RAF Kinloss in the very near future. This time our 'Herc' was in, and on time for the return flight up north to Iraq. The strange thing was that the plane had to make a quick stop at Ali Al Salem AB to unload a couple of cargo pallets – the very place that ideally, we would have liked to have flown out of. But then again, we had to return to Umm Qasr, anyhow. In no time we were airborne again, this time leaving Kuwaiti airspace and heading for Basrah International Airport. As is true with anything, all good things must come to an end, and as the late afternoon sun started to set, our wheels glanced the tarmac of BIA, I wondered, "Had it all just been a dream?"

Once back over to our vehicles in the parking area, dusk was starting to fall rapidly. Again, we'd missed the chance to grab some food in the terminal building, so the Boss suggested that we crack open the good old MRE's … when all else fails, they'll do. Within about twenty minutes we were done, and decided it best to make all good speed back to Umm Qasr – taking into account all local traffic and road movement. Darkness came on quickly, and so we had to keep our eyes peeled. With weapons unwrapped, they were 'locked and loaded' as we proceeded down well-worn routes.

On the approach to every road junction, the two of us were straining like crazy to see if there was anything that was liable to suddenly pull out on us – whether it be mechanical, human or animal. What didn't help was the lack of working tail lights (or any lights for that matter) on vehicles, and road lighting was virtually non-existent. Basrah outskirts by day were one thing, but in full-on darkness they were something else. We passed one or two donkey carts that seemed to appear like apparitions out of nothing. I mentioned to Herbie, who was driving, that we didn't want to have to complete any 'RTA' paper-work or attend any enquiry with regards to an incident involving a British Forces Land Rover and a half-starved donkey who's owner would have been rubbing his hands at the thought of a wad of Iraqi Dinars coming his way, by means of compensation for a written-off beast of burden. Suddenly, off to the West of us, there was a burst of gunfire as streams of tracer rounds went sky-wards. It was probably nothing, maybe just celebratory gun-fire, or the locals getting a bit excited, we thought? It wasn't uncommon. However, we had no intention of finding out. So, with two pairs of eyes practically glued to the windscreen and watching our lead Rover's tail lights, we pushed on through and beyond the suburbs of Iraq's second city and into the more open areas, where desert took over.

On the last leg of our virtually straight route back to the port, we didn't actually see many oncoming vehicles thank goodness, and those that we did pass, their wildly skewing headlight beams just added to the eyestrain from which we were already suffering from. Although it has to be said that, of those headlamp beams that actually worked, they would have made great anti-aircraft search lights, which would have lit up a low-flying jet no problem, and provided any extremists with an easy target. Finally, we made the turning off the road, across the railway track and headed for the checkpoint.

After ID'ing ourselves, we unloaded our weapons one more time. Pulling into the parking area near our team accommodation, we breathed a huge sigh of relief as the noise of the engine died. We then gave ourselves a minute or two before we started to unloaded our kit. A very interesting week had gone by and now we were back again. As the four of us exchanged points on the sapping, 'hairy' drive back to base, Herbie piped up with; "Well, Boss, I reckon that drive back was at least worth a 'Mention In Dispatches', what d'you think?" It was said with the greatest respect, and if nothing else, it raised a much needed laugh.

With gear again stowed and a quick catch up of events with the rest of the team, it was a shower then 'gonk city', as it was already tomorrow.

Within a few days, the first of the new guys (and gals), who were to eventually take over from us, would be coming out into theatre. I, for one certainly wouldn't have wanted to be arriving as the summer was starting to take hold. This would be a hot 'breaking-in' for the poor sods.

We were alerted as to our tour finish dates, where a half-a-dozen of the team would be disappearing on or around July 14th, just on a month before the main team were to 'bug-out' (minus five of us, who were to stay on for an extra couple of weeks).

Over the next few days, some of the team were assigned different tasks, with Hooch and I volunteering to assist the radiological specialist who had come out from the UK to take 'DU' readings from the 'Chally 2' that had been mangled in the earlier mentioned 'blue on blue' incident, along with the two Scimitars that had also been mistakenly attacked by a pair of A10 'Tank-busters'.

The chassis of the 'Chally' was resting on a low-load trailer within the confines of one of the empty port hangers (its turret lay next to it, as it had literally been blown off, such was the force of the explosion).

So at least we weren't going to be working in the blazing sunlight at this point. Once the readings had been taken and the levels were deemed safe enough for us to literally 'gift-wrap' the chassis in Hessian, Hooch and I got suited up in the white hooded coveralls, (the same as police forensics teams use) complete with masks, and got on with the task of wrapping up the tank to make it as safe as possible to load on the ship, RFA *Sir Galahad,* which was about to dock in the port. *Sir Galahad* was to transport the hulk back to the UK, where further investigation, analysis and final disposal of the tank would be carried out. As we went about preparing the tank for its return to the UK, and despite us being in the shade, it was still damnably hot in the suits, bringing back vivid memories of having to hastily pull on 'noddy suits' when the NBC alerts were given some three or so months previously.

Finally, when all other safety measures and precautions had been taken, the tank was ready to be transported across the port and onto the *Sir Galahad,* which was not quite as easy a task as it sounded.

With our task complete, we were swept from head to toe with the monitoring equipment to ensure that we were contaminant free and that we were not likely to end up glowing in the dark at some future stage, then we literally peeled ourselves out of our white 'romper suits', and stood in the breeze to dry our t-shirts and trousers.

The following day, I found myself requested by the Sgt Major to 'ride shotgun' with a WO1 from the MSG, who's task was to head back down into Kuwait to 'Camp Coyote' to inspect some damaged rolling stock, then all the way up to Shaibah airfield to conduct a similar task up there. Well it would fill the day, and at least I was in the air-conditioned comfort of his Pajero. So, after having grabbed a couple of really chilled bottles of water from the fridge, we set off. It had been a while since I'd been down to 'Coyote' – on a quick stop-off when heading over to 'Ali' to see Jim Davidson.

Anyway, with our non-descript journey down to 'Coyote' completed, we parked up and made our way over to the vehicle repair area, where I picked out the sound of a Liverpudlian accent. After a quick 'hello' we instantly struck up a conversation. He was, as it turned out, a TA REME guy who like myself, had volunteered at the start of the Op. A brew was offered and graciously accepted, as we chatted for a few minutes before he had to disappear to go and attack something else with a wrench. As is usually the way when you travel half way round the globe and bump into somebody from your locality, he only lived a few miles away from me too – "Very small world," I thought.

I wasn't required until the Sgt Major and I were to leave, so I spent the next hour or so keeping as cool as I possibly could in the mess tent, whilst writing several 'Blueys'.

Back on the road again, we eventually rolled back across the border and up into Shaibah in the full-on heat of the afternoon. Again, there was little that I could do but wait around, and I didn't particularly want to sit there for a couple of hours with the Pajero engine idling in order to keep the air-con going, so I got out, requested a cold bottle of water from the unit we were visiting and promptly found some shade, whilst the Sgt Major went about his business of inspecting a piece of armour which had mysteriously caught fire, possibly through some electrical fault.

As the sun was heading for the horizon we were back to Umm Qasr – and just in time for evening meal too. Although, the way that things had been panning out, I did think at one point that we'd miss it. However, good fortune and good timing paid off. And, I was glad that I didn't have to rely on an 'MRE' on this particular occasion, as the food back at 'Sultan' was usually pretty good fare.

I was intent on doing very little this particular evening, except maybe having a gander at a new movie that one of the guys had got from 'Camp Doha'.

It wasn't the easiest thing to try and do – several bods trying to squeeze around the flat screen of a laptop PC, all vying for the best viewing spec.

But we managed it. After which, I was determined to get my head down slightly earlier, which was now a much easier prospect in the cooler confines of our modular sleeping quarters.

The next day, the WO1 had again requested the use of my services (I must have been popular?), and due to the fact that the new 'Tigers' were now in theatre, we didn't need too many bods on their familiarisation tour around the various locations within our area of operation, and besides which, we didn't have the space on the vehicles anyway. So, this in effect, freed a couple of us up to do other tasks. Anyway, this time, the Sgt Major and I were to head further south, down as far as Shuwaikh sea port – no drama really.

I wondered whether I would bump into any of the port-based 'Tigers' down there. The Sgt Major was more than happy to drive again, so I watched the scenery (well, miles of flat virtually featureless desert – until we reached the suburbs of Kuwait City) go by, with my A2 perched on my lap, "just in case". It was more or less the same 'MO' as the previous day, except that we wouldn't be hanging around at the port. In fact once we arrived, we were done and dusted and heading north again in just over half an hour, and I did manage to catch up briefly with one or two of the team down there as well. They'd also heard it on the grapevine that there was the slight possibility of a few individuals winding up their tour earlier than planned, to which I replied, "Don't hold your breath and don't build up your hopes, you know how these things have a habit of changing".

Back on the road, the Sgt Major and I started to get an attack of the 'munchies' as it was nearing mid-day. So it was decided that we'd head for the US Camp – 'Commando' just south of the Mutlah Pass, to grab a bite to eat. As we travelled up the Jahra highway, approaching the turn-off for the camp, the Sgt Major recalled his experiences of the first Gulf War, pointing up ahead to where the part of the battle group that he had been serving with came sweeping across the terrain somewhere in front of our position.

This particular route north would infamously be known as "the highway of death," from whence the retreating Iraqi's (mostly looters, or so it is alleged) were caught in their vehicles by 'A-10's which simply rained death and destruction from above, upon the last column of vehicles trying to flee northwards towards the border from Kuwait City.

The Mutlah Ridge was just up ahead of us, and it was now hard to imagine 12 years on, the scenes of utter carnage which were transmitted across the world's media at the time. That much, I do remember seeing.

Because of the long traffic jam that led out of the city, it made the vehicles easy targets for the pilots. The words; 'turkey shoot' were used to describe the situation at the time and, not surprisingly, the pilots that returned from that particular sortie, found much disapproval from their comrades.

As we approached the ridge, a road sign bearing the Arabic words for 'Mutlah Ridge' also happened to have a large black and yellow sticker plastered above which read, 'God bless American troops' which immediately made me think; 'God help anyone from American friendly fire!' more like.

As we pulled into 'Commando', I could see that the place looked like a right dust-bowl and could imagine what it would be like when the desert wind picked up, but we were only here for a very quick visit to 'Subway' to grab a sandwich and a coffee – this was lunch 'on the hoof'. So, we cracked on, and eventually rolled back into 'Sultan Lines' at mid afternoon.

Whilst the British Foreign Secretary, Jack Straw had maintained that the political and security situation in Iraq had started to improve, electricity and oil supplies had been sabotaged by those wishing to prove him wrong, and with little change, the sporadic attacks on the US forces were still taking place. But even stranger, a tape recording purportedly of Saddam had been broadcast to the Iraqi people, urging guerrilla fighters to continue with their resistance against the coalition. Whether the voice on the recording actually was Saddam's or not, it ensured that the Iraqi people remained somewhat jittery, as there were, no doubt, some who thought that if Saddam remained at large, then there was always that very remote possibility that he could return to power, and obviously, those that had opposed him would suffer even more. And sadly, another British freelance TV cameraman had been killed when a gunman opened fire in the centre of Baghdad. Apart from the Vietnam War and the Iran-Iraq War of 1980-88, the media had never suffered so many international news personnel killed in any comparable period of time – 16 in a space of less than 4 weeks, yet not all of the fatalities were attributable to direct military (enemy) action. Road crashes claimed several, whilst mines, suicide bombers and 'friendly fire' claimed most of the remainder.

Hooch and I had been given the task of transporting some computer kit up to BIA for the Paradigm engineers to install up there – no doubt in a bid to improve the welfare situation for those based up at the airport. But this time we didn't have the luxury of anything with 'air-con', or even a land rover. This was to be an 8-tonner, part of the reason why Hooch had been asked … .he had the category of license. Anyway with me riding 'shotgun' again, we rumbled our way up the all too familiar routes that lead to the airport, unloaded the equipment and headed into the terminal for a much needed thirst-quencher. Whilst there, we decided to have a look at the EFI shop, but there wasn't anything that particularly grabbed my attention.

I suppose that was one of the things that the Americans did have over us, even in their relatively small PX's, they stocked pretty much anything. So with nothing further to delay us, we headed for home.

On our return trip, we passed numerous pieces of Iraqi armour that had either been abandoned or 'taken out' by coalition forces. Some of which faced across the open expanses of the desert, whilst others were buried in their tank scrapes with only the hatches and barrels barely visible. Most of the armour would be removed or totally destroyed. We slowed as we spotted some of the local Iraqi's attempting to remove whatever they could from one of the 'T55's that may have been some value – copper wire, I would wager.

Alerted by a beep of the vehicle's horn, they looked over, paused, waved and then carried on with their scavenging. Obviously even the slight possibilities of 'DU' didn't put them off either.

After what was only my second night back in 'Sultan Lines', the Sgt Major informed myself, Herbie and Alex that we were to re-locate to 'Ali' the very next day, now that a number of the new team members were to stay put at . This time, we didn't mind as 'Ali' was certainly no bad place to finish the last part of our tour. It was just the initial thoughts of, "Moving again?!," and so soon. We'd waited weeks and weeks to enjoy the benefits of the relative comfort of the TDA, but here we were, off again.

Well, I suppose that looking back, we'd seen and experienced a fair bit more than some, so we started to pack up the old 'parrots and monkeys' once again. All that is, except my chair. It had been a stalwart piece of kit, but I decided to leave it for the next 'Tiger' who would be moving into my bed-space. As I'd said previously, "the best five quid I'd ever spent!"

Now that we were to head south again for what was more than likely the last time, the one place that I would have liked to have been able to visit, whilst we were up and down to Basrah (tasks, time and threat state allowing of course) was, the war cemetery. I would have liked to have paid my respects to those soldiers from previous generations that had been here and fought long before we ever got here. Although, having said that, apart from outright neglect, hundreds of grave stones had been deliberately desecrated and destroyed. (Later, troops from '19 Mechanised Brigade' would set about salvaging the surviving head-stones for safe storage until the Commonwealth War Graves Commission could undertake further comprehensive reconstruction at some point). And whilst mention-ing such, another badly overgrown British war cemetery at Al Kut had been discovered.

This was the last resting place of around 700 British and Empire troops who had fallen during the Mesopotamian Campaign of World War One. This was the scene of heavy fighting, during which, the British suffered a disastrous defeat in 1916, and then an important victory in 1917. But, alas, I would not get to see either of these cemeteries.

I realised that with the exception of Oman and the opportunities that the trip presented, that this was an operational tour, not a sight-seeing tour.

But, my own personal doctrine was, "when in a strange land, and wherever possible … ..Explore!"

Catching up on the news, the US were now offering $25million (roughly £15m) for conclusive information concerning the whereabouts of Saddam, and the equivalent of around £9million for each of his two sons, Uday and Qusay. Saddam's location had been a mystery ever since the US forces took control of Baghdad on April 9th, and it was not known whether the two missions that had been launched against him were successful or not.

But then again, all the latest reports regarding the recent taped broadcasts indicated that the voice on the tape was indeed that of Saddam, which would mean that he was still at large. And whilst on the subject of rewards, the US had also previously offered $15million for information regarding the whereabouts of al-Qaeda leader, Osama Bin Laden, and yet he was still nowhere to be seen either.

7. Home Stretch

6th July – 12th August

With a three-quarter tonne trailer 'loaded to the gunnels', we said 'Ciao' to our comrades at 'Sultan' and climbed in the rear of the Wolf. The next time we'd be back up this way again would be when we were to drive those team members who would be leaving theatre slightly earlier, up and over the border to BIA for their Blighty flight.

It was a good job that the Boss had decided not to take the trip down to 'Ali' with us, as was the original plan, as it really would have been 'sardine city' in the back, and anyway, due to Alex's long legs it was better for all concerned if he sat up front in the passenger seat. Ibby was 'pilot' and wasn't one for hanging about either. That was no bad thing under the current circumstances as it meant that we'd make the trip in pretty good time, enabling us to get out before the pair of us seized up in the back, what with all the gear piled in with us. The other reason for us heading south was also to give the (soon to be) outgoing team a chance to 'decompress' – the adopted army term for tempering things accordingly, prior to returning home. A more honed example of this could be applied to the situation that the Black Watch found themselves in during the early days of the conflict, when they had to scale things down from a war fighting role into a peace keeping role, where adrenalin is still pumped up and there is a need to temper things accordingly – not an easy thing to do with the flick of a switch. Although admittedly, our own experiences and circumstances did not in any way reflect the same kind of situation that the Black Watch found themselves in.

The 'Ali' team had had a re-shuffle round in their accommodation when they'd been told to expect the three of us, and so I just dropped my kit and grabbed the spare bed in the same portakabin that I'd left only a fortnight earlier. Herbie and Alex moved next door-but-one, but we each got ourselves comfortable again in no time. Being back in my original quarters, where the fridge was located (most important), improved the current situation no end, along with the communal 'rat pack' locker which was still pretty well stocked. Upon opening this galvanised tin locker, it was just like opening a treasure chest. When you lifted the lid, all manner of shiny foil packages glinted up at you invitingly. It also made for something of a lucky dip when trying to find something to ease a case of the 'munchies'.

When the guys opened the Brit ration packs, (as with the MRE's) there was usually something that somebody didn't want, so the cast-off's ended up in this tin chest. The one thing that I really enjoyed, and there seemed to be no shortage of, were the packs of fruit biscuits or 'Biscuits Fruit – S1', just right for a dunk in a mug of tea. Mind you, by the time you'd submerged your second biscuit, half your tea was gone due to 'soak-up'.

Late on, most evenings, one of the lads usually had a rifle through to find his chosen meal sachet (stew or other suspicious looking substance), and by bringing the kettle to the boil and then shoving it in above the element for a couple of minutes he had himself a hot supper … .pouch open, spoon in … sorted.

One of the things that I really loved about being back down 'Ali,' was not just the superb RAF grub overall, and that's not to say that the food was inferior at 'Sultan Lines' by any means, but the additional luxury of also being able to fry or poach your own eggs on the hot plate provided at breakfast times, where sometimes just simple egg on toast or an egg 'banjo' was just the ticket. And, add to that, the nearby laundry, which dobied and pressed your kit (even socks and 'Bill Grundies' ended up with a creases down them … .well, almost). Things were usually ready in a day or two, and when you handed your ticket over, your freshly laundered gear was returned to you on hangers, wrapped in plastic, just like 'Johnsons'.

So, from having to hand-wash any and all bits of kit and clothing in small bowls, to actually ending up having it steam-pressed as though you were expecting a visit from Her Majesty, was absolute 'quality'.

Over the next few days, we were tasked to head back up to 'Hammersmith' to visit '27 Transport Regiment', right back to where we'd re-located from Arafjan, just before the war kicked off. It had been estimated that it would probably only take a day to clear the work up there, as we had a good number of bod's out on the ground on this particular day, having combined the sub-teams for the task in hand. But, what a day.

As we descended on '27 Regiment', there was that tell-tale haze that a storm was brewing. In next to no time at all, strong winds began to pick up, blowing sand in swirling eddys and 'dust devil's which dramatically altered the whole of the location.

We were working in pairs in an attempt to cover our task area more effectively. After an hour or so, we all RV'd at the mess tent for a water and brew stop. Despite the fact that the sun was now a barely visible, diffused disc in the sky, it remained just as hot as the desert surface continued to radiate its heat.

It was debated as to whether we should call it a day and finish off the task the next day, but nobody particularly wanted to do an 'encore'. So it was decided that we'd have a very quick bite to eat and crack on – visibility permitting. All through the afternoon the wind would suddenly drop then pick up again just as fierce as before. Thank goodness for ski masks and goggles, for without them, it would have been useless to even think about carrying on. We were buffeted about a fair bit, but fortunately the storm didn't get any worse which meant that we had no need to don shemagh's for that 'Bedouin wrap-around look'. With our task in the area finally completed around 1630, we all jumped back in the rovers and high-tailed it for 'Ali'. As we hit the main route south for the airbase, the worst of the storm was left behind, thank goodness.

As the kilometres fell away, the thought of a chilled beer sprang into my head, complete with misty coating on the glass, just like John Mills in 'Ice Cold In Alex', as he sat at the bar eyeing up his glass of Carlsberg, and savouring the moment before downing the golden liquid in one. I tried to dismiss the thought as quick as I'd thought of it – it was almost too much to bear … ..sheer torture. But despite the intake of plenty of luke-warm H_2O, a 'Mountain Dew' straight out of the fridge would have to do instead.

We were alerted that some of the new team were to be heading down in the next week or so to start to take over the port team's operation, which would mean things easing back even more for us. But we had to make sure that the accommodation that had previously housed three Tigers with plenty of space, now had to accommodate several. So, a couple of hours were spent dragging spare beds and lockers over from the central store and doing a complete make-over of the interior. By the time we'd finished, it looked more like a mini dormitory with beds and lockers installed, side-by-side, in true military fashion. It was the most sensible way of utilising all the space practically. But, talk about bringing a sweat on.

Prior to the re-shuffle, on a downtime day, Herb had gone for a marathon stay-cool, surface-only-for-meals kind of session, where he watched all 10 episodes of 'Band of Brothers' back to back on one of

the laptop's. No wonder it was dark by the time he finally surfaced …
.some viewing session!

After evening meal, a few of us had taken to sitting outside as dusk rapidly fell, whilst sampling the delights of the different kinds of brews that one of the guys had been sent out from home.

At this point in the tour, the biggest decision of the day that any of us had to make down here, certainly in this neck-of-the-woods was, "Shall we have a Darjeeling, or an Earl Grey, or maybe the Orange Peko?"

Honestly, we were like something from the days of the old Raj, with the odd declaration of, "Yes, old fruit, I quite agree with you, the breakfast tea is dashed refreshing, but you should really try the Lapsang!" Although we didn't quite fully capture the image, decked out in shorts and tea shirts, with little fingers crooked above the handles of plastic thermal mugs, or a slightly more fitting china mug (albeit with 'Hard Rock Café – Baghdad' on the front). "Would one care for a little more 'Orang Peko' or just a soupcon of 'Pa-Pa' perhaps?" – Damion would enquire, whilst managing to keep the look of aloof sincerity on his face. "No thanks old chap, one's quite tickety-boo with the EG". The only things that were missing here were the smoking jackets and an old gramophone playing '78' records to match the mood.

It amused us no end, and seemed a fitting way to round off several evenings.

As I'd said previously, I'd already lost what remaining vestiges of sanity I'd once possessed … .long, long ago in the mists of time (five or so months ago). Anyway, this is how the 'Ali Al Salem Air Base Tea Club' was formed – like all of the other great institutions, it had to start somewhere!

Back home, the whole 'false war claim' business was starting to implode. It appeared that with every new piece of information that was divulged, any credible reasons for actually going to war with Iraq didn't seem to hold much water with the British public. Claims were being made of a deliberately 'sexed up' dossier according to a 'leading source' were foremost in the news.[5]

---

[5] Sadly, due to the source of the information being named (a leading MOD weapons expert – Dr David Kelly) by the BBC's then defence correspondent, Andrew Gilligan, the intense pressure brought to bear on Dr Kelly, would allegedly lead him to commit suicide. The manner in which Dr Kelly had been identified as the 'leading source' would be seen as one of the worst betrayals of trust by a modern British government.

There were a whole string of dubious statements and half-truths being aired by both the US and our own Government.

And now, looking back at all the pre-war rhetoric, the back-slapping, and the determined loyalty shown to George 'Dubya' by the PM, it certainly gave me the impression that 'we', the Brit's, were now like the popular guest who'd turned up for a function (invited by the Americans), but had now started to wear out our welcome. Most people would agree that we were definitely playing second fiddle. Overall, it was their show and no mistake.

So, what with the mud-slinging going on between the two nations over who had or hadn't disclosed essential and accurate information regarding this or that, I could see the whole heated debate surrounding the reasons and justification for the war continuing for a very long time. Of that, there was nothing surer.

At 1200 local time on the 11th July, 3 (UK) Div took over from 1 (UK) Div as the Brit Forces HQ in Iraq. 3 (UK) Div was now HQ for the new Multi-National Division (South East) which was comprised of; Italian, Norwegian, Romanian, Danish, Dutch, Czech, Portuguese, Lithuanian and New Zealand troops coming under its command. The Italian Brigade were also to assume command of the Dhi Qui Province at midnight on the 14/15th July.

The day came when the Sgt Major announced that we had a no-holds-barred day off, suggesting that the water park in Kuwait City seemed like a really good way to spend it (the fact that he'd come back down to 'Ali' for a day or two and would also be joining us, made it all the more official). Who were we to argue? "You've gotta take it when you can get it". So with a mini-bus signed out from the airbase, and the Pajero also at the team's disposal, we Tigers went-a-swimming. This was a little like the effect that the CSE show in the Omani hotel had had on me, it was so surreal, in that here we were, entering this watery wonderland, a million miles away from our initial encounters with the Middle East, with the daily threat of incoming missiles. This was time to be a kid again, and get me some fun in the sun … ..and not a sand storm in sight either.

So, we splashed, we swam and rode the inflatables on the water rides.

Dr Kelly's death would lead to the Hutton Inquiry, the outcome of which would vilify the BBC and yet clear the government almost wholly of any responsibility for Dr Kelly's death.

I also managed several circuits of the 'lazy river', lying atop a rubber ring, just content to be bobbing along under the warm rays of the sun, amongst a few tourists and a fair number of local Kuwaiti's doing likewise.

Whilst enjoying the drifting sensation as the man-made current took us along, one or two of the Kuwaiti youths were curious as to our nationality (despite us not appearing quite as pale as some of our other countrymen), and gave the thumbs up when we said that we were British. One little Kuwaiti looked at me with a big grin and said, "We like British … ..British verrrry good!" to which I replied with a "Shokran jezeelan" or "Thank you very much".

Well, you couldn't really top that I suppose. For those youngsters that weren't old enough to remember, they had doubtless been told by their parents that the British (and Americans) had come to their aid once before, to drive out 'Big Bad Saddam', and not that long ago either. As if to re-inforce this point, there was a sign we would pass on the way out of the city which read something like, "Kuwait, America and Britain will be friends forever," but at least it wasn't quite as cloying as the sign I'd spotted near the Mutlah Pass, but then again, some passing US convoy had most likely stuck that sticker on themselves. But as far as the Kuwaiti's were concerned, they appeared to be quite passionate about the whole thing.

A small beach ran from the edge of the water park and sloped away into the waters of the Gulf, and although it was netted off a little way out (no doubt to stop anything with teeth from sampling the humans), we had a swim there too. Later, as the sun had arced across the sky, a couple of us got dressed and took the route along the promenade to the swish looking shopping mall known as the 'Sharq Souq'. It was built around a reasonably attractive marina, complete of course with a fair few Dinars worth of boats moored alongside. As the glass doors of the mall slid aside, air-conditioning met our hot skin – a most welcome feeling. There was only one thing to do, and that was to find a place to sit and drink something cold.

We turned a corner, and what do you know? There facing us was a 'Starbucks' – two ice cold 'Frappucino's coming right up!

We made it back to the park to get in the last hour of sunbathing, got showered and changed, then headed off for the centre of Kuwait City for a pre-planned Chinese meal, at an eatery that some of the 'EFI' people back at 'Ali' had recommended. They weren't wrong – the nosh was excellent and very good value too. One or two people had steak, which came in sizzling on its own cast iron platter, and was so hot you feel the heat from it as passed. Someone enquired as to whether a first-aid burns kit had been brought with us, just in case.

Apparently, this little food haven was frequented quite a bit by people from the base, so it did have quite a reputation for being one of the best (and most reasonably priced) eateries around. It was discreetly tucked away up a side opening just off from the main street, and you could quite easily have walked past it without ever knowing it was there. We would get the chance to do this a few more times over the next couple of weeks, with an invite being thrown to the new team's Sgt Major and OC, which acted as a bit of an 'ice-breaker' for all concerned.

But very soon, a few of the old team would be heading back to Blighty, followed a little while later (with the exception of six of us), by the majority of 'Tiger'. Everyone could now most definitely be considered 'short-timers'.

One of the major events to happen since the start of the war took place, – certainly in terms of the impact that it would have on the Iraqi people; the whereabouts of Uday and Qusay Hussein had been discovered.

Their hideout had been located in the town of Mosul in Northern Iraq. (It was believed that a Ba'athist colleague had betrayed the brothers to collect the very enticing reward).

However, during the ensuing gun-battle with US Airborne Troopers (of the 101st), the brothers and one of Saddam's grandsons had been killed, along with a couple of Saddam's most feared lieutenants. The dilemma now, was in trying to convince those Iraqis who for so long, had wanted to see the last vestiges of the old regime swept away, and until there was absolute proof that the sons of Saddam were indeed dead, the Iraqi people would remain sceptical.

There was one individual who would no doubt have been rejoicing to learn of the demise of the two Hussein brothers, but in particular Uday – that individual is called Latif Yahia, the man "chosen" to act as Uday's *fiday* or double. In Arab culture it means so much more – a disciple, a fighter, a partisan, a serf who must always be prepared to give up his life for his master. Latif and Uday were at school together – that is, when Uday could be bothered to turn up (with his body-guards in tow), and the resemblance between the two was quite striking. Latif tried to distance himself from the controlling and completely unpredictable Uday, who was definitely his father's son (having been made to watch torture and executions since the age of ten). After many years, believing that he'd finally broken the link between Uday and himself, it was whilst he was serving as a young officer, fighting at the front during the Iran Iraq War, that Latif was summoned by Uday. It was then 1987.

From that moment, he found himself in the service of the President's son, not of course, that there was any way that he could refuse "this great honour". He tried to resist initially, but found to his cost that you do not refuse such a man as Uday. It was some four years later, with the onset of the Gulf War that Latif finally found an opportunity to escape. Latif's own personal story where he witnessed and suffered a cruel combination of terror and unbridled power at the hands of Uday, whilst also living a life of caged luxury, is a rather amazing one.

Anyway, the scepticism of the Iraqi people would be dispelled the following day when, in 'a grisly exhibition of death', the US released pictures of the Hussein brothers laid out in plastic body bags – dead for all the world to see. The news reports showed anti-Hussein Iraqi's slapping TV screens whilst the images were being aired. It reminded me of the not dissimilar scenes where jubilant Iraqi's removed their sandals to smack the toppled statues of Saddam, the day that the Americans rolled into Baghdad.

But although the TV images were quite stark, they were aired to prove that neither would follow their father back into power. Uday had once told Latif that if he ever took over as the ruling power in Iraq, he would eclipse his father in terms of cruelty and barbarism.

Fortunately, justice had been served.

One particular evening, whilst we still had a couple of hours before dusk, it was decided that a couple of us would take the Pajero and venture into down-town Kuwait and try our hand in the gold souq for those 'end of tour' presents. After grabbing a plate of all-in chinese from the food court in the 'Sharq Souq' shopping mall, we headed across to the central souq, where the gold market's tangle of streets ran into the fruit, veg and fish markets.

The variety and colour of the fish on offer was just as amazing and varied as the nationalities that inhabited and worked in the city – there were Iranians, Asians and of course Arabs. It was a melting pot of cultures, and yet they managed to live and work side by side. Now I'm sure there's a lesson in there somewhere?

As we passed the bountiful electrical goods stores full of the latest gizmo's, gadgets and 'must haves', we meandered our way to the gold quarter to see what could be had.

After several invitations into the proprietors shops, we started to get a feel for the average cost-per-weight of the different types of gold-ware on offer, but it was still an eye-goggling experience what with all the shiny stuff that filled the windows. The downside was that it was quite a time consuming business that took a fair amount of leg work and a fair bit of haggling, and we had to be back at 'Ali within reasonable time. But in the end we bought a couple of trinkets, satisfied in the knowledge that we'd got a reasonable deal, whilst at the same time keeping our vendor happy with the profit that he'd made.

Later, whilst on another expedition, we had virtually the same experience when trying to buy fragrances and perfume, but one of the lads had put me straight with regard to one particular trader who was willing to do a reasonable deal on a few bottles – making ideal gifts for the ladies in the family.

Mind you, with half a dozen of us all buying multiple bottles, he must have thought that he had hit the jackpot and was on his way to buying his first Mercedes. Although thinking about it, he probably had it parked round the back already. Taf recommended a particular men's fragrance he'd sampled previously, it was called 'FMJ'. "What's that?" I enquired. "Full Metal Jacket," said he. "Honestly, I'm not 'avin you on, that's what it's called and it's very nice!" I was thinking that it was possibly a bit too 'army barmy', what with its name and all. But after sampling it, I was suitably impressed enough to buy myself a bottle … .well, I'd gotten everyone else something, so it only seemed fitting to treat myself. Our vendor was now well on his way to having his own swimming pool installed!

But the funniest and most memorable thing about the whole expedition happened when our merchant tried to up his sales technique by informing us that his current best seller was … .'Dogshit Banana'! To which I did a double take, as though I'd surely misheard him?

It was really, 'Dolce Gabbana', but our little Kuwaiti's pronunciation of it sounded more like the former. Anyway, it had those of us within earshot rolling around with laughter, and it was so infectious that even our perfume salesman joined in. So now, I can never look at this particular brand of fragrance without a smile and a memory flash-back … .it will never be the same again.

The day finally dawned when the first batch of team members were due to fly back to Blighty, so the previous night was to be the final gathering of the tea club. In a way, it was a little sad really, but at the very least I'd promised to keep in touch with the 'Grand Tea Master' himself.

No doubt for those several heading home, it was an enormous relief, knowing that they would very soon be back on home soil. The next batch of Tigers to follow would only be a week or so behind them. When they touched down at Brize, they would be transported back to Chilwell for the handing in of weapons, kit and admin clearance as part of the de-mobbing process, which in total would take no more than around half a day.

So, next morning after breakfast, the rovers and trailers were 'loaded to the gunnels', but before we exited the base with our outward-bound 'Tigers', we had one final photo before we left;

We got up and over the border without incident and in reasonable time too, and unloaded our charges and all their kit at BIA. Those in charge of the pre-bundled weapons went to check in first.

Once we'd said our farewells, we were off, south again for Kuwait and 'Ali'. And, one of the things I desperately needed to do when we got back was book into the base medical centre to try and sort my feet out … .they were giving me a few problems. Everything else had survived the conditions out here, but my feet were now finally beginning to rebel. I just needed to nurse them through the next couple of weeks until 'end ex', unless of course things went 'pear-shaped' (and by that, I don't mean my feet, but referring to the slowly disintegrating situation in the north – nobody could say with absolute certainty that the plug wouldn't be pulled on our departure date.

But for the moment, things were going to get a lot quieter as time rolled around for the remainder of the old team to 'bug out'. But, a day or so before their departure, we managed one final trip into Kuwait City and the water park, followed by a meal in everybody's favourite eatery.

It wouldn't be long before the British element on the airbase were to be reduced considerably either.

Prior to the remainder of 'Old Tiger' heading for home, Hooch had wanted a last look around the airbase, and in particular, some of the parts he'd not visited before. So with some time to ourselves we jumped into one of the rovers, passing the storage hangers as we drove around the perimeter road. The exterior of some of the hangers had been 'graffitti'd up' with the trademarks of the various units stationed here who'd endeavoured to do the artwork – some of designs were on quite a grand scale.

In one part of the base, US heli-techs were doing routine maintenance on some of their aircraft. The 'tecchies' had no problem with us taking a few photos here and there.

Not far from the base re-fuelling point, lay a line of old fighter planes from around the time of the '91' Gulf War. Apparently they hadn't flown in a long time and were unlikely to either, due, from what I'd been informed, to a lack of spare parts. The wording on each fuselage 'FREE KUWAIT' couldn't have made much more of a statement I suppose.

Once we'd circumnavigated the base, we headed over to 'Snakepit' – the US Marines camp to check out the latest goodies that had come in – not to mention a packet of the good old beef jerky. It'd been a while since I'd had a chew on this tasty, albeit leathery stuff. Upon entering, what was probably one of the smallest PX's I'd been in, even by US standards, Hooch's greeting of an "Alreet Bud!" to our man behind the counter, left him with a somewhat bemused look. It probably left him thinking, "Shoot! I cain't never unnerstand what them Brits is sayin'!"

When we finally parked up back at 'Tiger Lines' I said, "Well Sir, that's the end of the Ali Al Salem open top bus tour, and if you've thoroughly enjoyed it, then maybe you would like to show your appreciation to the guide, as all donations are greatly appreciated". If I remember correctly, the reply was an uttering of early anglo-saxon Newcastle-ees, as the two of us dismounted the vehicle, laughing between ourselves. I wasn't too far out with the open-top bus business either, as the Rover had a soft top and we did have the rear flap up after all.

Next up on my personal 'to-do' list, was a hack and whizz around the bonce – it was that time again. I'd already been informed about the marvellous barber on the base (mainly because of the head and neck massage that formed an integral part of the whole process). The last time I'd had such a 'heavenly haircut' was several weeks ago and several hundred miles away in the Sultanate of Oman. In the meantime, 'Marcel' had been doing the business hair-wise, but no massage thrown in. I'd timed it just right, as I looked like being the last customer of the day. Once the meticulous shaving and trimming side of things had been completed, I was pummelled in a firm yet rather relaxing way, and again, as with my previous experience, I came away feeling slightly better than when I first walked in.

The situation regarding Iraq's stability had started to change, and sadly for the worse. A disconcerting number of insurgent and guerrilla attacks had started to build up, more so in the north of the country.

Little were we to know, that as we were preparing to leave Theatre, the country was about to spiral into a state of total anarchy that would see countless innocent Iraqi's killed, along with many more US and British soldiers.

The news bulletins from home showed that Tony Blair and a number of his ministers had been accused of crimes against humanity in prosecuting the war against Iraq – a case that had been lodged with the international court by Greek lawyers.

And, yet another tape recording purported to be by Saddam had been aired. He praised his dead sons and declared that they had died as martyrs for Iraq, pledging that the US would be defeated, as the fiery anti-US cleric, Muqtada al-Sadir, who was doing his best to become the unchallengeable leader of Shia opposition, was attempting to rally somewhere in the region of 1000 recruits to join an "Islamic Army" in the Holy city of Najaf.

Iraq was now becoming an ever increasingly dangerous place for any westerner who dared set foot in the country.

Within the next couple of days the two Hussein sons would be buried in the grey, sun-blasted earth of the village of al-Awja – the small, ugly place that Saddam himself had always hated. The strange thing is that Uday in particular, was hated by almost everyone who ever knew him and yet people would continue to visit the brother's graves – more than likely out of some kind of respect rather than for the love of great leaders.

This was the morning that all of the original members of Tiger were to head to Basrah for their 'Blighty flight'. Although things were rapidly deteriorating in the North of the country, an assessment had been made that it was deemed safe enough for us to take our comrades to BIA without heavily armed escort. Again, as with our previous sojourn up and over the border to the airport, there was nothing about this trip that would in any way distinguish it from that last (apart that is, from an unwarranted detour).

This time, it was a little harder saying goodbye to all those now leaving, as I'd spent nearly all of my time in the company of a good half of the team. So, I made sure that I got round each and every individual to say goodbye as they waited to check in their bags.

I knew that as I said farewell, that there would be maybe a handful of people with whom I would remain in touch. People invariably have good intentions, but after a while things naturally fall by the way-side, that's the nature of things. We'd shared the ups and downs, the uncertainty of what was to happen next as we spiralled towards conflict, and not least, the laughs along the way. As I shook hands with my old buddy, Tony, I said, "Boy, it seems like another life when we met at Crewe station and first set out for Chilwell – so much has happened". He threatened to have the cool beer that I'd fantasized about, on my behalf. Mind you as is typical, he did rub it in about being able to have that wonderful beer much sooner than me, and taking great delight as he did so. "You're buying!" I said in retort. However, we agreed that when I followed him home a couple of weeks later, he'd give me a chance to catch my breath then we'd meet up. Having said that, during our whole time in theatre, we'd only really spent a week or two in each other's company at the beginning and end of the tour, with maybe a couple of days here and there. Our geographical diversity throughout the tour meant that we both had been through different experiences and had very different stories to tell, that much was certainly true.

The boss indicated that we should make a move for the border, so with that, I swivelled on my heel and headed for the departure lounge doors with those left to return to 'Ali'.

As we headed out from BIA, I wondered just how many individuals would actually keep in touch. The Boss and a few others had talked about a 'Tiger' re-union at some point, but realistically, I think people realised that it would most probably not happen. For one thing, it would have to take place at a mutually agreed location that was reasonably central for those furthest north and south.

What with those of us staying on, the one thing that we would miss out on was the end of tour shin-dig that would take place once the team arrived back at Chilwell. That would be the last time that the majority of the old team would be together before they did a 'bomb-burst' to all points of the compass, once through the Chetwynd Barracks gate, the next day. But hey, we'd agreed to stay on a little while longer, so they were the breaks I guess.

In the meantime, because of the fact that we were stationed on a bloody big airbase with all sorts of aircraft flying in and out, we formulated an idea (with the ok from the boss of course) that a couple of us would approach the USAF guys in an attempt to jack-up a flight on one of their AC-130 Spectre's when they were due to go out on one of their live firing missions out over the desert, or failing that, going up for a 'cabby' in one of their heli's. It was a matter of speaking to the right people, so this was the plan for the next few days.

Word came to us through the OC that we were to hand over our accommodation, any time soon, as we were to be re-housed in the purpose-built living quarters across the way. There were no sighs of "Not Again!" this time, as the four man rooms and en-suite facilities were outstanding. despite the fact that the surrounding area was literally a Kuwaiti building site.

So, even from the reasonably comfortable surroundings that we currently occupied, we were moving up another star on the comfort and amenities rating … ..no better way to end a tour of duty as far as I was concerned.

It would transpire that due to other circumstances, the additional 2 to 3 weeks that we had originally volunteered to extend our stay by, had now been whittled to 10 days. The boss briefed us that we would more than likely be on a Blighty-bound flight at the beginning of the following week. That was of course if he could get the five of us on whatever air transport was leaving theatre. So, we basically had a few days notice to move and, just when we were getting used to our new 'des-res' too. Our 'Spectre' flight idea was also down the pan now as well.

To think that our next "pick up your parrots and monkeys and move out!," was to be our last. And, although I wanted to go home at some point in the near future, a part of me wanted to stay, for reasons which I'll probably never be able to fully explain.

Returning from my UN tour in Cyprus after 6 months was rather strange, initially. But, returning back to the world and "normality" after being out here in the Middle-East whilst we were at war was different again. It wasn't that I had any concerns for myself, but guess I wasn't sure what to expect this time round. I knew that my experiences out here hadn't particularly changed me, and fortunately, I had no personal horror stories to relate, but I did wonder how I would react to a civilian world around me … and in particular, a world which for the most part would have no clue or idea as to what I, and those around me had been through. As before, could I just flick the switch and just become 'Mr Joe Public Esq'?

One of the most disconcerting things I found as we were preparing to leave was the ever-increasing number of attacks by insurgents and the chaos that would ensue. It would probably have been a fitting end to the tour to have come out from the conflict with the old regime gone, the 'bad guys' having been sorted out, and the Iraqi people as a whole, now jubilant with thoughts of a unified country. And not least, those nations that had formed the coalition to be able to back off (in a militaristic way) and help the country re-establish itself. Alas, this was not 'Hollywood' and we certainly weren't riding off into the sunset, knowing we'd saved the day.

The many battles may have been won, but the fighting was far from over, as more recent events would show.

As had been confirmed by the boss a few days previously, we were to be on the 11th of August flight, just a few days away. So we five, started to prepare ourselves for heading home.

Our departure day dawned soon enough, and we struck out for the border once again – this time with some of the newer tigers accompanying us as escort. Only this time we weren't running straight on to Basrah International, but stopping for a while at 'UQ'. We had a few bits of admin to get squared away and in particular, handing in our body armour to the QM at 'Sultan Lines' as had previously been arranged, rather than having to transport and carry this additional and heavy piece of kit back on the plane and finally to RTMC at Chilwell. Whilst being glad to be free of it, the thought did cross my mind that we had to get from here to BIA safely and without incident.

Surely there would be no problems in not having our body armour with us?!

Anyway, after grabbing lunch we had plenty of time to get to the A-pod as our flight wasn't until the following morning. But doing it this way also meant that at least we wouldn't have to be getting up and on the road at 'daft oclock' in order to be at the airport in time for our Blighty flight.

We left the port and on to our well-worn route and as we passed the hamlets I waved to the roadside 'munchkins' for one last time as we made for Basrah International.

Finally we unloaded our kit and equipment and headed into the departure lounge. We had a long night ahead, and so we tried to amuse ourselves as much as possible, although apart from the large screen set-up showing some TV news and the occasional dvd. So realistically, all that we could do was 'view and brew'. There were a couple of briefings about 'returning to the world' kind of stuff to break the monotony and one or two questionnaires – one of which asked whether individuals may have come into contact with Depleted Uranium whilst in Theatre. I'd already decided that I'd request a 'DU' health check back at Chilwell. Despite our limited exposure to the 'Chally 2' that Hooch and I had 'gift wrapped' in Hessian, we considered it enough to warrant the testing once back in the UK.

Apart from going on the hunt for a sat phone in an attempt to do an 'ET' (and phone home), whatever else happened is now a haze except that is for trying to get some kip on a hard carpeted floor with my day sack for a pillow.

Most of the desert-suited passengers on the plane cheered as the undercarriage glanced the tarmac of Brize Norton – home soil. The whine of the engines died as we came to a halt in our parking slot and the clicking of safety belts as the light came on. Wow! we were home and it was quite hard to believe in some respects. And, although it may have sounded crazy, that minute part of me was already missing the Middle-East.

It was then just a case of picking up our 'p's and m's' from the baggage hall, then wait for the transport back to RTMC – Chilwell.

After some six months, give or take, we were back through the gates at Chetwynd Barracks, where weapons were cleaned and handed back in at the armoury, pre-release medicals were carried out (including my request for a DU test at some point in the near future), and anyone who had previously signed out any other kit at the outset could now hand it back in – providing of course, that they still had everything they had mobilised with. Everyone was then cleared through the admin process in good time. I would have liked to have been able to say goodbye properly to my compadrés, but due to the fact that we'd all gone through the different de-mobilisation points at slightly different times meant that everyone had headed off, homeward bound as soon as individuals had been given the clearance to do so.

In my previous search for the sat phone at 'BIA' the day before, I'd briefly managed to speak to Linda where she'd happily agreed to come and collect me from Chilwell – she'd take the day off work. This would dispense with the need for a hire car or train warrant, plus it would mean getting to see her that little bit quicker.

So with the whole de-mob process done and dusted, there was nothing more to do other than wait for her to arrive, I sat outside 'Fletchers' in the agreeable sunshine, with a mug of coffee to hand, trying to evaluate numerous thoughts and experiences of the last several months.

A short while later she pulled up into the parking area and I went across to greet her. We hugged, said our "hello's" and decided to grab a bite to eat before moving off for home.

I let Linda do most of the talking on the journey, as I didn't know where to start trying to formulate what had happened in the last three months since I'd flown home for Mum's funeral.

Anyway, an hour and a half later, we turned the key in the door as I lugged my heavy bags in, and that was it … . 'End Ex!'

In the words of Dorothy, "There's no place like home!"

And so it was, that on December 15th, a little over four months to the day that I stepped off my return flight onto the tarmac at Brize, that one Saddam Hussein al-Tikriti was finally in coalition hands.

Mohammed al-Musslit, one of Saddam's most loyal and best regarded bodyguards, had been captured by the Americans and had given them the whereabouts of his former boss. Initially, he had helped Saddam escape up the Tikrit road as the Americans had started to tighten the noose around Baghdad on April 9th 2003. As al-Musslit proceeded to spill the beans, he informed the Americans that he knew of a number of hideouts that had been prepared for such an eventuality. It is also alleged that of those individuals who had dug and prepared the secret underground refuges (not much more than holes in the ground really), all were believed to have been disposed of, so as not to be able to give away any specific details.

The Americans flew al-Musslit to Tikrit in order for him to give them the exact location of the former President, whence they called in 600 troops from the 4th Infantry Division to examine all of the sites. After nearly three hours of searching they found no sign of anything that could possibly hide the deposed leader.

As it grew dark, the soldiers were about to suspend the search, when they decided to look around a small unremarkable compound near the Tigris river which they had searched previously. They came upon two locals sitting near a makeshift lean-to, who appeared to be extremely jittery in the presence of the soldiers. Now apart from perhaps their outright dislike of the Americans, they had no particular reason to fear them. However, it was in this debris strewn area that a piece of carpet lay, surrounded by beaten earth, which raised the suspicions of one of the soldiers … ..something just didn't look right about it.

As the soldier lifted the carpet along with a mud-smeared piece of polystyrene just below it (no doubt in place to prevent the carpet from sinking), they were faced with a square hole. As one of the soldiers was about to toss a grenade in, his buddy stopped him just seconds before two hands appeared in the light of their torches.

As a dishevelled and bearded head came into view, its voice said, 'My name is Saddam Hussein … I am the President of Iraq, and I want to negotiate'. One of the soldiers replied, 'Regards from President Bush', as the rest of them laughed. Even now in this submissive state, Saddam still believed that he had something with which to negotiate. The former President had some *cojones*, I'll give him that. Once evicted from his rather cramped lodgings, a pistol, two AK-47s, $750,000 in cash and a briefcase full of rather sensitive documents were found. He'd been at large for 250 days.

Had he decided to shoot his way out, or if the grenade had rolled from the soldier's hand, Saddam would no doubt have entered into the history books as one of the Muslim world's greatest martyrs. In death his legend would have been magnified tenfold. Can you imagine how that might inspire and insight countless pro-Saddam Muslims across the world?

In an ironic twist of fate, Mohammed al-Muslit would see not a single cent of the $25m due to the fact that he had not divulged the whereabouts of Saddam willingly. This would mean that he (al-Muslit) would most probably spend the rest of his life looking over his shoulder for anyone that might decide to take revenge on him for his act of betrayal.

With his self-respect and honour in tatters, and no matter how tough an individual he had been when Saddam was in power, he was now more than likely a dead-man walking.

Around the time that Saddam was captured, we, 'The Four Musketeers' were safely back together again, as Derek had finally returned from his stint in the Gulf, none the worse for his experiences.

So our long planned RV took place in our old haunt, where we raised a glass to each other (and every other serving individual), swapped tales and told many a funny story. This was our "therapy" group if you like, but not in a rehabilitation or healing sense, it just gave us the freedom to be able to talk amongst ourselves about our experiences on exactly the same level – whether it be about our time spent in the Gulf or other theatres we had served in.

Epilogue

As I write the final paragraphs of this book, I wonder how long or how many more sacrifices it will take before our job is finished in Iraq, (and indeed elsewhere) is anyone's guess. Many lobby to bring the troops out, but what of the ordinary Iraqi people, do we leave them to fend for themselves 'to get on with it', or do we stay till the bitter end, no matter the cost?

Like many, I have friends and other colleagues who are serving in the Middle-East and Afghanistan at this moment in time. Nearly everyone knows somebody who has served or is currently serving in the Gulf, and one can only hope that they all return home safe, the better for their experiences, as Regular Units and other 'volunteered mobilees' gear up to act as outgoing replacements – and so the cycle continues.

As the world's benign and not so benign 'hot spots' require more and more resources to be thrown at them (in terms of military manpower), what with ever-increasing pressures being put upon on already over-stretched Regular Army units to be here, there and everywhere, the Territorial Army of today is constantly changing and adapting to its proven role on worldwide operations.

I quote (ex Lt Col, 1 Royal Irish) Tim Collins…[6]

When enquiring of a Sgt as to how the TA guys under him were doing (whilst on Op Telic) he said, "How are the lads?"

The Sgt replied in typical Belfast-ese, "Stickin' out." (Outstanding). "Sure, as you said yourself, when you are called up you are not TA any more, you're just part of the Army."

"And that's a fact," TC replied. He went on to add:

> "…they might have been mechanics, insurance salesmen or carpenters, but when they put on their uniforms they were like any other man in the battalion. I believe it is one of the great strengths of the nation that our soldier citizens will come when called – all volunteers – and perform as these have done. That was the strength of the British regimental system. It is the spirit that animated these men's forefathers in the Second World War and the First World War

---

[6] From his book *Rules of Engagement – A Life In Conflict.*

before that. It was certainly alive in these men as I watched them working, laughing then sipping from their water bottles against the immense heat and the strain of their exertions."

I certainly could not agree more.

SUPERBIO AD HABÊRE STIPENDIUM IN SUBULUM

(PROUD TO HAVE SERVED IN THE SAND)

Maritime, Land and Air Components Involved in Op Telic 2003

This is not an exhaustive or definitive list and only the British contingent is represented here.

Naval Task Group:

Rear Admiral David Snelson

HMS Ark Royal (aircraft carrier)
HMS Ocean (helicopter carrier)
HMS Liverpool (Type 42 destroyer)
HMS Edinburgh (Type 42 destroyer)
HMS York (Type 42 destroyer)
HMS Marlborough (Type 23 frigate)
HMS Richmond (Type 23 frigate)
HMS Chatham (Type 42 frigate)
HMS Grimsby (mine-hunter)
HMS Ledbury (mine-hunter)
HMS Brocklesby (mine-hunter)
HMS Blythe (mine-hunter)

HMS Turbulent (Trafalgar class submarine)

HMS Splendid (Swiftsure class submarine)

RFA Argus (hospital ship)
RFA Sir Tristram
RFA Sir Galahad
RFA Sir Percivale
RFA Fort Victoria
RFA Fort Rosalie
RFA Fort Austin
RFA Orangeleaf

Other RN and RFA vessels included:

HMS Bangor (mine-hunter)
HMS Ramsey (mine-hunter)
HMS Shoreham (mine-hunter)
HMS Sandown (mine-hunter)
HMS Roebuck (survey ship)
RFA Sir Bedivere
RFA Bayleaf
RFA Brambleleaf
RFA Grey Rover
RFA Diligence
RFA Sea Crusader

The Royal Marines amphibious force comprising some 4,000 from HQ3 Commando Brigade:

Brigadier Jim Dutton

40 Commando Royal Marines
42 Commando Royal Marines
45Commando Royal Marines
29 Regiment Royal Artillery (equipped with 105mm light guns)
539 Assault Squadron, RM
59 Commando Squadron, RE

Plus elements of the SBS (Special Boat Service)

Helicopter air groups deployed on board HMS Ark Royal and HMS Ocean: 845,846,847 and 849 Squadrons

Land Force

Major General Robin Brims

The Land force numbered some 26,000
The primary units deployed in whole or part included:

1 (UK) Armoured Division:

HQ and 1 Armoured Division Signal Regiment

- » 30 Signal Regiment (strategic communications)
- » The Queens Dragoon Guards (reconnaissance)
- » 1st Battalion The Duke of Wellington's Regiment (additional infantry capability)
- » 28 Engineer Regiment
- » 1 General Support Regiment Royal Logistic Corps
- » 2 Close Support Regiment Royal Logistic Corps
- » 2nd Battalion, Royal Electrical & Mechanical Engineers
- » 1 Close Support Medical Regiment
- » 5 General Support Medical Regiment
- » 1 Regiment Royal Military Police

Plus elements from:

- » 33 Explosive Ordnance Disposal Regiment
- » 30 Signals Regiment
- » 32 Regiment Royal Artillery (equipped with Phoenix UAV's)

7th Armoured Brigade:

Brigadier Graham Binns

Headquarters and Signals Squadron:
- » Royal Scots Dragoon Guards (equipped with Challenger 2 Tanks)
- » 2nd Royal Tank Regiment (equipped with Challenger 2 Tanks)
- » 1st Battalion The Black Watch (equipped with Warrior infantry fighting vehicles)
- » 1st Battalion Royal Regiment of Fusiliers (equipped with Warrior infantry fighting vehicles)

- » 3rd Regiment Royal Horse Artillery (equipped with AS90 self-propelled guns)
- » 32 Armoured Engineer Regiment

Plus elements from various units including:
- » Queens Royal Lancers (equipped with Challenger 2 tanks)
- » 1st Battalion Irish Guards (equipped with Warrior infantry fighting vehicles)
- » 1st Battalion The Light Infantry (equipped with Warrior infantry fighting vehicles)
- » 26 Regiment Royal Artillery
- » 38 Engineer Regiment

16 Air Assault Brigade:

Brigadier Jacko Page:

Headquarters and Signals Squadron:
- » 1st Battalion The Royal Irish Regiment
- » 1st Battalion The Parachute Regiment
- » 3rd Battalion The Parachute Regiment
- » 7 (Para) Regiment Royal Horse Artillery (equipped with 105mm Light Guns)
- » 23 Engineer Regiment
- » Household Cavalry Regiment (1x armoured reconnaissance squadron)
- » 3rd Regiment Army Air Corps (equipped with Lynx & Gazelle helicopters)
- » 7 Air Assault Battalion, Royal Electrical & Mechanical Engineers
- » 13 Air Assault Support Regiment, Royal Logistic Corps
- » 16 Close Support Medical Regiment
- » 156 Provost Company RMP

102 Logistics Brigade:

Brigadier Shaun Cowlam

Headquarters 2 Signal Regiment
- » 36 Engineer Regiment
- » 33 Field Hospital
- » 34 Field Hospital

- » 202 Field Hospital (Volunteer)
- » 4 General Support Medical Support Regiment
- » 3 Battalion, Royal Electrical & Mechanical Engineers
- » 6 Supply Regiment, Royal Logistic Corps
- » 7 Transport Regiment, Royal Logistic Corps
- » 17 Port & Maritime Regiment, Royal Logistic Corps
- » 23 Pioneer Regiment, Royal Logistic Corps
- » 24 Regiment, Royal Logistic Corps
- » 5 Regiment, Royal Military Police
- » specialist Royal Engineer teams
- » airfield engineer support units from 12 Engineer Brigade
- » elements from 11 Explosive Ordnance Disposal Regiment
- » elements from additional Royal Logistic Corps Regiments

Air components

Air Vice Marshal Glenn Torpy

(approximate numbers: 100 fixed-wing aircraft, 27 support helicopters, 7,000 personnel).

Aircraft types involved included:
- » Sentry AEW1 command & control aircraft (from 8 and 3 Sqns)
- » Tornado GR4 bomber/reconnaissance aircraft (from 2, 9, 12, 31 and 617 Sqns)
- » Jaguar GR3 attack/reconnaissance aircraft (from 6, 41 and 54 Sqns)
- » Harrier GR7 attack aircraft (from 1, 3 and 4 Sqns)
- » Tornado F3 air defence aircraft (from 43 and 111 Sqns)
- » VC-10 tanker aircraft (from 10 and 101 Sqns)
- » Tristar tanker aircraft (from 216 Sqn)
- » C-17 transport aircraft (from 99 Sqn)
- » Hercules transport aircraft (from 24, 30, 47 and 70 Sqns)
- » Nimrod aircraft (from 51, 120, 201 and 206 Sqns)
- » Canberra PR9 reconnaissance aircraft from (39 1 PRU Sqn)
- » Chinook helicopters (from 7, 18 and 27 Sqns)
- » Puma helicopters (from 33 Sqn)

RAF Regiment units provided ground defence for the force.

The Army's 21 Signal Regiment provided communications support for the Joint Helicopter Force.

Abbreviations and Slang

AFV	Armoured Fighting Vehicle
APC	Armoured Personnel Carrier
AOR	Area of responsibility
Bergen	Soldiers Large pack
Berm	A Hindi word to describe an earthwork rampart
'Bomb Up'	To charge or load up a weapon magazine
Boonie's	(Boondocks) The middle of knowhere
'Bug Out'	To Leave or Depart
Bukshee	Arabic (Bakhshish) for anything free
Bundook	Hindustani (Banduq) for rifle
CasEvac	Casualty Evacuation (aka 'dust-off')
CO	Commanding Officer
'Dobi'	To wash
DU	Depleted Uranium
Egg Banjo	An Egg Sandwich
EOD	Explosive Ordinance Disposal
'End Ex'	The end of the exercise – finish for the day
EFI	Expeditionary Forces Institute (UK version of an American PX)
Gonk	Sleep
GPMG	General Purpose Machine Gun also known as a 'Gimpy'
GPS	Global Positioning Satellite
Growlers	Sausages (particularly Compo Sausages)
Gucci Kit	Top of the range kit and equipment
'Head Shed's	Top Brass/Senior Military Personnel
HLS	Helicopter Landing Site
IPE	Individual Protective Equipment (NBC Kit & ancillaries)
JFLogC	Joint Force Logistics Component
K's	Kilometres
MALEESH	Arabic for; never mind, it doesn't matter.
MFO	Movement Freight Overseas
MCCP	Military Clearance Check Point
MSG	Maintenance Supply Group
MSR	Main Supply Route
NAPS	Nerve Agent Pre-Treatment System
NBC	Nuclear Biological Chemical

'Noddy Suit'	Protective Chemical Warfare Suit (as above)
OPFORS	Opposing Forces
OC	Officer Commanding (or simply 'Boss')
PLCE	Personal Load Carrying Equipment
PX	American Military Store/Shop
QRF	Quick Reaction Force
'Rat Pack'	Ration Pack (Not Frank Sinatra and his buddies!)
'Recce'	(Reconoitre) to scout or explore
'Rezzie'	Respirator or Gas Mask (also known as a 'Gasperator')
RMP	Royal Military Police
RP	Regimental Police
RPG	Rocket Propelled Grenade
RV	Rendez Vous (To meet up)
'Scratcher'	Sleeping Bag (also known as a 'Maggot' or 'Gonk Bag')
SOP's	Standard Operating Procedures
Spams	Alternative name for American Soldiers
Stickies	Cakes and Pastries
UNFICYP	United Nations Force In Cyprus
UXB's	Unexploded Bombs
WMD	Weapons of Mass Destruction
WMIK	Weapons Mounted Installation Kit (or heavily armed stripped-down Land Rover
Z's	Sleep